100 THINGS
YANKEES FANS
SHOULD KNOW & DO
BEFORE THEY DIE

David Fischer

TRIUMPH
BOOKS

The Library of Congress has catalogued the previous edition as follows:

Fischer, David, 1963–
  100 things Yankees fans should know & do before they die / David Fischer.
      p. cm.
  ISBN 978-1-60078-669-3
  1. New York Yankees (Baseball team)—History. 2. New York Yankees (Baseball team)—Miscellanea. I. Title. II. Title: One hundred things Yankee fans should know and do before they die.
  GV875.N4F54 2012
  796.357'64097471—dc23
                                              2011049496

This book is available in quantity at special discounts for your group or organization. For further information, contact:
  Triumph Books LLC
  814 North Franklin Street
  Chicago, Illinois 60610
  (312) 337-0747
  www.triumphbooks.com

Printed in U.S.A.
ISBN: 978-1-62937-547-2
Design by Patricia Frey
Photos courtesy of AP Images unless otherwise indicated

To all the players, from David Aardsma to Paul Zuvella,
who proudly wore the Yankees uniform

Contents

Introduction

For those who avidly follow the New York Yankees, a series of momentous events begins to form over time in the mind's eye. It's a common repository, if you will. The fan who would think nothing of paying $500 for a ticket near the dugout and the one who would rather spend $10 on a bleacher seat both remember or have heard of certain compelling moments in Yankees history: Don Larsen pitching the only perfect game in World Series history. Roger Maris hitting 61 home runs in 1961. The afternoon a dying man with courage and dignity, Lou Gehrig, did indeed feel like the luckiest man on earth.

Over the years, these shared moments evolve into a kind of canon of Yankee fandom. Hard-core fans and casual followers alike know many of the elements. David Cone pitching a perfect game while Larsen and Yogi Berra looked on is part of the canon. So is Derek Jeter reaching 3,000 hits and Aaron Judge breaking the single-season rookie home run record. The season when pitcher Ron Guidry won an incredible 25 games is also included. And yes, so is the achingly sad 2001 World Series, when emotions of the September 11 terrorist attacks were still raw.

The words and photographs you have in your hands catalog this memory book from 1 to 100. I have chosen what in my judgment are the most compelling players, the most important events, and the most rewarding excursions. In attempting to choose the greatest games and most influential individuals, I accepted three premises: That news value is primary. That some events become more compelling when viewed with hindsight. And that the world of baseball cannot be interpreted apart from the society and the era in which it exists. Hours of thoughtful analysis went into making the choices. And so difficult was limiting the selections to 100, it is understood that there may be a player, a game, or a thing to do that your personal list might include but here goes missing. Yet that's okay, too. Because whether you start at the beginning and read this book in order, or if you prefer to hop around and find the moments that are most meaningful to you, you will no doubt rediscover the rich history and tradition that makes the New York Yankees franchise so legendary.

1 Ruth's 714 Home Runs

Babe Ruth was baseball's first great home run hitter. He hit his first as a member of the Boston Red Sox on May 6, 1915, off New York Yankees pitcher Jack Warhop. Five years later, in 1920, he was sold to the Yankees, where he became an outfielder and gained fame as "The Bambino" for his power hitting. He will always be known as the man who made the home run famous.

In the early 1900s baseball was dominated by pitching and speedy base runners. Frank "Home Run" Baker earned his nickname by leading the American League with 11, 10, 12, and 9 homers in the years from 1911 to 1914. When Ruth hit 29 in 1919, he stunned the baseball world. The next-highest home run total that year was 12. The following year the player they would call "The Sultan of Swat" smashed 54 home runs in a year in which nobody else hit more than 19. Ruth knocked more balls out of the park than any other *team* in the league. The next year the Babe did even better, belting a mind-boggling 59 homers to break his own single-season home run record for the third year in a row. During the 1921 season, in just his seventh major league season, Ruth had become the top home run hitter in the history of baseball.

Ruth—already the first batter to slug 30, 40, and 50 home runs in a season—became the first man ever to hit 60 home runs in a season in 1927. He also had a .356 batting average with 164 RBIs, even though he was walked intentionally game after game. Ruth hit his record-breaking 60th home run off Tom Zachary of the Washington Senators at Yankee Stadium on September 30, the next-to-last day of the 1927 season. The ball rocketed into the right-field bleachers, now called Ruthville. When he went to his

1

position in right field in the top of the ninth inning, fans waved handkerchiefs and the Babe responded with military salutes. In the clubhouse after the game, Ruth boasted, "Sixty, count 'em, sixty. Let's see someone match that." Nobody took the invitation for 34 years.

Ruth was also the first hitter to reach 200, 300, 400, 500, 600, and 700 career homers. (Hank Aaron and Barry Bonds have since also passed the 700 mark.) He hit home run No. 500 on August 11, 1929, and No. 600 just two years and 10 days later. In July of 1934, Ruth hit home run No. 700. Asked if he followed any superstitions after hitting a home run, the Babe replied, "Just one. I make certain to touch all four bases." In all, Babe led the American League in home runs 12 times, including six consecutive seasons from 1926 through 1931, when he averaged more than 50 home runs per year.

Spurred on by his fantastic long balls, fans flocked to ballparks to watch the Babe in action. Yankee Stadium was built to hold the large crowds that came to see him. Fittingly, Ruth hit the first home run there, in 1923. He won his first and only Most Valuable Player award that season and led the Yankees to the first of their record 27 world championships.

Babe Ruth changed the very way the game was played. He ushered out the age of the singles hitters and turned baseball into a power hitting game. Ruth's on-field record speaks for itself: 714 career home runs, a .342 batting average, 2,062 bases on balls, and the MLB-record 72 games in which he hit two or more home runs. His hitting ability was so awesome, it is sometimes forgotten that he began his career in 1914 as a pitcher for the Boston Red Sox. He was so talented that had he remained a pitcher for his entire career, he probably would be celebrated today for his skill on the mound. He pitched for the Red Sox from 1914 to 1919, posting an 89–46 record. He threw 29 consecutive scoreless innings in the 1916 and 1918 World Series.

Going, Going, Gone!

To understand just how unique Ruth's home run production was during his greatest seasons, consider this: in 1920 and again in 1927, Ruth single-handedly hit more homers than any team in the league (54 in 1920, 60 in 1927). That represented more than 15 percent of all the homers hit in the league those seasons. The league-leading home run hitters today, hitting 40 to 50 homers, represent about 2 percent of all the homers hit in their leagues.

Although Hank Aaron and Barry Bonds eventually broke Ruth's career home run record, Bonds needed nearly 1,500 more at-bats and Aaron needed nearly 4,000 more at-bats. Ruth belted his 714 home runs in only 8,399 at-bats. If Ruth had maintained his home run pace (one every 11.8 at-bats) and come to the plate as many times as Aaron did, he would have hit more than 1,000 homers.

The Babe retired in 1935, and the following year, he was one of the first players elected to the National Baseball Hall of Fame, along with Honus Wagner, Christy Mathewson, Walter Johnson, and Ty Cobb.

Jeter's 3,000 Hits

With one out in the third inning, Derek Jeter came to bat in a game against the Tampa Bay Rays at Yankee Stadium on Saturday, July 9, 2011. Not a single person visited the concession stand or the bathroom. Every spectator was in the ballpark, off their seat, standing on toes, or craning necks for what they hoped would be the best view of history.

Jeter had come into the game needing two hits for 3,000 in his charmed career, which would make him the 28th major league player, and the first as a Yankee, to record 3,000 hits. Flame-throwing left-handed pitcher David Price was on the mound for Tampa. In his first at-bat Jeter worked the count to 3-2 and Price threw a 95-mph fastball that Jeter smacked to left field for hit No. 2,999. The fans roared their approval. They wanted to witness history.

Two innings later, Jeter connected on a full-count curveball, swinging his shiny black bat and sending the ball into the left-field bleachers to reach the 3,000-hit mark in the most thrilling way possible—by hitting a home run. It was magical that on his second hit of the day, in his second at-bat, Jeter—No. 2—reached his historic milestone at 2:00 PM. He is just the second player to do so with a home run, joining Wade Boggs, and it was Jeter's first homer at Yankee Stadium in nearly a year.

His teammates jumped joyously over the dugout railing and poured onto the field. Even the relievers ran in from the bullpen. All of them were waiting to celebrate at home plate as their captain rounded the bases. Raising a fist quickly in the air, Jeter ran head down, suppressing the urge to smile. Jorge Posada was the first to greet Jeter at home plate. Posada was Jeter's best friend on the Yankees, a teammate since they played Class A ball in Greensboro, North Carolina in 1992. The two friends met in an overpowering embrace.

"I told him I was proud of him," said Posada.

Mariano Rivera, the third remaining Yankee from the dynasty teams of the 1990s, was right behind Posada, as was a receiving line of welcoming teammates. The applause and acclaim from the Yankee Stadium crowd of 48,103 lasted about four minutes. Jeter responded to the rousing ovation with a pair of curtain calls, turning to each corner of the stadium to accept the congratulations. Then Jeter tipped his batting helmet to his family in a private box high above the first-base line with his right hand.

"If I would have tried to have written it and given it to someone, I wouldn't have even bought it," said Jeter. "It's just one of those special days."

Yankees captain Derek Jeter notched his franchise-record-breaking 3,000[th] career hit against the Tampa Bay Rays on July 9, 2011.

But Jeter was far from done. He doubled in the fifth inning, singled in the sixth, and drove in the go-ahead run with another single in the eighth, matching a career high by going 5-for-5 as the Yankees beat the Rays 5–4.

"The thing that means the most to me is that I've been able to get all these hits in a Yankee uniform," said Jeter. "No one's been able to do that before, which is hard to believe. I've grown up with these fans. They've seen me since I've been 20 years old."

Jeter recorded 2,914 hits from 1996 to 2010, the most in baseball in that span. He has amassed more hits as a Yankee than Gehrig, Ruth, DiMaggio, and Mantle. As were Gehrig's before him, Jeter's name and reputation are similarly exalted in today's game, and the kid from Kalamazoo who loves his parents and respects the game is sure to be a first-ballot Hall of Famer when his name comes up for election in 2019.

Jeter retired with 3,465 hits, sixth best in Major League Baseball history. He averaged 204 hits a season over a 20-year career. "It's unbelievable what he does," said former manager Joe Girardi. "He's so consistent. He gets 200 hits a year, every year. They're normal Derek Jeter years, but all those normal years add up to greatness."

3 DiMaggio's 56-Game Hit Streak

Of all the legendary Yankees batting records that once seemed unconquerable—Babe Ruth's 714 career home runs and Roger Maris' 61 home runs in a season—only Joe DiMaggio's hitting streak in 1941 has stood the test of time. "Joltin' Joe" hit safely in 56 games in a row. The closest anybody has come to matching DiMaggio's feat is a 44-game hitting streak by Pete Rose in 1978.

DiMaggio began the incredible streak with a single against the Chicago White Sox on May 15, 1941. A DiMaggio base hit was no surprise. Having won batting titles in 1939 and 1940, baseball fans were used to seeing him hit safely. DiMaggio got a hit in the next game, and in the next, and in the game after that. Pretty soon he had strung together a lengthy hitting streak. Over the next two months, he would get at least one base hit in every game in which he played.

Newspapermen covering the Yankees flocked to the center fielder's locker after he set the club record of 29 games in a row on June 16. DiMaggio said he became conscious of the streak when it stretched to 25 straight games on June 10. Amid the hubbub, the unflappable DiMaggio never changed expression, perhaps because of his impressive 61-game hitting streak as an 18-year-old playing for the San Francisco Seals of the Pacific Coast League (a rung beneath the major leagues) in 1933.

"The Yankee Clipper" broke Rogers Hornsby's National League mark of 33 straight games on June 21. The next record to fall was George Sisler's single-season mark of 41 consecutive games with a hit, which DiMaggio passed on June 29 against the Washington Senators. Official scorers admitted to feeling the pressure (they didn't want to end or prolong the streak on a questionable play). The final standing mark was shattered on July 2 when DiMaggio passed Willie Keeler's major league record of 44 games, set in 1897.

DiMaggio's streak reached 50 games on July 11, as he pounded out four hits against the St. Louis Browns. On July 16, he got three hits off two Cleveland pitchers, Al Milnar and Joe Krakauskas, marking game No. 56. The sensational streak finally ended on July 17, 1941, before 67,463 people in Cleveland's Municipal Stadium. Indians left-hander Al Smith retired DiMaggio on two hard smashes to third baseman Ken Keltner, who made two outstanding plays to rob potential hits. DiMaggio walked in his third plate appearance. Coming up for the last time against a knuckleballer, Jim Bagby, with one out and bases loaded, DiMaggio needed a hit to keep the streak going. DiMaggio rapped a Babgy pitch at shortstop Lou Boudreau who threw to start a double play. The streak had ended at 56 games. During that time, DiMaggio had 91 hits and batted .408 with 15 home runs and 55 runs batted in—not a bad *season* for some players.

An undeterred DiMaggio remained hot. He hit safely in the next 16 games, making his streak 72 out of 73 games. He won the Most Valuable Player award that year, beating out Ted Williams in a season in which Williams batted over .400. For the season, DiMaggio batted .357 with 30 homers and a league-leading 125 runs batted in.

The summer of 1941 belonged to Joe DiMaggio, even though baseball was merely a footnote to world events. President Franklin Delano Roosevelt had warned the nation of Hitler's plan to extend his Nazi domination to the western hemisphere. To receive the latest news, people flocked to radios and newspaper stands. Soon the entire nation was also checking DiMaggio's performance in

Listen to Simon and Garfunkel's "Mrs. Robinson"

At his peak, Joe DiMaggio was often saluted in the popular culture. In addition to being serenaded in song as "Joltin' Joe DiMaggio" by Les Brown, he was immortalized in print by Ernest Hemingway in *The Old Man and the Sea* when the main character Santiago says, "I would like to take the great DiMaggio fishing; maybe he was as poor as we are and would understand."

DiMaggio was also mentioned in films and Broadway shows; the sailors in *South Pacific* sing that Bloody Mary's skin is "tender as DiMaggio's glove." Years later, he was remembered in song by Paul Simon, who wondered: "Where have you gone, Joe DiMaggio? Our nation turns its lonely eyes to you. What's that you say, Mrs. Robinson? Joltin' Joe has left and gone away."

The song "Mrs. Robinson," written by Paul Simon and performed by Simon and Garfunkel, won the Grammy Award for Record of the Year in 1969. The reference to DiMaggio is "one of the most well-known lines that I've ever written," said Simon, who grew up a fan of Mickey Mantle. When asked why Mantle isn't mentioned in the song instead of DiMaggio, Simon explained that the number of syllables in DiMaggio's name fit the beat.

For his part, DiMaggio, sensitive to any derogatory public comment that could affect his legacy, was puzzled by Simon's lyric, saying he hadn't gone anywhere, and sought an answer to the meaning of the song when he and Simon were dining at the same New York restaurant. Only when Simon explained his motives to express a feeling that true heroes are a thing of the past, and that the line was meant as a sincere tribute to DiMaggio's grace and dignity, was DiMaggio mollified.

When DiMaggio died in 1999, Simon performed "Mrs. Robinson" at Yankee Stadium in DiMaggio's honor.

the morning papers and getting radio bulletins on every at-bat. DiMaggio was more than a baseball idol. He was a national celebrity. The song called "Joltin' Joe DiMaggio," lyrics by Alan Courtney and performed by Les Brown and His Orchestra, with Betty Bonney on vocals, hit No. 12 on the pop charts in 1941.

Led by DiMaggio, the Yankees won the World Series in 1941. In all, he played on nine World Series champions. He won three MVP awards (1939, 1941, and 1947), and was elected to the Hall of Fame in 1955. DiMaggio was especially a hero in the Italian American community and he remained a beloved national celebrity until his death in 1999 at the age of 84.

4 Maris' 61 Homers in '61

In 1961, Roger Maris began a march on Babe Ruth's season record of 60 home runs, the most famous record in baseball. Maris had a compact, left-handed swing that was perfect for the short right-field porch at Yankee Stadium. As it became apparent that the 27-year-old Maris would challenge Ruth's record, baseball commissioner Ford C. Frick announced that since Ruth's record was set in a 154-game season—and the Yankees in the expansion era of 1961 were playing 162 games—Maris would not be recognized as the one-season home run champion if he hit his 61st homer after the 154-game mark. A home-run record accomplished after the team's 155th game, according to Frick's infamous ruling, would receive second billing to Ruth.

As Maris reached 50 home runs, it looked as though Ruth's record *might* be broken within the 154-game period. By game 130, Maris had 51 homers. At that same point, Ruth had belted out

Roger Maris broke Babe Ruth's single-season home run record in 1961 and had his No. 9 retired by the Yankees in 1984.

49. With 57 homers, Maris was one ahead of Ruth's pace for 150 games. In game 152, he hit his 58th homer. Maris conceded the odds were against him, and the pressure of making a run at one of baseball's most cherished records was so intense that it made his hair fall out in clumps.

Maris hit No. 59 during the 155th game. According to Frick's ruling, Ruth's record still stood. Four games later Maris hit No. 60. On the final day of the season, the Yankees played the Boston Red Sox in Yankee Stadium. There wasn't even a sellout at the Stadium, with only 23,154 fans in attendance. In the fourth inning, on a 2-0 count, Maris connected with a Tracy Stallard fastball and sent it flying over the right-field wall. The new home run king rounded the bases with stoic grace, got a handshake from third-base coach Frank Crosetti, and was convinced by teammates in the dugout to make a reluctant curtain call. "I knew it was gone the minute I hit it," Maris said. "I can't explain how I felt. I don't know what I was thinking as I rounded the bases. My mind was blank."

Maris' 61st home run in '61 was one more than Ruth hit in 1927—though the milestone homer didn't erase Ruth's record. Frick, true to his word, had Maris' accomplishment listed after Ruth's feat in the record books, in effect telling Maris that he was second fiddle to Ruth. No asterisk in the baseball record book noting that Roger Maris set his single-season home run record in 163 games (statistics from one postponed game also counted in 1961) while Babe Ruth reached his in 154 really ever existed—the records were simply listed separately. But the twin listing itself ignited a controversy, implying to some that Maris' record was somehow inferior. The humble man from Fargo, North Dakota, was no folk hero like Ruth, but he deserved credit for his amazing performance. "As a ballplayer, I would be delighted to do it again," he said. "As an individual, I doubt if I could possibly go through it again."

In all, Maris hit 275 homers in a 12-season career from 1957 to 1968. In 1961, he led the American League in runs (132), runs batted in (141), and, of course, home runs (61), and was the American League's Most Valuable Player for a second straight season, a testament to his all-around ability.

"Roger Maris was the best all-around baseball player I ever saw," said Mantle. "Roger was a great fielder, he had a great arm, he was a great base runner, he was always mentally in the game, and he never made a mistake throwing too high or to the wrong base. Roger was as good as there ever was."

Maris hit 33 homers the year after his record-breaking season, and though he never topped 26 again, he was a winner. No one in the 1960s appeared in more World Series than Maris, who played in seven that decade. Five came with the Yankees; the last two in 1967 and '68 came with the Cardinals.

No matter how it was cataloged in the record book, fans have always recognized Maris as the true record-holder, the first player in major league history to hit more than 60 homers in a regular season. In 1991, baseball commissioner Fay Vincent made it official, announcing that a MLB committee on statistical accuracy had voted to remove the distinction, giving the record fully to Maris. Sadly, he did not live to see the change, having died of cancer in Houston at age 51 in 1985.

Maris held the single-season home run record for 37 years—longer than Ruth had held it—until Mark McGwire of the St. Louis Cardinals surpassed the mark with 70 homers in 1998. His record was subsequently broken when the San Francisco Giants' Barry Bonds hit 73 home runs in 2001.

5 Reggie Becomes Mr. October

When Reggie Jackson arrived in New York for the 1977 season, he instantly made friends with Yankees fans who had been starving for a winner since 1964. But Jackson wasn't liked by all of his teammates. Years before he arrived in New York, Jackson boasted that if he were ever to play in the intense media glare of that city, he would end up with a candy bar named after him. He did.

"I didn't come to New York to be a star," Reggie once said. "I brought my star with me."

The tempestuous Jackson combined with fiery manager Billy Martin and other stubborn and egotistical personalities in the Yankees organization to form a volatile mix that threatened to undermine the team's fortunes. The clubhouse was dubbed "The Bronx Zoo" because of the constant bickering among Jackson, Martin, catcher Thurman Munson, owner George Steinbrenner, and others. In the end, though, the team fed off the atmosphere to win its first World Series in 15 years.

Eat a Reggie! Bar

Reggie Jackson famously boasted that if he ever played in New York, they'd name a candy bar after him. Sure enough, after his memorable performance in the 1977 World Series, he got his wish. Manufactured by Standard Brands Confectionary, the Reggie! candy bar was a round, 25-cent patty of chocolate-covered caramel and peanuts. Cracked teammate Catfish Hunter, "When you unwrap a Reggie! bar, it tells you how good it is."

Prior to the 1978 Yankees home opener, Standard Brands handed out free Reggie! bars as a sales promotion gimmick to the 44,667 fans who passed through the turnstiles. The home opener also marked the day that Roger Maris ended his 12-year exile by returning to the Bronx. In a pregame ceremony, Maris and Mickey Mantle raised the team's first world championship flag in 15 years.

In the game's first inning, Jackson, who had homered on his last three swings of the 1977 World Series at Yankee Stadium, connected again on his first cut of the home season, smashing a three-run homer off Chicago's Wilbur Wood in the Yankees' 4–2 win over the White Sox.

When Reggie took his position in right field to start the second inning, the fans threw thousands of Reggie! bars onto the field in tribute. The game was delayed about five minutes while groundskeepers gathered the candy.

New York, which had won 100 games during the regular season to edge the Baltimore Orioles and Boston Red Sox by 2.5 games in the American League's Eastern Division, outlasted the Kansas City Royals in a taut ALCS. The Yankees scored three runs in the ninth inning of the fifth and final game to win 5–3 and wrest the pennant from the Royals' clutches.

Jackson struggled against Kansas City's pitching in the ALCS, but he made the World Series against the Los Angeles Dodgers his personal stage, on which he batted .450 with five home runs and eight runs batted in. The Yankees won in six games, and Jackson's performance in the finale—when he blasted three home runs—was one of the most memorable in World Series history.

Reggie Jackson was a star both on and off the field after signing with the Yankees as a free agent in 1977.

Jackson's reputation as a star in the postseason earned him the nickname "Mr. October," and his dramatic play in Game 6 of the 1977 World Series was a signature performance. After receiving a base on balls in his first plate appearance that night against the Dodgers, Jackson belted a two-run home run off Los Angeles staring pitcher Burt Hooton in the fourth inning to put the Yankees ahead for good. The next inning, he slugged another two-run homer off reliever Elias Sosa that left the park in the blink of an eye. "I overwhelmed that baseball by the sheer force of my will," said Jackson.

Then, in the eighth, with the Yankees' title well in hand, he punctuated the night with a solo home run off Charlie Hough that landed deep into the far-away center-field bleachers. The beauty of Jackson's performance was that he blasted each of his three home runs on the first pitch against three different pitchers.

"I must admit," said Dodgers first baseman Steve Garvey, "when Reggie hit his third home run and I was sure nobody was looking, I applauded in my glove."

As Jackson crossed home plate, the 56,407 exuberant hometown fans paid tribute to one of the greatest individual performances in baseball history by screaming, "Reg-gie, Reg-gie," until their hero popped out of the dugout for a curtain call, nodding to the appreciative crowd. He became the first player since Babe Ruth to hit three homers in a Series game. His five homers in the Series, including four in a row, were also a record.

It was no surprise that Jackson was such a World Series star; he thrived in the spotlight. For his career, Jackson batted .357 with 10 home runs in 98 World Series at-bats. He was the World Series MVP in 1973 (while with the Oakland Athletics) and 1977, set a career record for slugging percentage (.755), and played on five championship teams.

Jackson was an all-or-nothing showman who belted 563 career home runs, but also struck out an incredible 2,597 times, the most in major league history. He helped carry 10 teams to the playoffs in a 12-year span from 1971 to 1982, but he also put off teammates and fans with his bragging.

When Jackson signed a $3 million contract with the Yankees in 1977, he became baseball's highest-paid player and proclaimed himself "the straw that stirs the drink" in New York. He quickly alienated established Yankees stars with the remark. Eventually, though, he may have proved himself right.

6 Larsen's World Series Perfection

Not every great pitching accomplishment in baseball is the work of a superstar like Whitey Ford or Roger Clemens. In fact, the most remarkable pitching feat in baseball history was achieved by a man who will be remembered for what he did in a single game. The classic pitching performance occurred in the 1956 World Series between the New York Yankees and the Brooklyn Dodgers.

In Don Larsen's first World Series appearance, in 1955, the Dodgers beat him up, scoring five times in his four innings of work. In 1956, the 27-year-old right-hander had a good regular season, going 11–5 despite battling control issues. Starting Game 2 of the Series, he was staked to a 6–0 lead after an inning and a half. But after an infield error and a couple of walks, he was gone. The Yankees relievers didn't stem the tide and Larsen's log after 1⅔ innings was four runs allowed. Brooklyn won 13–8.

Yankees manager Casey Stengel later admitted his second-inning hook of Larsen might have been too hasty. "However," said Stengel, "it might also help to get him really on his toes the next time he starts."

Three days later, Larsen had pinpoint control, going to three balls on just one hitter. In the early innings, few Dodgers even came close to reaching base. By the middle of the ballgame, the Yankee Stadium crowd of 64,519 fans woke up to the fact that Larsen might pitch a perfect game. The tension mounted as the game rolled on.

"In the seventh inning I noticed no one on the bench was talking to me," said Larsen.

The tension reached its peak in the ninth inning. Carl Furillo was the first hitter Larsen faced. He was out on an easy fly ball. Roy Campanella, the next hitter, grounded out. The crowd hushed as it was now obvious that all that stood between Larsen and a history-making game was the pinch hitter, a left-handed batter named Dale Mitchell.

"Ball one!" was the call on the first pitch.

Larsen rocked forward on the mound. His arm flashed downward.

"Stee-rike!"

Larsen kicked and fired again. Mitchell lashed at the ball and missed. It was strike two. Mitchell swung at the next pitch. This time he connected. The ball went foul.

The umpire threw a new ball into play. Larsen rubbed the slickness from the cover. He glanced around the diamond, took a deep breath, and stepped on the rubber.

Then Larsen's 97th pitch, a fastball on the outside corner, was called strike three by umpire Babe Pinelli, sending catcher Yogi Berra jumping into Larsen's arms to celebrate the only perfect game in World Series history.

"It never happened before, and it still hasn't happened since," said Berra.

Of course, Larsen had plenty of support, including a one-handed running catch by the fleet Mickey Mantle in center. A hard liner by Jackie Robinson off the hands of third baseman Andy Carey was alertly snapped up by shortstop Gil McDougald and turned into an out. Larsen also struck out seven batters in the 2–0 victory.

The Yankees went on to win the Series in seven games, thanks to a journeyman pitcher who had triumphed at a time when the Yankees needed it most with one of the most spectacular achievements in baseball history. Indeed, the Series will forever belong to an imperfect man who pitched a perfect game.

"It can't be true," he said after the game. "Any minute now I expect the alarm clock to ring and someone to say, 'Okay, Larsen, it's time to get up.'"

His career lasted 11 more seasons with six different teams. He never again approached the glory of October 8, 1956. But who could?

7 Ironman Lou Gehrig

Lou Gehrig became known as "The Iron Horse" for setting a record of playing in the most consecutive games. The streak began on June 1, 1925, when Gehrig came into a game as a pinch hitter. The next day, regular first baseman Wally Pipp sat out a game with a headache and Gehrig started in his place. Gehrig did not leave the Yankees starting lineup for the next 14 years. The Yankees captain played in 2,130 consecutive games. The record stood until 1995, when Cal Ripken Jr. played in his 2,131st straight game for the Baltimore Orioles.

Gehrig himself ended the streak on May 2, 1939, when he told his manager Joe McCarthy not to play him in Detroit because he was tired. Gehrig would never play again. Gehrig had taken himself out of the lineup "for the good of the team." The Yankees first baseman knew that something was wrong. A lifetime .340 hitter, Gehrig had slumped to .295 in 1938 and was batting a miserable .143 through the 1939 season's first eight games. After a teammate applauded him for making a simple put-out at first base, Gehrig knew it was time to sit down. "When guys start feeling sorry for you…" he said.

Recite Gehrig's Farewell Speech

There are those who believe Lou Gehrig knew he was dying as he spoke at Yankee Stadium on that memorable day. If this is true, his brief speech points out the selflessness and bravery of the man. He said simply:

"Fans, for the past two weeks you have been reading about the bad break I got. Yet today I consider myself the luckiest man on the face of this earth. I have been in ballparks for 17 years and have never received anything but kindness and encouragement from you fans.

"Look at these grand men. Which of you wouldn't consider it the highlight of his career just to associate with them for even one day? Sure, I'm lucky. Who wouldn't consider it an honor to have known Jacob Ruppert? Also, the builder of baseball's greatest empire, Ed Barrow? To have spent six years with that wonderful little fellow, Miller Huggins? Then to have spent the next nine years with that outstanding leader, that smart student of psychology, the best manager in baseball today, Joe McCarthy? Sure, I'm lucky.

"When the New York Giants, a team you would give your right arm to beat, and vice versa, sends you a gift—that's something. When everybody down to the groundskeepers and those boys in white coats remember you with trophies—that's something. When you have a wonderful mother-in-law who takes sides with you in squabbles with her own daughter—that's something. When you have a father and a mother who work all their lives so you can have an education and build your body—it's a blessing. When you have a wife who has been a tower of strength and shown more courage than you dreamed existed—that's the finest I know.

"So I close in saying that I may have had a tough break, but I have an awful lot to live for."

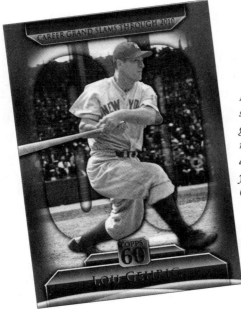

Lou Gehrig's incredible streak of 2,130 consecutive games played was one of the most hallowed records in all of sports. It lasted for 56 years until it was broken by Cal Ripken Jr. in 1995.

Two months later, he was diagnosed with amyotrophic lateral sclerosis (ALS), an incurable neurological disease. It underlines Gehrig's stature, not only in baseball but also in the national spotlight, that ALS would come to be known as Lou Gehrig's Disease.

To express their admiration, the Yankees designated the doubleheader against the Washington Senators on July 4, 1939, as "Lou Gehrig Appreciation Day." Gehrig's teammates, past and present, including Babe Ruth and all the members of the superb 1927 team, as well as 61,808 fans, came to honor the man they called "The Pride of the Yankees."

The tribute between games of the doubleheader lasted for more than 40 minutes. There were speeches by Mayor Fiorello La Guardia and Postmaster James A. Farley. Then manager Joe McCarthy spoke to Gehrig: "Lou, what can I say except that it was a sad day in the life of everybody who knew you when you came to my hotel room that day in Detroit and told me you were quitting as a ballplayer because you felt yourself a hindrance to the team. My god, man, you were never that."

It was as if Gehrig, in the words of sports columnist Paul Gallico, was "present at his own funeral." Each of the many dignitaries on the field spoke in glowing terms of their stricken former teammate. Gehrig, never one to seek the spotlight, stood with his head bowed, hands placed deep into the rear pockets of his uniform pants, scratching at the turf with his spikes.

After being showered with gifts and praise, it was finally Gehrig's turn to speak. The crowd chanted, "We want Lou! We want Lou!" He was so shaken with emotion that at first it appeared he would not be able to talk at all. The Yankee Stadium crowd, sitting in absolute silence, watched as the Iron Horse, obviously sick and walking with a slight hitch in his gait, approached the microphone. Although he probably knew he was dying, Gehrig said he considered himself a lucky man with a lot to live for. When he finished speaking, Ruth threw his arms around the big first baseman and hugged him. Gehrig's sincere, humbled words and Ruth's impulsive show of affection brought tears to many pairs of eyes.

At season's end the Yankees retired Gehrig's No. 4, making his the first retired number in baseball. (Since then, more than 120 numbers have been retired.) To this day Gehrig is the only Yankees player ever to wear the number. The Hall of Fame, whose building opened earlier the same year in Cooperstown, New York, waived its five-year eligibility requirement for Gehrig and voted him into the Hall of Fame immediately. He died two years later, on June 2, 1941, at his home in the Riverdale section of the Bronx. He was just 37 years old.

8 Dent's Monster Moment

The Yankees' light-hitting shortstop Bucky Dent lifted a seventh-inning fly ball over the left-field wall at Boston's Fenway Park for a three-run homer, propelling the Yankees to a tension-filled 5–4 victory over the Red Sox in a one-game playoff that decided the 1978 American League East Division championship.

The victory capped the Yankees' amazing comeback from a 14-game July deficit and earned them a chance to play Kansas City for the AL pennant. The playoff became necessary when Boston won its final regular season game and the Yankees lost to Cleveland.

The Red Sox broke out to a 2–0 lead against 24-game winner Ron Guidry on Carl Yastrzemski's second-inning home run and Jim Rice's sixth-inning RBI single. The Yankees could manage only two hits through six innings off Boston starter Mike Torrez, a Yankees free agent defector. But Chris Chambliss and Roy White singled in the seventh. That brought up Dent, a .243 hitter who was allowed to bat only because the Yankees were short on extra infielders and could not pinch-hit.

Before his home run, Dent painfully fouled a ball off his foot. As he grimaced and hopped around in obvious pain, the trainer came out to take a look. With time out, Mickey Rivers, the on-deck batter, noticed that Dent was using a cracked bat. Rivers handed his bat to a batboy. "Give this to Bucky," said Rivers. "Tell him there are lots of hits in it. He'll get a home run."

Dent switched to the new bat despite being in the middle of an at-bat. Then it all happened. On the next pitch, Dent lifted a fly ball that seemed like a harmless pop-up to left field. Torrez swears he thought it was an easy out, just like most everyone else did. But the ball got a boost from the wind and settled onto the screen atop

Fenway's Green Monster. It was a crushing blow; Dent had hit only four other homers all year. A double by Thurman Munson that scored Mickey Rivers provided another seventh-inning run for the Yankees, this one off Bob Stanley, who had replaced Torrez.

Guidry, pitching on two days' rest, didn't overwhelm the Red Sox, but he pitched well enough for the Yankees to have a 4–2 lead when he departed during the seventh inning. To preserve the lead, the Yankees called on relief ace Rich "Goose" Gossage. Soon he had a 5–2 lead on Reggie Jackson's decisive homer into the center-field bleachers in the eighth. "It was a fastball right over the plate," said Jackson, who detoured on his way back to the dugout to shake hands with Yankees owner George Steinbrenner.

The Red Sox rallied for two eighth-inning runs off Gossage to narrow the lead to 5–4 going into the ninth. With one out, Rick Burleson walked and Jerry Remy singled. Lou Piniella lost Remy's low liner in the glare of the late-afternoon sun, but the right fielder stabbed the ball with his glove, holding Burleson, the tying run, at second. To protect the lead, Gossage now had to face Jim Rice— who would be chosen the league's MVP because of his 46 homers and 139 runs batted in—and Carl Yastrzemski, the Red Sox future Hall of Famer.

"I wasn't worried out there," said Gossage, who earned his 27th save of the season. "If I got beaten I was going to lose on my own effort."

Rearing back, Gossage fired his fastball. Rice lifted a soft fly to Piniella, and then Yaz popped a high foul that Graig Nettles caught near third base to end the game.

"We've come back from bigger deficits," said Nettles. "It was nothing to worry about. The best part was that we did it against Torrez. He's been bad-mouthing us all season, ever since he left the Yanks."

As for Dent, he was not worried about his injured foot. "A little ice and champagne will fix that," he said smiling.

The Yankees went on to defeat the Kansas City Royals in four games in the ALCS. They won the World Series in six games over the Los Angeles Dodgers after losing the first two games. Dent, who continued his surprising offensive production by batting .417 with seven runs batted in, was named the World Series MVP.

Chambliss Delivers the 1976 Pennant

The remodeled Yankee Stadium was unveiled in 1976, and just as they had in 1923, the New York Yankees opened their new stadium in grand style by reaching the World Series. New York first baseman Chris Chambliss sent the hometown fans into a frenzy with a dramatic home run in the bottom of the ninth inning against the Kansas City Royals in the decisive Game 5 of the American League Championship Series to deliver a pennant to the Bronx for the first time since 1964.

The 1976 Yankees acted like the Yankees of old, winning 97 games to run away with the AL East Division title by a 10-game cushion. The Yankees were four seasons into the ownership reign of George Steinbrenner and in the first full season with former Yankees second baseman and World Series hero Billy Martin as manager. "The Yankees belonged in the World Series," Martin said. "That's the way it was when I played with the Yankees and that's the way I want it to be as I manage the Yankees."

The Yankees and Royals were tied at two games apiece and the score was knotted at 6–6 in the decisive game when Chambliss stepped in to face Kansas City reliever Mark Littell to open the home half of the ninth. Chambliss smashed Littell's first pitch over the right-field wall, touching off a wild celebration at Yankee

Chris Chambliss' game-winning home run in Game 5 of the 1976 ALCS inspired Yankees fans to rush the field while the first baseman was still circling the bases.

Stadium. New York fans had grown accustomed to seeing their Yankees win pennants almost at will over the years. But New York's 11-season drought from 1965 to 1975 was its longest since winning its first American League title in 1921. And so, when Chambliss' blast landed in the right-field bleachers, it triggered a mad rush as thousands of joyous fans poured onto the field in celebration to mob their new hero as he circled the bases. Chambliss, in fact, was knocked to the ground by overzealous fans between second and third base. "I was in the middle of a mass of people, and when I fell to the ground, it was scary," he said. Chambliss was escorted off the field and into the clubhouse, then returned later to touch home plate.

Despite Chambliss' heroics, the world championship trophy remained in Cincinnati for another season. The defending champion Reds had little trouble dispatching the Yankees in four games in the World Series. Cincinnati second baseman Joe Morgan homered in the bottom of the first inning of Game 1, and the Reds never looked back, steamrolling to 5–1, 4–3, 6–2, and 7–2 victories. Game 2 at Cincinnati's Riverfront Stadium psychologically deflated the Yanks. On the mound was their ace pitcher, Jim "Catfish" Hunter, with the score tied 3–3 going into the bottom of the ninth inning. With two outs and nobody on, speedy Ken Griffey Sr. bounced a ground ball to Yankees shortstop Fred Stanley, who threw wildly for a two-base error. Following an intentional walk, Cincinnati first baseman Tony Perez lined Hunter's first pitch into left field for the game-winning hit.

Reds designated hitter Dan Driessen—this was the first World Series to allow the new rule—went 3-for-3 with a home run and a double in Game 3 at Yankee Stadium. Following the 6–2 defeat, Billy Martin vowed the Yankees would win the next four in a row. The Yankees led only once in the Series, when they took a 1–0 lead in the first inning of the fourth, and final, game. Cincinnati erased that deficit and went on to win 7–2 to complete the sweep.

"This won't happen again," said Martin. "We'll be a better team next year."

Reds catcher Johnny Bench was the star of the World Series, batting .533 with two home runs and six runs batted in. The one real bright spot for the Yankees was catcher Thurman Munson, who hit .529 with a Series-best nine hits, including hits in his last six at-bats. Jim Mason, a defensive replacement in Game 3 for the Yankees, hit a home run, becoming the first player to homer in his only Series at-bat.

10 Count the Rings at the Yogi Berra Museum

For pure staying power, no dynasty compares to the New York Yankees' version of 1949 to 1964. Those Yankees won nine World Series in 14 tries over 16 seasons, including a record five straight championships from 1949 to 1953. The constant of that era was their catcher, Yogi Berra. So integral was Berra to the Yankees' fortunes that he was voted the American League's MVP three times (1951, 1954, and 1955) over a five-year span in a league that boasted such future Hall of Fame stars as Mickey Mantle, Ted Williams, and Al Kaline. Even more impressive, from 1950 to 1956, Berra never finished lower than fourth in the MVP voting.

Bridging the team's transition from Joe DiMaggio to Mantle, Berra was a member of all 14 pennant winners during that prodigious stretch. He is the only player in history to play on 10 World Series championship teams. He holds World Series records for at-bats (259), games (75), hits (71), and doubles (10). He played 19 years in the majors and was selected to the All-Star Game 15 consecutive years. When he retired, his 313 career home runs as a catcher (358 overall) stood as the record for catchers until Johnny Bench, Carlton Fisk, and then Mike Piazza broke it. He was elected to the Hall of Fame in 1972 and was chosen to baseball's All-Century Team for the 1900s.

Lawrence Peter Berra grew up in an Italian section of St. Louis called "The Hill." He got his nickname as a kid after his friends saw an Indian actor in a movie who reminded them of Berra. From that point on, Larry was Yogi (a Hindu word for teacher). Berra began his career in the Yankees farm system in 1943. He served in the U.S. Navy during World War II from 1944 to 1946, then joined the Yankees' top minor league team in Newark, New Jersey, where

Lawrence Peter "Yogi" Berra is the only man in baseball history to have played on 10 World Series championship teams.

Mel Ott, the New York Giants manager, saw him play. "He seemed to be doing everything wrong, yet everything came out right," said Ott. "He stopped everything behind the plate and hit everything in front of it."

When Berra joined the Yankees in 1946 he was a backup player, sharing the catching duties and occasionally playing left field. In Yankee Stadium, left field is notorious for its late-afternoon shadows. "It gets late early out there," he once said.

Berra was squat and clumsy when he joined the Yankees. One writer said he looked like "the bottom man on an unemployed acrobatic team." Some teammates dubbed him "The Ape" and mocked him by hanging from the dugout roof by one arm. But manager Casey Stengel believed in Berra from the start. Berra knew how to call a game, and Stengel called him "my assistant manager." Yankees catcher Bill Dickey had just finished his Hall of Fame career, and he took the young Berra on as a student. Dickey was a great teacher, showing Berra the basics of catching, and Berra proved to be an excellent pupil. "Bill is teaching me all his experience," said Yogi.

In 1949, Berra became the Yankees' full-time starting catcher, a job he would hold for 10 years. Behind the plate Berra was one of the top defensive catchers in the game and a great handler of pitchers. The jug-eared catcher who was built like a fire plug had cat-like quickness. "He springs on a bunt like it was another dollar," said Stengel. Berra led the league in games caught eight times, led in turning double plays six times, and went the entire 1958 season

Yogi-isms

Yogi Berra is known to many people as the inventor of "Yogi-isms," Berra's own brand of rearranging the English language and warping logic. It's ironic that the master of Yogi-isms was managed for most of his Yankees career by baseball's other great reinventor of the English language, the originator of "Stengelese," Casey Stengel. Here is a list of some of Berra's most famous Yogi-isms:

- "If you can't imitate him, don't copy him."
- "I knew I was going to take the wrong train, so I left early."
- "I want to thank you for making this day necessary."
- "Baseball is 90 percent mental. The other half is physical."
- "You can observe a lot by watching."
- "A nickel ain't worth a dime anymore."
- "If the world were perfect, it wouldn't be."
- "It's déjà vu all over again."
- "Nobody goes to that restaurant anymore; it's too crowded."
- "Slump? I ain't in no slump. I just ain't hitting."
- "I made a wrong mistake."
- "If you come to a fork in the road...take it."
- "In baseball, you don't know nothing."
- "You should always go to other people's funerals; otherwise, they won't come to yours."
- "It ain't the heat; it's the humility."
- "If the fans don't come out to the ballpark, you can't stop them."
- "I always thought that record would stand until it was broken."
- "I really didn't say everything I said."

without an error behind the plate. He called two no-hitters thrown by Allie Reynolds in 1951 and caught Don Larsen's perfect game in the 1956 World Series.

Playing for the Yankees, Berra had the opportunity to show his talents year after year in the World Series. Berra's great catching played a big part in the team's success, and so did his solid bat. He was one of the great clutch hitters of his day, "the toughest man in baseball in the last three innings," said Paul Richards, who managed the Orioles and White Sox during the 1950s. Berra was an amazing bad-ball hitter. Berra was skilled at reaching for balls out of the strike zone and hitting them out of the park. Yet for all his aggressiveness at the plate, he rarely struck out—only 414 times in 7,555 at-bats. In 1950 he fanned only 12 times in 597 at-bats. During that 1950 season, though not one of his MVP seasons, he hit a career-best .322 with 28 homers and 124 runs batted in. Berra drove in at least 90 runs nine times during his career.

By the late 1950s, with the emergence of Elston Howard at catcher, Berra had moved to left field to save his legs. From there, he helped the Yankees win two more World Series in 1961 and 1962—bringing Yogi's record total to 10 World Series rings won as a player. You can count those rings on display at the Yogi Berra Museum and Learning Center, in Little Falls, New Jersey.

11 Play Air Guitar to "Enter Sandman"

A flicker of anticipation ran through the grandstand as an excited crowd of 43,201 inched forward in their seats. The Yankees were holding on to a four-run lead against the Toronto Blue Jays at Yankee Stadium on May 25, 2011. The game moved to the top of the ninth inning with the home team just three outs away from a victory—the three toughest outs in baseball to record. Entering the game was Mariano Rivera, a reedy right-handed relief pitcher from Panama with a steely focus and a sense of mental calm so great he could sleep through a hurricane.

If there is one relief pitcher in the last decade who might personify the word *closer*, a stadium full of baseball experts would pick Rivera. Few, if any, relief pitchers enjoy the immensely positive reputation for finality that Rivera has earned with the Yankees. As team captain Derek Jeter said, "When he comes in the game, the mind-set is, it's over."

The game against the Blue Jays was a typical appearance. The 41-year-old reliever faced four batters, got three outs, and threw just 12 pitches, 10 for strikes. But it was not a typical appearance; it was special, for Rivera became the first pitcher in MLB history to have appeared in 1,000 games for one team (and the 15th to reach the plateau overall).

"It's a blessing to be able to be on the same team and do that. It's not too often you see that. But the most important thing is that we won," Rivera said after retiring the side in the ninth inning of the Yankees' 7–3 win over Toronto.

The vision of Rivera bursting through the bullpen door is enough to give even the most malevolent opposing hitters serious pause. With the Yankee Stadium sound system blaring Metallica's "Enter Sandman," and the fans raucously cheering in anticipation, he jogs across the outfield grass, strides gracefully to the mound, fires seven or eight warm-up pitches, stares blankly at his target with shark-like eyes, and then gets down to serious business.

"The song starts playing, the game's over," said former teammate Jason Giambi.

Despite the perilous situation and the swelling crowd noise, whether for him or against him, whenever Rivera arrives for his rescue act, he resists the pressure simply by ignoring it. Occasionally

A beloved member of the Yankees' "Core Four," Mariano Rivera has saved a whopping 42 postseason games with a miniscule 0.70 earned-run average.

he isn't even aware of the identity of the man swinging the bat at home plate. In former manager Joe Torre's opinion, he has the ideal temperament for a closer.

"He's the best I've ever been around. Not only the ability to pitch and perform under pressure, but the calm he puts over the clubhouse," Torre said.

Rivera doesn't quarrel with that view.

"I don't get nervous. I trust God. If I get nervous, I can't do my job," he said.

More than anyone else, it was Rivera doing his job that propelled the Yankees to World Series championships five times, as he was on the mound to record the final out in four clinching games in 1998, 1999, 2000, and 2009. October after October, the 6'2", 185-pounder held precarious leads the Yankees had scratched together. He literally attacked rival hitters with one pitch: an unsolvable cut fastball that has been called a combination of thunder and location.

Rivera's impact is hard to understate. His lifetime postseason earned-run average of 0.70 is the major league record. During the Yankees' memorable 1998 season, Rivera did not give up a run in the postseason. He did the same again in 1999, when he was named the World Series MVP. More impressive still, his record 42 postseason saves, including 11 in the World Series, are 24 more than his next-closest competitor, Brad Lidge (18), which explains why Rivera's teammates act as if they are about to inherit the family trust fund.

"Our whole game plan [was] to get a lead and give the ball to him in the ninth inning," said ex-teammate Paul O'Neill.

Rivera became the king of all closers after passing Trevor Hoffman with a record-setting 602nd save by pitching a perfect ninth inning in a 6–4 win over the Minnesota Twins at Yankee Stadium on September 19, 2011. After he had been mobbed by his teammates, his longtime catcher Jorge Posada pushed Rivera back out to the mound so the crowd could salute him one more time. Asked to describe that moment, Rivera said, "Oh, my god. For the first time in my career, I'm on the mound alone. There's no one behind me, no one in front of me. I can't describe that feeling because it was priceless."

Final inventory figures for his career will show that all other relief pitchers will be shooting at his mark of 652 career saves for a long time to come. But Mariano Rivera's contributions go beyond mere numbers, impressive as the numbers happen to be. It's the form as well as the substance that makes Rivera a star in the grand old Yankees tradition: humble, gracious, poised, and commanding. The fact that he's also a spiritual and faithful man makes him all the more valuable as an inspiration to his teammates and his opponents.

"On the field and off the field, he's a Hall of Famer," said opposing manager Ozzie Guillen. "Young people should look up to him. He's the perfect player. God bless Mariano."

To Yankees fans, Guillen is preaching to the choir.

12 Mickey Mantle

Few players in the history of baseball had as much talent as Mickey Mantle. The blond, broad-shouldered switch-hitter from Commerce, Oklahoma, could blast the ball for tremendous distances from either side of the plate. He also had a fine throwing arm and great speed—he could run from home to first base in 3.1 seconds. Mantle's natural talent once prompted his manager, Casey Stengel, to say of the slugging center fielder, "He should lead the league in everything."

In 1956, he did. That season, Mantle won the MVP award and became the only switch-hitter to win the batting Triple Crown—leading the league in batting average, home runs, and runs batted in. He hit .353 to Ted Williams' .345 for the Red Sox; his 52 homers were far ahead of Vic Wertz's 32 for the Indians; and his 130 RBIs topped Al Kaline's 128 for the Tigers. He also led the league in runs scored (132), total bases (376), slugging percentage (.705), extra-base hits (79), and most times reaching base safely (302). Then he capped off his great season with three homers in the 1956 World Series, won by the Yankees over the Brooklyn Dodgers in seven games. Mantle was just 24 years old.

Mantle continued his offensive prowess in 1957 and repeated as the league's MVP, batting a career-high .365, with 34 homers and 94 RBIs. In 1961, he battled teammate Roger Maris (they were known as "the M&M Boys") not only for the AL home run crown but also for a shot at Babe Ruth's single-season home run record of 60. Mantle started off red-hot, but by the middle of the summer, Maris had pulled ahead after hitting 24 homers in a 38-game span. In the middle of September, injuries forced Mantle to drop out of the race with 54 homers. Maris went on to hit 61.

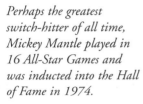

Perhaps the greatest switch-hitter of all time, Mickey Mantle played in 16 All-Star Games and was inducted into the Hall of Fame in 1974.

"The Mick" played his first major league game when he was 19 years old. He played for 18 seasons beginning in 1951, when he was a rookie for the Yankees' World Series champs. He suffered a serious knee injury in the outfield during Game 2 of the Series against the New York Giants that year. The injury robbed him of much of his speed and troubled him throughout the rest of his career. As teammate Jerry Coleman said, The Mick had "the body of a god. Only Mantle's legs were mortal." Still, he managed to belt 536 career home runs—the most ever by a switch-hitter.

Despite an injury-riddled career, Mantle put up impressive numbers. He played in 16 All-Star Games, led the league in home runs four times, and hit .300 or better 10 times. He was a three-time American League MVP and finished in the top five another six times. He played on 12 pennant winners and seven world championship teams. He holds World Series records for home runs (18), runs scored (42), RBIs (40), walks (43), extra-base hits (26), and total bases (123). "He is the best one-legged player I ever saw play the game," said Stengel.

In his final World Series, the 1964 Fall Classic against the St. Louis Cardinals, Mantle hit three round trippers, drove in eight runs, and batted .333. That season marked the end of the lengthy Yankees dynasty that had started in the 1920s with Babe Ruth and peaked in the years from 1949 to 1964. Mantle's fortunes sank along with those of his team. By 1968 he could no longer take the pain of playing every day, and his numbers reflected it. At 37, he had undergone seven surgeries in his career. On the eve of the 1969 season, Mantle decided that he did not want to sign a contract and retired.

The team and fans paid tribute to the last great superstar of the Yankees dynasty by retiring his uniform jersey No. 7 at a Mickey Mantle Day ceremony at Yankee Stadium on June 8, 1969. In his speech, Mantle spoke of the Yankees' tradition. "To retire my number with Nos. 3, 4, and 5 tops off everything," he said. "I often wondered how a man who knew he was dying could get up here and say he's the luckiest man in the world. Now I think I know how Lou Gehrig felt."

Mantle was elected to the Hall of Fame in 1974. As the first baseball star Yankees fans could watch on television, he remains a fan favorite and is still one of baseball's most popular superstars even 50 years after playing his last game. Early in 1995 he was diagnosed with liver cancer, brought on by his years of hard drinking. He had a liver transplant but died in August of that year at age 63.

13 Dynasty Years 1949 to 1953: Five in a Row

In 1949, rookie manager Casey Stengel's Yankees clung to the heels of the hot Boston Red Sox despite a long series of injuries to key players. Star center fielder Joe DiMaggio, who had a sore heel, didn't play his first game until June 28. Juggling the lineup to keep his players fresh, Stengel somehow kept the team in the thick of the pennant race. On the last weekend of the season, the Red Sox were set to play two games against the Yankees. If the Yanks could win both games they would take the flag. Boston's Ted Williams was having another great year. The Sox's two best pitchers, Ellis Kinder and Mel Parnell, were rested and ready for the Yanks. But the Yankees upset all the odds. They won the two games and the pennant. Afterward, a humble Stengel said, "I couldn't have done it without my players."

The first two games of the Yankees-Dodgers World Series were as tight as the pennant race. The Yankees won the opener 1–0 on a homer by Tommy "Old Reliable" Henrich. The Dodgers won the second game by the same score on a double by Jackie Robinson and a single by Gil Hodges. But the Yankees won the next three games to give Casey Stengel his first World Series championship. It was just a hint of things to come.

In 1950, with DiMaggio and shortstop Phil Rizzuto having great years at the plate, and pitcher Vic Raschi's 21 wins second in the league, the Yankees again took first place, this time fighting off Detroit. As for the World Series, the Yankees swept the Philadelphia Phillies, known as the "Whiz Kids," in four straight games for their second consecutive world title. When asked about his theory of managing, Stengel said, "The secret of managing is to keep the five guys who hate you away from the five who are undecided."

Cleveland was the main threat to the Yankees in 1951, as fire-balling right-hander Bob Feller proved to be the best pitcher in the league and one of three pitchers to win 20 or more games for the Indians. The Yankees had two 21-game winners in Vic Raschi and Eddie Lopat. Allie Reynolds also pitched two no-hitters. But the team's hitting was very weak. Only one player—Gil McDougald, a rookie infielder—hit over .300. Yogi Berra, however, had 88 runs batted in to lead the team. The Yanks suffered a severe blow when DiMaggio was injured toward the end of the year. To replace him, Stengel daringly dipped into the Yankees farm system and called on a converted shortstop named Mickey Mantle. Overcoming all their shortcomings, the Yankees finished five games ahead of Cleveland. The World Series against the Giants went to six games, but the results were the same as in the previous two years—another Yankees triumph in the Fall Classic.

When DiMaggio retired prior to the 1952 season, Stengel reshaped the team around catcher Yogi Berra, pitcher Whitey Ford, and Stengel's special protégé, Mickey Mantle. As the season got under way, fans and sportswriters realized that Stengel and the Yankees had a chance to equal a record by winning four World Series in a row. This had only been accomplished by Joe McCarthy's 1936–39 Yankees. To take the pennant in 1952, the Yanks had to fight off Cleveland's powerful pitching staff of three 20-game winners—Early Wynn, Bob Lemon, and Mike Garcia. But the Yankees did win the pennant, even though Mantle and outfielder Gene Woodling were the only two players to hit over .300. The Yankees then triumphed over the Dodgers in the Series to tie McCarthy's Yankees record of the 1930s.

Now that they had tied the record, could Stengel's Yankees do what had never been done—capture the pennant and the World Series for the fifth time in a row?

The answer was a resounding yes.

The 1953 Yankees, stronger than the year before, won the pennant easily, finishing in front of Cleveland by 8.5 games. Left-handed starting pitchers Whitey Ford and Eddie Lopat won 34 games between them. In the World Series against the Brooklyn Dodgers, play was dominated by Billy Martin, the Yankees' aggressive second baseman. He hit two homers, two triples, a double, and seven singles as the Yankees won the Series in six games. Mantle also swung a potent bat, driving in seven runs with five hits, including a grand slam home run.

The Yankees threatened to make it six World Series wins in a row in 1954, but the Indians, still getting great pitching from Wynn, Lemon, and Garcia, beat them out for the pennant. To do it, however, Cleveland had to win 111 games, a record for the American League. (The 1998 Yankees would better the mark with 114 wins.)

Over the next six years, the Yankees won five more American League titles. Their record of 10 pennants and seven World Series victories in 12 years (1949–60) made them the dominant team of the 1950s and the most successful baseball dynasty in history.

14 Whitey Ford

Edward Charles "Whitey" Ford was the ace of the New York Yankees pitching staff in the 1950s and early '60s. The only Yankees pitcher of that era to make it into the Hall of Fame, Ford is the club's all-time leader in wins, games started (tied with Andy Pettitte), innings pitched, shutouts, and second to Pettitte in strikeouts.

Ford's lifetime record of 236–106 gives him a career winning percentage of .690, the highest among any major league pitcher since 1900 with 200 or more wins. Ford changed his pitch speeds expertly, mixing up a solid fastball, a sharp breaking curve, and a very effective change-up. A top-notch fielder, he also had one of the league's great pick-off moves. All this resulted in a consistently low earned-run average that stayed at or below 3.00 in 11 of his 16 major league seasons, never rising higher than 3.24 throughout his career. Ford led the American League in victories three times and in earned-run average and shutouts twice. He won the Cy Young award in 1961, when pitchers in both leagues competed for only one trophy.

Ford saved his most impressive performances for when they counted most—in the World Series. The Yankees won 11 pennants during Ford's years with the club, and he helped the Yankees win six World Series titles. "You kind of took it for granted around the

Whitey Ford is the Yankees' all-time leader in wins, games started, innings pitched, shutouts, and second in strikeouts, remarkable achievements considering the franchise's illustrious history.

Yankees that there was always going to be baseball in October," said Ford.

The left-hander still holds several important World Series pitching records, including most Series (11), most games (22), most opening-game starts (8), most innings pitched (146), most strikeouts (94), and most wins (10). He allowed only 44 earned runs in his 22 World Series starts. "If the World Series was on the line and I could pick one pitcher to pitch the game, I'd choose Whitey Ford every time," said teammate and lifelong pal Mickey Mantle.

In 1960 and 1961, Ford started four World Series games, won them all, and allowed no runs. On his way to his fourth straight World Series shutout in Game 4 of the 1961 Series, Ford injured his ankle and had to leave the game. He departed that contest with a streak of 32 consecutive scoreless innings, having broken Babe Ruth's World Series record. (As a Boston Red Sox pitcher, the Babe pitched 29 consecutive scoreless innings in the 1916 and 1918 World Series. Ruth would often say this was his proudest accomplishment in baseball, greater than any of his batting feats.) In the 1962 Series, Ford continued his streak, ending up with 33 consecutive scoreless innings—still a World Series record for a starting pitcher.

Paul Krichell was a Yankees scout for 37 years, and it was Krichell who first spotted and signed Ford (as well as Lou Gehrig and Phil Rizzuto in previous years). Krichell found the 17-year-old first baseman in Astoria, Queens, not far from Yankee Stadium. Ford was only 5'9" and 150 pounds in high school and was too small to be a position player in the majors. So he switched to pitching full time. Ford made the Yankees squad midway through the 1950 season, and he won his first nine games on his way to a 9–1 rookie record, helping the Yankees win the pennant his first season. That year, in his first of many World Series, Ford pitched 8⅔ innings without allowing an earned run, winning Game 4 of a four-game Yankees sweep of the Philadelphia Phillies.

Ford spent 1951 and 1952 in military service. He returned in 1953 and went 18–6, followed by a 16–8 record in 1954. His 18–7 record in 1955 tied him for most wins in the American League. He led the league with 18 complete games and finished second in earned-run average (2.63), earning his first of eight All-Star selections. The next season he went 19–6, leading the AL in win percentage (.760) and earned-run average (2.47). He also won the ERA title in 1958 with a 2.01 mark.

Yankees manager Casey Stengel limited Ford's starts, resting him four or five days between appearances and saving him for use against the better teams in the league. Stengel would hold out Ford against cellar-dwelling teams such as the Washington Senators and Philadelphia Athletics, so he could start against division rivals such as the Cleveland Indians and Detroit Tigers. Only once during the decade under Stengel did Ford start more than 30 games in a season. But in 1961, when Ralph Houk took over as the Yankees manager, he moved Ford into a regular four-man rotation and the durable lefty thrived on the heavier workload. In 1961, Ford led the league with 39 games started—10 more than the year before—and innings pitched (283). He posted a spectacular 25–4 record to lead the major leagues in wins and winning percentage (.862). That season, he won his only Cy Young award and then earned the World Series MVP award. Two years later, at the age of 34, he started 37 times and went 24–7. It's possible that Stengel's conservative use of Ford might have robbed the pitcher of at least 40 more career wins.

In 1963, Ford, who was known as "The Chairman of the Board," again led the league in wins (24), winning percentage (.774), games started (37), and innings pitched (269⅓). The World Series that season between the Yankees and the Los Angeles Dodgers provided a showcase for the game's top two left-handed pitchers. Ford was the premier lefty in the American League. The Dodgers' Sandy Koufax had posted a 25–5 record and was the best lefty in the National League. The pitchers met in Game 1. In the first inning, Ford struck out two Dodgers and got the other out on an easy ground ball. Koufax struck out the first five Yankees batters and outpitched Ford all afternoon. The Dodgers won 5–2, as Koufax struck out 15 Yankees to set a Series record. Ford and Koufax met again in Game 4. This time Ford gave up just two hits in seven innings, but an error by Yankees first baseman Joe Pepitone proved costly and the Dodgers won the game 2–1 to complete a Series sweep.

After 13 straight seasons of at least 11 victories, Ford suffered his first losing seasons in 1966 and '67, his final major league campaigns. Still, he sported impressive earned-run averages of 2.47 and 1.64, respectively. After retiring following the 1967 season, Whitey and his good buddy Mickey were enshrined in the Hall of Fame together in 1974.

Following his playing career, Ford admitted to throwing illegal pitches, primarily by having his catcher Elston Howard scuff the baseballs with mud before throwing the ball back to him on the mound. Ford also used a wedding ring with a sharp edge to nick the ball, causing the ball to sink more than his usual pitches. "I didn't begin cheating until late in my career, when I needed it to survive," Ford admitted. "I didn't cheat when I won the 25 games in 1961. I don't want anyone to get any ideas and take my Cy Young award away. And I didn't cheat in 1963 when I won 24 games." Then he added with a sly smile, "Well, maybe just a little."

15 The House That Ruth Built

The arrival of Babe Ruth in New York City caused the turnstiles to spin like never before at the Polo Grounds, which the Yankees had shared with the New York Giants since 1913. Spurred on by his fantastic long balls, fans flocked to ballparks to watch the Babe in action. In 1920, Ruth's first season with the Yankees, they became the first major league team to draw more than 1 million fans (officially 1,289,422) in a single season.

As landlord, the New York Giants were not happy playing second fiddle to their guests, and notified the Yankees to vacate the premises as soon as possible. When the Giants told the Yankees to leave the Polo Grounds, Colonel Jacob Ruppert, co-owner of the New York Yankees, declared, "I want the greatest ballpark in the world." He got his wish.

In February of 1921, the Yankees purchased 10 acres of property from the estate of William Waldorf Astor at 161st Street and River Avenue in the west Bronx, directly across the Harlem River from the Polo Grounds. Yankees owners Ruppert and Tillinghast Huston announced the construction of baseball's first triple-decked structure. With a capacity of over 70,000, it would also be the first structure to be called a "stadium."

The Osborn Engineering Company of Cleveland designed the park. In addition to being the first ballpark to have three decks, it was also the first to ring its grandstand with the 16-foot copper façade which became its trademark, the first to house as many as 60,000 seats, and the first to have a flagpole and monuments in the field of play.

The White Construction Company of New York broke ground on the site on May 5, 1922. Incredibly, the stadium was built in only 284 working days and at a price of $2.5 million. The steel framework eventually involved 2,200 tons of structural steel and more than 1 million brass screws. Materials used to form the playing field included 13,000 cubic yards of earth, topped by 116,000 square feet of sod.

Yankee Stadium would favor left-handed power hitters with a right-field foul pole only 295 feet from home plate. Because it was widely recognized that Ruth's tremendous drawing power had made the new stadium possible, Fred Lieb of the *Evening Telegram* called the stadium The House That Ruth Built, and the name stuck.

Yankee Stadium opened on April 23, 1923, with all the pomp and circumstance befitting the new king of baseball stadiums. According to *The New York Times*, 74,217 fans packed themselves inside, and thousands more were turned away by the fire department "convinced that baseball parks are not nearly as large as they should be."

During the pregame festivities, John Philip Sousa and the Seventh Regiment Band raised the Stars and Stripes and the Yankees' 1922 pennant at the flagpole in deep center field. New York's governor, Al Smith, threw out the first pitch. Ruth had told a reporter, "I'd give a year of my life to hit a home run today."

Fittingly, he did. Ruth, always able to rise to the occasion, christened the new ballpark in the Bronx by slamming the first home run in Yankee Stadium history—a three-run shot off Howard Ehmke to help Bob Shawkey and the Yankees capture a 4–1 victory over the Red Sox, Ruth's former team.

The Yankees, led by manager Miller Huggins, punctuated the new stadium's first season by reaching the World Series. Ruth batted .368, walked eight times, scored eight runs, and walloped three home runs. Said owner Ruppert, "Now I have the greatest ballpark *and* the greatest team."

16 Louisiana Lightning Strikes Out 18

Perfect games and no-hitters have been pitched at Yankee Stadium, but it is safe to say that no pitcher was more dominant in the Bronx than Ron Guidry was on June 17, 1978, the memorable night when he turned the California Angels' bats into sawdust.

Guidry struck out a team-record 18 batters. The 27-year-old from Lafayette, Louisiana, allowed four hits on the way to a 4–0 victory. At the time, it was the most strikeouts in baseball history thrown by a left-handed pitcher. The record has since been surpassed by Randy Johnson.

Although Guidry struck out two California batters in the first inning, he feared a struggle after two innings. "Believe it or not, I didn't think I was going to get out of the first inning of that game because I couldn't get my slider in the strike zone," said Guidry, who was known as "Gator" to his teammates. "I kept bouncing it, and when I got it over the plate, it was always high. I couldn't throw my fastball for strikes when I was warming up either. I saw [Yankees relief pitcher] Sparky Lyle when I came in from the bullpen, and I asked him, 'What's the earliest you've ever come into a game? I don't feel like I have good stuff tonight.' And Sparky said to me, 'You've got good stuff. It's just a little high. Just go out there, and eventually it will come.'

"When I went out in the third inning, things started to change," Guidry continued. "The Angels were just swinging and missing. When I threw balls down the middle of the plate, they were taking. When they'd swing, it would be out of the strike zone. I had them off-balance. After the third inning, guys were just striking out."

Somehow, despite his wiry 5'11", 160-pound frame, Guidry could throw a fastball 95 miles per hour, and his slider handcuffed

Clap for a Strikeout Thrown by a Yankees Pitcher

Ron Guidry established a franchise record by striking out 18 batters in the Yankees' 4–0 win against the California Angels on June 17, 1978. This was also the game that began the Yankee Stadium tradition of fans getting up on their feet and rhythmically clapping for a strikeout whenever an opposing batter has two strikes against him. On this night against the Angels, the boisterous hometown crowd of 33,162 kept getting up on its feet every time Guidry got two strikes on a California batter. And more times than not, he rewarded them with the third strike.

"When they start hollering and screaming, you just get pumped up that much higher and you try harder," Guidry said. "I felt I disappointed them when a guy hit a ball with two strikes. I thought I made a mistake."

To this day, whenever an opposing batter gets two strikes against him, Yankees fans will rise to their feet and methodically clap for a strikeout.

and tormented right-handed hitters. "He caught a lot of teams by surprise because of his size," recalled third baseman Graig Nettles. "They didn't expect him to throw that hard."

On this night, Guidry's fastball pounded the catcher's mitt so loudly that the television announcer, Phil Rizzuto, began calling him "Louisiana Lightning."

The Yankees scored all their runs in the first three innings. After that it was zeroes for both teams, and the way Guidry was pitching, they could have played 20 innings and the Angels weren't scoring. Through six innings he had 14 strikeouts—meaning that only four of the 18 outs had come on balls that were put in play.

By the time Guidry was done, he had struck out the side three times and had struck out every Angels batter at least once. The victims: Bobby Grich twice; Rick Miller once; Dave Chalk twice; Joe Rudi four times; Don Baylor twice; Ron Jackson once; Merv Rettenmund once; Brian Downing twice; and Ike Hampton three times. As California's Joe Rudi, who fanned four times, said afterward, "If you saw that pitching too often, there would be a lot of guys doing different jobs."

Guidry improved to 11–0 with his win over the Angels. He would win his first 13 decisions of the 1978 season and go on to finish 25–3 with nine shutouts. His 25th win came in the Yankees' victory over the Red Sox in the one-game playoff at Fenway Park to win the American League Eastern Division title. Then the Yankees went on to win their second World Series title in a row. In postseason honors, Guidry won the Cy Young award and was runner-up to Boston's Jim Rice in the Most Valuable Player voting.

17 Boone Homer Wins 2003 Pennant

Aaron Boone played in 54 regular season games as a Yankee, but will be remembered in New York forever. His 11th-inning home run capped a dramatic comeback win over the archrival Boston Red Sox in Game 7 of the 2003 American League Championship Series, sending the giddy Yankees to their sixth World Series appearance in eight seasons.

Prior to hitting that legendary home run, Boone was famous for being a third-generation major league ballplayer. He is the son of former catcher Bob Boone (1972–1990), and the grandson of former infielder Ray Boone (1948–1960). His brother, Bret, also had a solid career as a major league infielder (1992–2005). The Boone family is the only family with three generations of All-Star players.

Aaron Boone came to New York from Cincinnati at the July 31 trading deadline to play third base. He hit .254 with six homers and 31 runs batted in for the Yankees. His bat was slumping awfully at season's end, and his offensive frustrations continued into the postseason. In the first six games of the ALCS against Boston, Boone was just 2-for-16, an anemic .125 batting average. Both hits were groundball dribblers that never left the infield. Manager Joe Torre benched Boone in the series-deciding seventh game in favor of Enrique Wilson, who hit .216 in four seasons with the Yankees.

The Red Sox came out swinging against New York starting pitcher Roger Clemens, knocking him out in the fourth inning already leading 4–0 and with two men on base and nobody out. The Red Sox seemed poised to turn the game into a blowout. Only three brilliant shutout innings by Mike Mussina (making the first relief appearance of his career after 400 starts) kept the Red Sox at bay. Boone sat on the bench watching for six innings. The Yankees trailed 4–1 and had managed just three hits against Boston's masterful pitcher Pedro Martinez.

Finally, in the seventh inning the Yankees flexed a little muscle. Jason Giambi hit his second solo home run of the game to close the deficit to 4–2. In the top of the eighth, David Ortiz homered to restore Boston's three-run cushion. The Yankees were six outs away from losing the pennant. Martinez had given Boston seven strong innings of work, and though the Red Sox bullpen had been lights-out all series, manager Grady Little decided to stick with his ace and sent Martinez back to the mound to pitch the bottom of the eighth inning.

The eighth inning started innocently enough, with Martinez retiring the first batter to face him. With one out and nobody on base, Derek Jeter doubled and Bernie Williams singled him home, prompting Little to walk to the mound to consult with his pitcher. Now, it seemed clear to all, Little would replace his tiring ace with a fresh arm. But Martinez must have assured his manager he still had something left in the tank, because Little remained confident in the pitcher who had won three Cy Young awards. Little allowed Martinez to stay in the game to face Hideki Matsui, a controversial move that will be forever debated among baseball fans. Matsui ripped a double down the right-field line and Jorge Posada followed with a two-run double to tie the game 5–5. Finally Little signaled to the bullpen to replace Martinez.

The contest was far from over as both bullpens went in lockdown mode. Mariano Rivera came on for the Yankees in the ninth and pitched three shutout innings. Boston's Mike Timlin pitched a scoreless ninth and Tim Wakefield pitched a scoreless 10th. As the game moved into the bottom of the 11th inning, Boone, who had entered earlier as a pinch runner, was set to lead off against Wakefield, a knuckleballer who had already won two games in the series.

"All I wanted," Boone would say later, "was to get on base, to make contact."

In one of the most dramatic scenes in baseball history, Boone launched Wakefield's first pitch into the left-field seats for a pennant-winning home run, propelling the Yankees into the World Series and once again breaking hearts across Red Sox Nation. As Boone jumped on home plate with both feet, Rivera, the ALCS MVP, raced to the pitcher's mound and collapsed atop the rubber—part joyous celebration, part exhaustion—before being carried off the field on his teammates' shoulders.

"You always emulate these moments in your backyard," Boone would say. "I still can't put the feeling into words…I'm floating."

On December 6, 2017, Boone was re-introduced to Yankees fans as the club's 35th manager in franchise history.

18 The Pine Tar Game

The Pine Tar Game is certainly one of baseball's most bizarre and controversial finishes. On July 24, 1983, the Kansas City Royals were at Yankee Stadium to play the Yankees in just another regular season game. The Yankees were leading 4–3 in the top of the ninth inning with two outs when Royals third baseman George Brett smashed a two-run homer off Yankees relief pitcher Rich "Goose" Gossage, giving the Royals a 5–4 lead. Or so everyone in the stadium thought.

Yankees manager Billy Martin protested to the umpires that Brett had used an illegal bat because it had too much pine tar on it. (Pine tar is a sticky brown substance batters apply to their bats to give them a better grip.) Baseball rule 1.10 (b) allows a player's bat to have 18 inches of tar from the end of the bat handle.

"I was feeling pretty good about myself after hitting the homer," Brett recalled. "I was sitting in the dugout. Somebody said they were checking the pine tar, and I said, 'If they call me out for using too much pine tar, I'm going to kill one of those SOBs.'"

The umpires didn't have a ruler to measure the pine tar on Brett's bat, so they placed the lumber across home plate, which measures 17 inches across. When they did, they saw that the pine tar exceeded the legal limit. The four umpires huddled up again, and then home-plate umpire Tim McClelland signaled that Brett was out, meaning his potential game-winning home run was nullified. The game was over, and the Yankees won 4–3.

"I couldn't believe it," said Brett.

"I can sympathize with George," Gossage remarked after the game, "but not that much."

An enraged Brett sprang from the dugout, his eyes bulging like a madman, and he was screaming obscenities as he raced toward

The Yankees' Longest Game

In the longest game in Yankees history, Jack Reed hit a two-run home run in the top of the 22nd inning off Detroit's Phil Regan to give the Yankees a 9–7 win over the Tigers on June 24, 1962. The Yankees had a 7–3 lead after two innings, but were then held scoreless for 19 straight innings before Reed hit his homer. It was the only home run Reed hit in his 129 major league career at-bats, and it came at an opportune time. The game lasted exactly seven hours, the longest game by elapsed time in Yankees history. The longest nine-inning game the Yankees ever played took 4 hours, 45 minutes against the Red Sox at Boston's Fenway Park on August 18, 2006. The Yanks won 14–11.

McClelland. The umpires' crew chief, Joe Brinkman, intercepted Brett before he reached McClelland, grabbing him around the neck and trying to calm him down. "In that situation," said Brinkman, "you know something's going to happen. It was quite traumatic. He was upset."

"It knocks you to your knees," said Royals manager Dick Howser. "I'm sick about it. I don't like it. I don't like it at all. I don't expect my players to accept it."

Meanwhile, Royals pitcher Gaylord Perry, who had long admitted throwing an illegal spitball, grabbed the bat from McClelland and was halfway up the tunnel toward the team locker room to hide the evidence when stadium security personnel grabbed him and the bat. The bat was given to Brinkman and presumably went on its way to the American League office for inspection.

"I didn't know what was going on," said Howser. "I saw guys in sport coats and ties trying to intercept the bat. It was like a Brink's robbery. Who's got the gold? Our players had it, the umpires had it. I don't know who has it—the CIA, a think tank at the Pentagon."

The Yankees had won the game by a score of 4–3—or so everyone who left the stadium had thought. But the Royals protested the umpires' decision, arguing that Brett had no intentional plan to cheat and that he therefore did not violate the spirit of the rules.

Four days later, American League president Lee MacPhail upheld the Royals' protest. Acknowledging that Brett had pine tar too high on the bat, MacPhail explained it was the league's belief that "games should be won and lost on the playing field, not through technicalities of the rules." MacPhail overruled the umpires' decision, overturning the events on the field, and reinstated the outcome of Brett's at-bat, putting the Royals back in front 5–4. The contest was then declared "suspended."

Following this incident baseball's rulebook was amended to prevent a similar situation from occurring again. The rule now states that the protest must occur before the bat is used in play.

Yankees owner George Steinbrenner was miffed. "I wouldn't want to be Lee MacPhail living in New York!" he snapped.

Twenty-five days after it began, on August 18 (an open date for both teams), the Pine Tar Game resumed at Yankee Stadium in front of only 1,245 fans. To show their annoyance and mock the proceedings, for the final out of the top of the ninth inning, the Yankees played pitcher Ron Guidry in center field and first baseman Don Mattingly (a left-handed fielder) at second base. Guidry played center field because the Yankees had traded away Jerry Mumphrey, who had come into the game for defensive purposes. When the game resumed, in protest of the protest, Martin appealed at both first base and second base, claiming Brett had missed touching the bags on his home run trot around the bases. Then New York's George Frazier struck out Hal McRae for the third out of the inning. In the bottom of the ninth, Royals reliever Dan Quisenberry was able to retire Mattingly, Roy Smalley, and Oscar Gamble in order, and the Royals won by the same 5–4 score.

When Brett was elected to the Hall of Fame in 1999, the famous pine tar bat went to Cooperstown with him, where it was placed on display.

19George Steinbrenner

George Steinbrenner, a ship builder from Cleveland, led a group of investors in buying the New York Yankees from the Columbia Broadcasting System (CBS) in 1973 for a bargain-basement price of $8.7 million. "It's the best buy in sports today," said Steinbrenner, who also vowed to be the prototypical hands-off owner.

"I won't be active in the day-to-day operations of the club at all," he said the day the sale was announced at Yankee Stadium. "I can't spread myself so thin. I've got enough headaches with my shipping company."

The once-proud Yankees franchise was floundering, following nine consecutive losing seasons and dwindling attendance. Aided by the coming of free agency, Steinbrenner would return the Yankees to prominence. Under his tenure—the longest ownership in team history—the Yankees won 11 pennants and seven World Series championships.

The man known simply as "The Boss" was known for several things, most notably an intolerance for losing and a short fuse. He hired and fired managers with abandon, especially early in his ownership. Incredibly, the fiery Billy Martin was re-hired five times.

In 1974, baseball commissioner Bowie Kuhn suspended Steinbrenner from baseball ownership for two years after The Boss was indicted for making illegal contributions to President Richard Nixon's re-election campaign and then covering it up. The suspension was lifted after 15 months, with Steinbrenner returning to the Yankees in 1976. Under Steinbrenner's watchful eye, the Yankees won three consecutive pennants beginning in 1976, and won the 1977 and 1978 World Series, albeit in a turbulent environment dubbed by pitcher Sparky Lyle as "The Bronx Zoo."

In 1990, Steinbrenner was suspended again, this time for life, by commissioner Fay Vincent after the owner had hired a known gambler to dig up dirt on outfielder Dave Winfield after the outfielder didn't perform in the clutch to Steinbrenner's liking. Steinbrenner was reinstated in 1993, and the Yankees have been a model franchise ever since.

The Yankees returned to the playoffs in 1995, the first of 13 consecutive postseason appearances. Steinbrenner had mellowed, allowing Joe Torre to remain in the manager's office for 12 seasons, and leaving personnel decisions to his organizational brain trust. With World Series titles in 1996, 1998, 1999, 2000, and 2009, the Yankees have won 27 world championships, more than any other franchise.

In addition to the team's on-field success during Steinbrenner's ownership reign, the Yankees topped the American League in attendance for a record eight straight seasons from 2003 to 2010. The Yankees are also the only franchise in baseball history to draw more than 4 million fans at home in four consecutive seasons (2005–08).

The Yankees are now worth more than $1 billion, thanks to Steinbrenner's astute business tactics. He was the first owner to sell broadcast rights of his team's games to cable television, an idea which has grown into the Yankees' own YES Network. Steinbrenner spearheaded a renovation of Yankee Stadium in the mid-1970s and then oversaw the building of a new Yankee Stadium that opened for the 2009 season, keeping the team in the Bronx.

In 2007, The Boss, age 77 and in failing health, ceded control of the team to his two sons, Hank and Hal. George Steinbrenner died in 2010 after 37 years as principal owner, during which time the Yankees posted a MLB-best .566 winning percentage. Steinbrenner's 37 years of ownership is the most of any other New York Yankees owner by 13 years (Colonel Jacob Ruppert owned the Yankees from 1915 to 1939, a total of 24 years). Steinbrenner's tenure brought a level of stability to the Yankees that other franchises only dream about. Since the Steinbrenner family took over the Yankees, the other 29 major league teams have had more than 100 owners while the Yankees have had just one.

20 Study the History of the Pinstripes and the Interlocking NY

The Yankees' interlocking NY monogram is the most recognizable insignia in all of sports. But when the Yankees, then called the Highlanders, began play in 1903, their uniform jersey sported a large N on the right breast and a large Y on the left breast. In 1905, the N and Y were merged on the left breast, creating a prototype of the now-legendary emblem. Four years later, the monogram made its first appearance on the players' caps and left sleeve of the Highlanders' jerseys for the 1909 season.

The interlocking NY was a design created by Louis C. Tiffany in 1877 for a medal to honor the first New York City policeman shot in the line of duty. Bill Devery, one of the club's early owners and a former New York City police chief, may have adopted the design for the organization.

In their final season at Hilltop Park the Highlanders made a fashion statement in the 1912 home opener by taking the field wearing pinstripes for the first time in franchise history. Pinstripes were a popular look at the time, as eight of the 15 major league teams wore striped uniforms. The Highlanders abandoned the pinstripes during their first two seasons sharing the Polo Grounds with the New York Giants, but by 1915, the pinstripes on the home uniform were back for good.

The Yankees removed the NY monogram from the jersey in 1917—though the NY remained on the cap—and for the next two decades the team favored the pinstripes-only look. It wasn't until 1936 that the interlocking NY was restored to the Yankees uniform, meaning that Babe Ruth, who played for the Yankees from 1920 to 1934, played his entire Yankees career without ever sporting the club's legendary insignia on his jersey. The Yankees home uniform has remained mostly unchanged for more than 80 years.

The Yankees wore differently styled caps from 1903 to 1921, including a white cap with pinstripes in 1921, before finally settling on the team's signature look in 1922, a solid navy cap with interlocking NY insignia.

The club's road uniforms—solid gray with NEW YORK in block letters across the chest—have remained relatively unchanged since 1918. Teams wear dark uniforms for road games to help fans tell the visiting team from the home team. This tradition began around 1890. Back then, baseball teams chose to wear gray during road games for another reason, too: they rarely had places to wash their uniforms on road trips. The gray color hid dirt and stains—sort of. Fans still complained that visiting teams looked grubby, and players complained about the aroma in the visitors' dugout.

In 1929, the defending world champion New York Yankees and the Cleveland Indians became the first teams to wear permanent numbers sewn onto the backs of their uniforms. Starting players were given numbers that matched their usual place in the batting order. That's why Babe Ruth, who normally batted third, wore No. 3.

The numbers and corresponding names were listed in the club's scorecards, and so, perhaps, also marked the first time ballpark vendors called out, "Scorecards, get your scorecards, here! You can't tell the players without a scorecard."

Other major league teams quickly adopted the idea and, by the late 1930s, uniform numbers became standard for all teams.

Bill Veeck introduced player names to the back of his Chicago White Sox jerseys during spring training in 1960. The idea was an immediate success, brought about by the popularity of baseball on television, and today, every big league team has adopted the practice with one notable exception. Despite being the first major league club to adopt permanent uniform numbers, the tradition-minded New York Yankees have yet to don a uniform (home or road) adorned with player names.

21 Babe's Called Shot

The 1932 World Series was Babe Ruth's seventh Series appearance in 13 years with the Yankees. He was at his best in these October showdowns, and his most famous home run of all came in this Series. It occurred on October 1 at Wrigley Field in Chicago. Ruth took one look at the park's cozy dimensions and salivated. "I'd play for half my salary if I could hit in this dump all the time," he said.

The Yankees were playing the Chicago Cubs in Game 3 of the World Series. Charlie Root was pitching for the Cubs with the score tied 4–4. Ruth had already hit a three-run homer in the first inning, much to the pleasure of New York governor and Democratic presidential nominee Franklin D. Roosevelt, who was at the game.

When Ruth approached the plate in the top half of the fifth inning, the 51,000 Wrigley Field fans, who had heckled him lustily all day, now yelled insults about his age and weight. Some fans started throwing vegetables at him, while others tossed lemons. According to folklore, the Cubs bench also directed taunts at the Babe in the form of racial slurs.

What followed depends on whose version of the tale you believe. Root threw strike one, which the fans cheered. Ruth supposedly held up one finger and, according to Cubs catcher Gabby

Promises, Promises

Babe Ruth's called shot in the 1932 World Series was not the first Series home run he dared promise to hit. In 1926, the Yankees had won the pennant by three games over the Cleveland Indians. Ruth was a major factor in that winning season. He belted 47 home runs with 150 RBIs and a .372 batting average. Though the Yankees lost the World Series in seven games to the St. Louis Cardinals, Babe's mark on the series was indelible.

Prior to Game 4, Babe sent an autographed baseball to Johnny Sylvester, an 11-year-old boy who had survived a horseback riding accident. To make Johnny feel better, the Babe promised to hit a home run for him in the next game. That game was the first Series game ever broadcast on national radio.

Ruth hit one home run, then another, and then a third, becoming the first man to hit three home runs in a single World Series game. The record-breaking third homer was also the first ball ever hit into the center-field bleachers at Sportsman's Park in St. Louis. When the ball finally came down, an excited radio announcer Graham McNamee called, "What a home run! That is a mile and a half from here." An impressionable Johnny Sylvester would make a full recovery from his injuries.

Hartnett, said, "It only takes one to hit it." Root followed by throwing a pair of balls, and then a called strike. The count stood at 2-2. Wrigley Field was ready to explode if Ruth struck out.

Ruth stepped out of the batter's box. Raising his right arm, the Babe pointed. Did Ruth "call" his home run? Did he really predict that he would hit it? No one knows for sure. He may have been pointing to the pitcher, or showing the crowd that he still had one more strike. Another possibility is that he might have been gesturing at the Cubs bench, which was filled with players who were teasing him. Or, as legend has it, was he pointing at the outfield fence to indicate where he would hit Root's next pitch?

With the fans on the edge of their seats, the big-swinging lefty launched that next pitch straight over the center-field fence to that exact spot, a towering hit that measured 435 feet. It was the longest home run ever hit at Wrigley Field. It was also Ruth's 15th, and last, World Series home run. But did Babe really call his shot? No one can be sure, though there was no shortage of opinions.

"Ruth did point, for sure. He definitely raised his right arm. He indicated [where he'd already] hit a home run. But as far as pointing to center...no, he didn't," said Mark Koenig, the Cubs shortstop and Ruth's former Yankees teammate.

Pitcher Charlie Root firmly denied Ruth had pointed at the fence before he swung. Root said, "If he had made a gesture like that, well, anybody who knows me knows that Ruth would have ended up on his [backside]." In 1948, when asked to play himself and re-create the scene for the film biography *The Babe Ruth Story*, Root flatly refused.

Lou Gehrig, who was in the on-deck circle and followed with another homer on the next pitch, said, "Did you see what that big monkey did? He said he'd hit a homer, and he did."

The one man who could definitively answer the question was not saying. "Why don't you read the papers?" Ruth liked to say while flashing a sly smile whenever he was asked if he had called the home run. "It's all right there in the papers."

The Babe never said he did and he never said he didn't. But it does not really matter whether he actually called that home run. Whatever the facts may be, it is absolutely certain that Ruth always had a flair for the dramatic, and it was heroic enough that in the face of abusive taunts from a large, hostile crowd he came through in the clutch and delivered the crushing blow that defeated the Cubs. The battle over what truly happened in that one moment of time so long ago may never be settled. Still, Babe's called shot remains one of the most legendary home runs in World Series history. The Yankees went on to sweep the Cubs, the third straight time they won a Series without losing a game.

22 Tour New Yankee Stadium

If you want to learn the history of the New York Yankees, there is no better way than to take a guided tour of Yankee Stadium with Tony Morante. One of Yankee Stadium's longest-serving employees, Morante began working at the original Yankee Stadium in 1958 when he was just 14 years old.

The Yankees are in Morante's blood. Like his father, also named Tony, Morante started working in the stadium as an usher, but then moved into the group and season ticket sales office. The younger Morante created and gave his first official tour of the renovated Yankee Stadium in 1979, and he hasn't stopped since. He has been the team's director of stadium tours (and unofficial historian) since 1998. He has given thousands of tours at the old stadium, and now approximately 120,000 people take Morante's new stadium tour every year.

Morante gives individual tours each day beginning at 11:00 AM; prices range from $20 to $25 for adults and kids. The price is a bit cheaper for group tours. "The revenue from the tours goes into the Yankees Foundation, which has programs that benefit children in the city and throughout the New York metropolitan area," said Morante.

The tour lasts about an hour. Guests enter the stadium through the Babe Ruth Plaza. Located along East 161st Street between Gates 4 and 6, it honors the life of the legendary Yankees slugger through a series of porcelain images and storyboards displayed on light posts. Once inside the stadium, the tour starts off in the Great Hall. This 31,000-square-foot concourse between Gates 4 and 6 features huge double-sided banners of 20 Yankees greats, from Joe DiMaggio and Yogi Berra to more modern stars such as Don Mattingly and Paul O'Neill.

From there, Morante leads guests to the Yankee Museum located on the main level, near Gate 6. The museum features World Series trophies, displays on Ruth and Lou Gehrig, Thurman Munson's locker, and autographed baseballs. There are also video screens showing old games, a revolving model of the stadium, and a tribute to Don Larsen's 1956 World Series perfect game. Then tourists are taken to Monument Park, located in center field behind the outfield fence. All plaques and monuments for the 22 Yankees who have had their numbers retired are on display for fans.

Morante walks backward as he speaks, and his style is that of a fellow fan leading you around the stadium. His stories are filled with personal memories, such as working as a member of "the suicide squad," a group of men hired to help protect Mickey Mantle by escorting him from center field after each home game and preventing adoring fans from jumping over the rails and mobbing him.

"We'd say, 'Here we go, Mickey, let's move,'" Morante recalled. "Here I am, with one of my idols, helping to get him to the dugout safely."

The tour continues as Morante takes his groups down to the field and into the dugout for a 10-minute lesson on the pinstriped uniform jerseys the Yankees have worn for nearly 100 years. And then it's into the team's clubhouse, where he points out the lockers used by Aaron Judge and Gary Sanchez. Finally, the tour ends in the Great Hall.

Those looking for a unique private tour of Yankee Stadium as well as a fine dining experience can take advantage of the Yankee Stadium Twilight Tour. Twilight Tours are reserved for groups of 20 people or more and cost $100 per person. That includes a private group tour of Yankee Stadium followed by dinner at NYY Steak, the Yankees premier steak house located at Yankee Stadium.

Tours are booked based on availability and must be reserved in advance by calling (646) 977-TOUR or (212) YANKEES, or via e-mail at tours@yankees.com.

23 Lefty Gomez

Vernon Louis "Lefty" Gomez was known as much for his colorful, eccentric personality and his good humor and wit as he was for his pitching ability. He combined with Red Ruffing to form a formidable lefty-righty starting pitching duo for the Yankees' dynasty teams of the 1930s. Gomez was an ace. His blazing fastball and sharp curve helped lead the Yankees to five World Series championships, including four in a row from 1936 to 1939. Gomez twice led the American League in wins, winning percentage, and earned-run average, and he led the league in strikeouts and shutouts three times, and in innings pitched once. He always led the league in laughs.

Lefty was known to his teammates as "Goofy" for his warped logic, such as the time he came up with a new invention. "It's a revolving bowl for tired goldfish," he said, sure it would save the fish the trouble of swimming. Gomez was also a favorite of sportswriters, who could always count on him for a good quote. "My first name was Quits," he said one day. "When I was born my father took one look at me and said to my mother, 'Let's call it quits.'"

Opposing hitters didn't think it was too funny when Gomez averaged 22 victories during his first four full major league seasons. He had established himself as an ace left-hander in 1931, when he had a 21–9 record with a 2.67 earned-run average. The next year he had a 24–7 record and won the first of five World Series rings. Gomez was dominant in the Fall Classic. His perfect 6–0 mark is the most wins in World Series history without a loss.

Gomez was picked as the American League's starting pitcher in the inaugural All-Star Game on July 6, 1933. The exhibition game, created by *Chicago Tribune* sportswriter Arch Ward to coincide with the celebration of Chicago's Century of Progress Exposition, was billed as the "Game of the Century," with Connie Mack managing the AL squad and John McGraw guiding the NL. The pregame introduction of baseball's greatest sluggers awed many fans, yet it was Gomez, a notoriously poor hitter, who owns the distinction of knocking in the first run in All-Star Game history, with a two-out single in the second inning that scored Jimmy Dykes of the Chicago White Sox. Babe Ruth's two-run homer in the third inning gave the AL a 3–0 lead. The AL held on to win 4–2, with Gomez earning the historic victory. Gomez was a seven-time All-Star—and the starting pitcher four times in five years. He holds the record with three wins in All-Star Games.

Gomez was 6'2" and 173 pounds, but his slender frame was no indication of the great speed of his fastball. He used a very high leg kick and a whip-like arm movement to propel his pitches toward home plate. Yankees general manager Ed Barrow thought Gomez could throw with more velocity if the pitcher put on more weight. Gomez arrived for the 1933 season 20 pounds heavier, but after his wins total dropped to 16, he quickly lost the extra weight and reached a career-best 26 victories in 1934. That season, he won the pitching Triple Crown, leading the American League in wins, earned-run average (2.33), and strikeouts (158). He duplicated that feat in 1937, with 21 wins (against 11 losses), a 2.33 ERA, and 194 strikeouts.

Gomez won at least 20 games four times, and he still ranks as one of the premier pitchers in franchise history. He is fourth on the team's all-time list with 189 victories, and fifth in strikeouts with 1,468. For all his success, Gomez feared pitching to Jimmie Foxx. He said the formidable slugger had "muscles in his hair" and claimed that the intimidating Foxx "wasn't scouted, he was trapped." During one game, Gomez held onto the ball rather than pitch to Foxx. When exasperated catcher Bill Dickey ran to the mound to find out what pitch he wanted to throw, Gomez replied, "None. Let's just stall and hope he gets a phone call and has to leave." According to the story, Foxx belted the next pitch into the grandstand.

There were many laughs for Gomez and the Yankees as they breezed to a fourth straight World Series triumph, and second straight sweep, in 1939. Then Gomez developed arm trouble in 1940, when he appeared in only nine games for a 3–3 record. "I'm throwing as hard as I ever did, the ball's just not getting there as fast," he said. So Gomez learned to win with finesse, and rebounded nicely in 1941 with a 15–5 season, leading the league in winning percentage (.750). That season he pitched a shutout while allowing 11 walks, the most walks ever issued in a shutout.

Gomez continued to pitch for the Yankees through the 1942 season and lost one game for the Washington Senators in 1943 before retiring from baseball. While filling out a job application, when asked why he had left his previous position, Gomez, in typical fashion, wrote, "I couldn't get anybody out."

He was elected to the Hall of Fame in 1972. A plaque for Gomez was unveiled in Yankee Stadium's Monument Park in 1987. It reads: "Known for his excellent wit as he was fast with a quip and a pitch."

24 Alex Rodriguez

Before he became the New York Yankees' third baseman, Alex Rodriguez was far and away the most productive shortstop of all time. A-Rod, as he is known to his many fans, became a full-time major league player in 1996 with the Seattle Mariners when he was 20 years old, and that year he won the batting title with a .358 average. He was the first American League shortstop in more than

50 years to lead the league in hitting. His .358 average was the highest mark by a right-handed batter in the AL since the legendary Joe DiMaggio hit .381 in 1939.

In 1998, Rodriguez hit 42 home runs and also stole 46 bases, becoming just one of four members of the 40 home runs/40 stolen bases club. The others in this special group combining power and speed are Jose Canseco (Oakland Athletics, 1988), Barry Bonds (San Francisco Giants, 1996), and Alfonso Soriano (Washington Nationals, 2006). That year Rodriguez began a record-setting streak for a shortstop of six straight seasons of 40 or more homers.

"He's the type of kid you build an organization around," said Seattle right fielder Jay Buhner.

Rodriguez's contract with the Mariners ended after the 2000 season, making him the most attractive free agent in baseball. He made huge headlines on December 11, 2000, by signing a 10-year, $252-million contract with the Texas Rangers, the biggest contract

Alex Rodriguez took over at third base for the Yankees in 2004 and the next year hit a league-leading 48 home runs.

All-Star Switch

Alex Rodriguez was named the American League's starting shortstop in the 2001 All-Star Game. Cal Ripken Jr., a shortstop for most of his career, was set to start at third base, where he had moved four seasons earlier. Ripken had announced he would retire after the 2001 season. Before the first pitch of the All-Star Game, Rodriguez, with the okay from AL manager Joe Torre, urged Ripken to switch positions with him. Rodriguez wanted to pay tribute to his hero by letting Ripken play his final All-Star Game at the position for which he was most famous. At first Ripken didn't want to trade places, but he agreed after Alex gave him a gentle push toward the shortstop position. Soon after Rodriguez's classy move, Ripken hit a home run and was voted the game's MVP.

in sports history. Rangers owner Tom Hicks thought Rodriguez was so great that he agreed to pay the 25-year-old shortstop $2 million more than he had paid to buy the entire team, including the ballpark, just three years before.

The $252 million contract was the talk of the sports world. His huge paycheck put him in a special class. In return, Rodriguez was expected to transform a last-place team into a World Series contender. It would be a difficult standard to live up to. Playing for a new team, a new manager, and with new teammates in a new ballpark, he started his time in Texas with three of the greatest seasons in baseball history. In 2001, he hit 52 home runs, breaking the all-time record for most homers hit by a shortstop in one season (Ernie Banks had hit 47 homers in 1958). In 2002, he surpassed his own record by hitting 57 home runs, while also winning a Gold Glove as the best defensive player at his position. At 6'3" and 225 pounds, he is one of the biggest men ever to play the position on a regular basis. And he played the position superbly; he is quick, flashy, and has a strong and accurate throwing arm.

Rodriguez was honored with his second consecutive Gold Glove, and won his first Most Valuable Player trophy, in 2003.

That season he hit 47 homers to lead the American League for a third straight season. However, the Rangers finished in last place all three years. Following the 2003 season, they traded Rodriguez to the New York Yankees. The best player in baseball was bringing his skills to the most famous stage in all of sports: Yankee Stadium.

Even though he had won two Gold Gloves as the Texas shortstop, Alex agreed to switch positions and become a third baseman when he joined the Yankees so Derek Jeter could remain at short. Alex was the best shortstop in the majors, but he knew the Yankees would be a better team with him and Jeter playing together. So like his hero, Baltimore Orioles star Cal Ripken Jr., he moved to third. But Ripken moved to third because he had gotten older and slower; Rodriguez was still in the prime of his career. His position switch was the selfless act of a team player.

Besides switching positions, Alex also had to switch uniform numbers. He had worn No. 3 his entire career as a tribute to another one of his idols, former Atlanta Braves star Dale Murphy. But No. 3 is retired by the Yankees in honor of Babe Ruth, so Rodriguez chose to wear No. 13. It proved to be lucky for the new Yankees third baseman, as Rodriguez finished the 2005 season with a league-leading 48 homers. He won the AL Most Valuable Player award for the second time in three seasons, and became the only player to win the award for two different teams at two different positions.

In 2007, A-Rod hit 54 homers and won his third MVP. His mark of 54 homers is the most homers ever hit in a season by a third baseman. Rodriguez holds the records for most home runs in a single season at two positions, shortstop and third base.

25 Tony Lazzeri

In the greatest run-producing day in American League history, Tony Lazzeri drove in a league-record 11 runs in a 25–2 victory over the Philadelphia Athletics at Shibe Park on May 24, 1936. New York's second baseman became the first player to club two grand slam home runs in one game. Lazzeri also hit a third homer and a triple. A day earlier, Lazzeri had three homers and five runs batted in during a doubleheader sweep, giving him an incredible six home runs and 16 RBIs in a three-game span.

Lazzeri, who played 12 years for the Yankees from 1926 to 1937, is the greatest second baseman in team history. He drove in 100 runs seven times and won five World Series rings. He hit .300 or better five times. In 1929, he hit a career-high .354. His reputation for driving in clutch runs earned him the nickname "Poosh 'Em Up" Tony. In the 1928 World Series sweep of the St. Louis Cardinals, he had three hits in the clinching game, and in the 1932 World Series he finished off the Chicago Cubs with two home runs in the clinching Game 4 victory. In the 1936 Series against the Giants, won by the Yankees, Lazzeri hit a grand slam in Game 2 off Giants pitcher Dick Coffman; it was only the second grand slam ever hit in Series competition.

Despite his reputation for timely hitting, Lazzeri is most remembered for striking out in Game 7 of the 1926 World Series. The Cardinals led the Yankees 3–2 in the seventh inning of the seventh game at Yankee Stadium, but starting pitcher Jess Haines was having trouble controlling his knuckleball. Earle Combs led off with a single, and Mark Koenig bunted him to second. Haines walked Ruth intentionally, then Bob Meusel hit into a force play before Gehig walked to load the bases. With the rookie Lazzeri due up next, Rogers Hornsby, the Cardinals' player-manager, decided to make a pitching change. He waved in 39-year-old Grover Cleveland Alexander, the once-great, aging pitcher who had been in baseball since 1911. There were whispers that "Ole Pete" was washed up. But Hornsby showed his faith in Alexander by naming him the starting pitcher in the sixth game. The veteran responded beautifully with a complete game. The Cardinals won a laugher 10–2, tying the Series at 3–3. After the game, Alexander celebrated, certain he wouldn't be called to pitch in the final game. Hornsby, however, decided to have him in the bullpen just in case.

Now, at the key moment of the Series, as the fans buzzed, Alexander methodically threw his warm-up tosses. He took his time in hopes of unnerving the rookie. The day before, Lazzeri had gone 0-for-4 against Alexander. Now Lazzeri stepped up to the plate. The first pitch was low for ball one. The second pitch was a called strike. On the next pitch, Lazzeri swung and cracked a ball deep toward the left-field stands. The fans and players held their breath. "Foul ball!" cried the umpire. Alexander and the Cardinals sighed in relief. The ball was foul by inches. Lazzeri swung at Alexander's next pitch and missed for strike three. Baseball fans talked about Lazzeri's strikeout for years. When Alexander went into the Hall of Fame in 1938, Lazzeri was still an active player, but he earned the distinction of being the only player to have his name on someone else's Hall of Fame plaque. That's because Alexander's plaque, in part, reads: "He won the 1926 world championship for the Cardinals by striking out Lazzeri with the bases full in the final crisis."

The popular Lazzeri was a hero in Italian American communities around the United States. He helped draw thousands of newly arrived immigrants to ballparks and helped foster an interest in baseball in many of America's newest citizens. Manager Miller Huggins called him the type of player that comes along "once in a generation." Known as a quiet leader, Lazzeri suffered from epilepsy, although he was never affected by the disorder during a game. In 1946, he died of a heart attack, likely induced by a seizure, at age 42. In 1991, Lazzeri was elected to the Hall of Fame and finally received a well-deserved bronze plaque of his own.

26 Imitate Jeter's Flip Play

Game 3 of the 2001 American League Division Series featured Derek Jeter's most famous highlight: his sprint across the field and backhanded flip relay to Jorge Posada which nailed Oakland's Jeremy Giambi at the plate in the seventh inning to preserve the Yankees' 1–0 win.

"It was like Superman flying out of the sky to save the season," said general manager Brian Cashman.

The Yankees, winners of the American League East by 13.5 games, entered the postseason as the three-time defending champion and heavy favorite in the American League Division Series against the Oakland Athletics. But the Yankees got off to a rough start, losing the first two games of this best-of-five series in the Bronx. The dynasty looked dead as the Yankees traveled to Oakland with history against them. No team had ever won a best-of-five series after losing the first two games at home.

In the seventh inning of the third game, New York was clinging to a 1–0 lead thanks to catcher Jorge Posada's homer. Mike Mussina was making his first playoff start for the Yankees, but his Oakland counterpart, Barry Zito, had held the Yanks to just two hits, one of which had left the yard for the game's only run. With Oakland's Jeremy Giambi on first base and two outs, Terrence Long ripped Mussina's 100th pitch for a double down the first-base line. As the ball rattled off the wall, Giambi ran around third base heading for home. Though not fleet of foot, Giambi seemed a sure bet to score the tying run.

Outfielder Shane Spencer retrieved the ball in the right-field corner and fired a throw that sailed over the head of the first cutoff man, second baseman Alfonso Soriano, and the second cutoff man, first baseman Tino Martinez. Standing at his infield position, Derek Jeter saw the situation developing, and that's when the 27-year-old shortstop decided to dash across the infield grass and chase down a throw he realized was too high for either Soriano or Martinez to catch. Nobody knows why Jeter was in position to react that way. "It was my job to read the play," Jeter said later.

Jeter caught the ball on a bounce on the first-base line about 20 feet from home plate, running toward the first-base dugout and away from Posada. Jeter, with his momentum taking him away from home plate, had the presence of mind to flip the ball to Posada so the catcher would receive it on the third-base side of home plate. For some reason, perhaps expecting a collision, Giambi did not slide—he ran across the plate standing up. Posada caught the ball and slapped a tag on Giambi's right leg a blink of an eye before Giambi's right foot landed on home plate. Umpire Kerwin Danley signaled Giambi out at home. "If he slides," Posada said, "I don't have a chance."

Mariano Rivera held the A's scoreless over the final two innings to secure the Game 3 victory, and the Yankees won again the next day to force a deciding Game 5 in the Bronx. Prior to the game, Yankees Hall of Fame shortstop Phil Rizzuto followed up his ceremonial first pitch by pulling a second ball out of his pocket, trotting toward the first-base line, and then flipping the ball back to the catcher in a perfect Jeter imitation.

The Yankee Stadium crowd loved it, but not as much as they loved the original. The Yankees were leading the decisive final game 5–3 with one out in the eighth and Oakland's Eric Chavez on first. Terrence Long, the same batter whose Game 3 double led to Jeter's flip play, lifted a high foul ball behind third base. Jeter chased after it, and reached for the ball far into the stands. Jeter's momentum caused him to flip over the railing headfirst and land against the cement floor of the photographers' pit. The crowd of 56,642 gasped when Jeter disappeared from view, fearing for the shortstop's safety. Jeter suffered only a cut on his elbow, but more important, he had caught the ball. As Jeter climbed back over the railing and onto the field, the fans chanted his name. "It felt good," Jeter said of the chant.

Rivera again pitched the final two scoreless innings, and the Yankees became the first team to lose the first two games of a best-of-five at home and then win the series. Jeter delivered big. He batted .444 in the series and saved the Yankees from near-certain elimination with his instincts in Game 3.

"We definitely win the series if Jeter doesn't make that flip play," said Oakland's J.P. Ricciardi.

27 2001 World Series: Mystique and Aura

The New York Yankees dropped the first two games of the 2001 World Series to the Arizona Diamondbacks, but they were coming home to the Bronx to play the next three games at Yankee Stadium. After the Yankees won a hard-fought 2–1 victory in Game 3, Curt Schilling, who would be on the Yankee Stadium mound as Arizona's Game 4 starting pitcher, was asked to comment on the mystique and aura of Yankee Stadium, as evidenced by the team's unprecedented championship tradition.

"Mystique and aura," Schilling said of the idea of Yankees magic, "those are dancers in a nightclub."

Presidential Pitch

The national mourning in the aftermath of the September 11, 2001, terrorist attacks had resulted in the extension of that year's baseball season, so Game 3 of the 2001 World Series, played on October 30, marked the latest date that a Major League Baseball game had ever been contested.

Moments before game time, a tall right-hander from Texas popped out of the Yankees dugout and began striding toward the pitcher's mound to thunderous applause from the 55,820 fans cheering "U.S.A.! U.S.A.!" George W. Bush, the 43rd president of the United States, waved to the New York crowd, and toed the Yankee Stadium pitcher's slab.

For the first time in 45 years, a sitting president would throw out the ceremonial first pitch at a World Series game. Only four other presidents had ever thrown out the ceremonial first pitch at a World Series game while still serving in office, and none had made a Fall Classic pitch since Dwight Eisenhower did before the opening game of the 1956 Series at Ebbets Field in Brooklyn.

With little question, security at a World Series game has never been of more paramount concern than for President Bush's appearance at Yankee Stadium in 2001. Though no one realized it at the time, there was an extra umpire on the field for the pregame ceremony, a Secret Service agent working undercover.

As the president reared back into his throwing motion, stretching his sweatshirt emblazoned with FDNY, a tribute to the New York City Fire Department, the outline of a bulletproof vest became visible. Seemingly unencumbered, the president fired a strike to Yankees backup catcher Todd Greene. Suddenly, a convoy of Air Force military jets flying in a V-formation screamed over the stadium light stanchions.

Then the night's other marquee Texan, Roger Clemens, took the mound for the Yankees and overpowered the Diamondbacks with his fastball and sinker. The Rocket came up huge in a gut-check game, giving up only three singles and striking out nine Arizona batters in seven innings. Mariano Rivera got the final six outs with four strikeouts to nail down a crucial 2–1 victory, setting the stage for the unbelievable endings to Games 4 and 5.

He couldn't have been further off base.

On October 31, 2001, Yankee Stadium hosted the first Major League Baseball game ever played on Halloween. Appropriately, the game had a bizarre finish. Schilling had stymied the Yankees for seven innings and left the game with a two-run lead. Arizona's sidearming relief pitcher Byung-Hyun Kim entered the game to record the final six outs. He dispatched the Yankees quickly in the eighth, and with two outs in the ninth inning, the Yankees were one out away from going down in the Series 3–1. Paul O'Neill was on first base and Tino Martinez, hitless in his previous 11 plate appearances, was in the batter's box. Kim seemed unhittable, and the Yankees needed a miracle. They got one. On Kim's first pitch, Martinez swung and lashed a line drive that carried over the right-center-field wall for a dramatic home run to tie the score. The stadium's upper tiers were rocking and the concrete floor was rolling. A fan's poster said it all that night: WE'RE BACK. How true it was. Just weeks after the September 11 tragedy, New Yorkers were counting mightily on the Yankees to help restore the pride and spirit of their indomitable city. And now a critical game so perilously close to being lost had new life.

As the game went into extra innings, the stadium clock struck midnight. It was now November 1—the first time a World Series game had ever been played in November. The Yankees captain, Derek Jeter, fouled off three tough pitches from the South Korean reliever before running the count full. Then Jeter smacked Kim's next pitch toward the right-field corner. The ball snuck inside the foul pole and landed in the first row of seats for a game-winning home run to even the Series at 2–2. The crowd erupted with a primordial scream lasting several minutes as Jeter trotted around the bases, his right fist raised in the air, before jumping onto home plate and into the waiting arms of his jubilant teammates.

The gravity of the moment was not lost on Jeter.

"I've never hit a walk-off homer," said the Yankees' new Mr. November. "I don't think I hit one in Little League. That was huge."

The next night, in Game 5, Arizona again held a two-run lead in the ninth inning, and once more, manager Bob Brenly called on Kim to protect it. Jorge Posada was on second base with two outs, and the Yankees were again down to their last out, just as they were when Martinez tied Game 4 with a homer off Kim. This time, Scott Brosius played the hero, connecting on Kim's second pitch and propelling the ball deep beyond the left-field wall. It was the second time in as many nights the Yankees had come back from the brink of defeat by hitting a two-run home run with two outs in the ninth to tie the game.

"It's Groundhog Day," said Joe Torre. "This is the most incredible couple of games I've ever managed."

As Brosius began to celebrate his two-run homer, the rampant emotion throughout the Stadium crackled like lightning, and the buzzing didn't stop until the smoke had cleared in the 12th inning, when Alfonso Soriano singled home Chuck Knoblauch with the winning run for a 3–2 Yankees Series lead.

A fan sitting behind the Arizona dugout unfurled a banner that read MYSTIQUE AND AURA APPEARING NIGHTLY. The Yankees had done it again.

Sadly, the magic didn't last. Despite taking a 2–1 lead on an Alfonso Soriano solo homer in the eighth inning of Game 7, the Yankees allowed two runs in the ninth and lost one of the most thrilling World Series of all time.

28 Lou Gehrig

Lou Gehrig was born in New York City in 1903, and never strayed too far from his roots. He attended Columbia University and signed with the Yankees in 1923. After a handful of games on the major league level in 1923 and 1924, Gehrig became the Yankees' starting first baseman in 1925, and from then until 1932, he and Babe Ruth were the two greatest hitters ever to play together. Ruth and Gehrig finished first and second, respectively, in the home run race each season from 1927 to 1930, then tied for the lead in 1931. They scared opposing pitchers in a way two batters had never done before.

Gehrig had good seasons in 1925 and 1926, but it was in 1927 as part of the famous "Murderers' Row" Yankees lineup that Gehrig exploded as a superstar. He batted .373 with 47 homers and 175 runs batted in. Gehrig was chosen as the American League's Most Valuable Player that year. The 1927 Yankees—considered by many to be the greatest team of all time—swept the Pittsburgh Pirates in the World Series that year.

For the rest of his career Gehrig was the picture of consistency and offensive production. He drove in at least 100 runs in 13 consecutive seasons, topping 150 RBIs seven times and setting the American League record with 184 RBIs in 1931. He had at least 100 RBIs and 100 runs scored in every full season of his career.

After sweeping another World Series in 1928, this time from St. Louis, the Yankees took a back seat to Connie Mack's Philadelphia Athletics for three years. On June 3, 1932, Gehrig became the first AL player to hit four home runs in a game. That year, the Yankees were back on top, sweeping the Cubs in four for the championship. The Yankees finished second from 1933 to 1935, but in 1934,

Gehrig achieved the batting Triple Crown by leading the league in home runs (49), RBIs (165), and batting average (.363).

Though Gehrig and Ruth would be a terrific tandem through 1934, Gehrig was often overshadowed by his teammate's outsized personality. Still, baseball history regards him as the greatest first baseman ever. In his career, he hit 493 home runs (including 23 grand slams, a record held until Alex Rodriguez bested the mark in 2013) and had a .340 batting average. He was a member of six World Series champions. Yet Gehrig always played in Ruth's enormous shadow. Gehrig batted fourth in the powerful Yankees batting order, protecting Ruth in the lineup. His homers didn't fly quite as high or as far. Because he played second fiddle to Ruth, Gehrig's offensive exploits are often overlooked. For example, when Gehrig blasted four home runs in the 1928 World Series, Ruth made history by whacking three in one game for the second time in his career.

When it was suggested that Gehrig try to be more colorful, he said, "I'm not a headline guy. I knew that as long as I was following Babe to the plate I could have stood on my head and no one would have noticed the difference. When the Babe was through swinging, whether he hit one or fanned, nobody paid any attention to the next hitter. They all were talking about what the Babe had done."

By 1935 Babe Ruth was no longer a Yankee, but 1936 brought the arrival of Joe DiMaggio, who helped Gehrig and the Yankees win World Series titles in 1936, 1937, and 1938. The Yankees won the 1939 World Series, too, but without Gehrig. He had been diagnosed with amyotrophic lateral sclerosis, forever after known as Lou Gehrig's Disease. It was incurable and fatal. He died two years later at the age of 37.

29 See Thurman Munson's Locker at the Yankees Museum

The New York Yankees boast a legendary history, and sadly, that history has occasionally been touched by tragedy. On August 2, 1979, Yankees catcher and team captain Thurman Munson, only 32 years old, was killed when the private plane he was piloting crashed shortly after takeoff near his home in Canton, Ohio. Munson had used a day off in the team's schedule to fly home to see his family. The unexpected death of the fiery, gruff, but very popular player shocked all New York baseball fans.

For nearly three decades, Munson's locker in Yankee Stadium remained unoccupied in tribute. When the team moved across the street to the new Yankee Stadium, Munson's locker was carefully removed and transported from the old stadium and placed in the Yankees Museum, located on the main level near Gate 6.

Munson is still a revered figure in Yankees history. A seven-time All-Star selection, Munson hit for a .292 average over 11 seasons and was at his best in the clutch, batting .357 in 30 post-season games between 1976 and 1978. Munson had a tough outer shell, but his teammates knew him as a leader, the heart and soul of three consecutive American League pennant winners and two World Series championship teams.

Drafted out of Kent State and after less than one season in the minors, Munson earned the starting catching job in spring training of 1970. That season, the Yankees won 93 games with a rookie catcher. It was their best season since 1964. Munson won the American League's Rookie of the Year award, receiving 23 of 24 first-place votes. His .302 batting average ranked eighth-best in the league. He was also quickly establishing himself as a quality defensive catcher with a take-charge attitude.

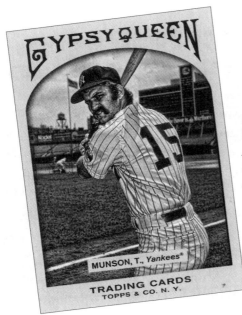

Catcher Thurman Munson was a two-time World Series champion and seven-time All-Star selection before losing his life in a tragic airplane crash in 1979.

Munson hit his stride in 1973, batting .301 with 74 runs batted in and a career-high 20 homers. He also won the first of three Gold Glove awards for fielding excellence. In 1975, he hit .318 with 102 RBIs, establishing himself as one of the game's best clutch hitters. For his career, Munson batted .302 with runners in scoring position. He was also named the first Yankees team captain since Lou Gehrig four decades before. Like Gehrig, Munson is also remembered as a tragic figure.

In 1976, Munson earned the AL Most Valuable Player award, finishing with a .302 average, 17 home runs, and 105 runs batted in. The Yankees breezed to the AL East division title, and Munson hit .435 against the Kansas City Royals in the American League Championship Series. The Yankees returned to the World Series for the first time in 12 years, but the Cincinnati Reds swept the Yanks in four games. Munson did his part, however, batting .529 with nine hits in the series.

In 1977, the Yankees won a second straight pennant and Munson hit .308 with 18 homers and 100 RBIs. He was the first major leaguer in 13 seasons—and only the second catcher—to compile three straight seasons batting .300 while knocking in at least 100 runs. The Yankees won the World Series, beating the Los Angeles Dodgers in six games, for the franchise's first world title since 1962. As the defending champions in 1978, the Yankees trailed the division-leading Boston Red Sox by as many as 14 games in mid-July, but rallied with a great stretch run to win the division crown. New York faced the Kansas City Royals in the playoffs. In Game 3, with the series tied 1–1, Royals third baseman George Brett hit three home runs off Yankees starting pitcher Jim "Catfish" Hunter and the Royals led 5–4 in the top of the eighth inning. In the bottom of the inning, with a runner on base, Munson blasted a 430-foot shot over Yankee Stadium's Death Valley in the left-center-field bullpen off Doug Bird which proved to be the difference-maker for the Yankees. New York ousted Kansas City for the third consecutive year to advance to the World Series. The Yankees then overcame a 2–0 deficit to the Dodgers by winning four straight games to capture the team's 22nd title.

Now 31 years old, the wear and tear of catching was eroding Munson's power. Playing on sheer guts during the 1978 season, he kept his batting average near .300, finishing at .297, but his production was way down, with six homers and 71 RBIs. The decline continued in 1979. On August 1, after 97 games, Munson was hitting .288 with three homers and 39 RBIs. There was talk of retirement due to balky knees and an aching right shoulder. Most of all, he sorely missed his family. The life of a ballplayer is travel and time spent away from family. Munson found a way to spend more time with his wife, Diane, and their three children. He earned a pilot's license a few years earlier, and in 1979 he bought a twin-engine Cessna Citation. The Yankees finished a road trip in Chicago the night of August 1. He flew home to spend the off-day

Yankees Captains

Player	Position	Tenure
Hal Chase	First base	1912
Roger Peckinpaugh	Shortstop	1914–1921
Babe Ruth	Outfield	May 20, 1922 to May 25, 1922
Everett Scott	Shortstop	1922–25
Lou Gehrig	First base	April 21, 1935 to June 2, 1941
Thurman Munson	Catcher	April 17, 1976 to August 2, 1979
Graig Nettles	Third base	January 29, 1982 to March 30, 1984
Willie Randolph*	Second base	March 4, 1986 to October 2, 1988
Ron Guidry*	Pitcher	March 4, 1986 to July 12, 1989
Don Mattingly	First base	1991–95
Derek Jeter	Shortstop	June 3, 2003 to 2014

*Co-captains

Babe Ruth's tenure as Yankees captain didn't last long. Just five days after being named captain, Babe was stripped of the title for his boorish behavior on the field. Ruth had been called out at second base, and he proceeded to toss dirt at umpire George Hildebrand. Babe then had to be restrained from going into the stands after an unruly spectator.

with his family. He was practicing takeoffs and landings at the Akron-Canton airport. That afternoon, his plane crashed short of the runway and burst into flames. Munson was dead, but miraculously, the co-pilot and a passenger survived.

The team flew to Ohio for the funeral service. Munson's close friends and teammates, Bobby Murcer and Lou Piniella, each delivered tearful eulogies. The night of the funeral the Yankees returned to Yankee Stadium to play a game against the Baltimore Orioles. When the Yankees took the field, the catcher's box was left unmanned. Reggie Jackson wept openly during the pregame ceremony. The game was one for the ages. The Yankees overcame a 4–0 deficit to win 5–4, with all the runs driven in by Bobby Murcer, who hit a three-run home run in the seventh inning and a two-run single in the ninth that gave the Yankees a dramatic walk-off victory. Murcer was so emotionally drained from the day that he nearly fainted on the field after the winning run crossed home plate.

The Yankees wore black armbands for the remainder of the season. Munson's uniform No. 15 was retired, and he was honored with a plaque in Monument Park in a commemorative ceremony in Yankee Stadium on September 20, 1980. The plaque reads: "Our captain and leader has not left us—today, tomorrow, this year, next... Our endeavors will reflect our love and admiration for him."

30 Original Stadium Renovation

By the 1970s, Yankee Stadium had become an aging ballpark in need of modernization. When the team signed a 30-year lease with New York City on August 8, 1972, the agreement called for Yankee Stadium to be completely renovated in time for the 1976 season. After completing the Stadium's 50th anniversary season in 1973, a complete remodeling began. The 1974 and 1975 Yankees played in Shea Stadium for two years while Yankee Stadium was torn down and rebuilt.

Significant improvements were made to the original Yankee Stadium. Ten new rows of seats were added to the upper deck, and the steel columns supporting the second and third decks were removed in the renovation. This gave the already grand Stadium an even more majestic look. Workers replaced the old wooden seats with wider plastic ones and erected a replica of the famed Stadium façade atop a 560-foot-long scoreboard that would stretch across the rear of the center-field bleachers. The state-of-the-art board had the first "Telescreen" to show fans instant replays of the action. The renovated park accommodated only 54,000 fans, but nearly every seat was a good one.

The Stadium's exterior was also changed dramatically, as three escalator towers were added, one at each of the main entrances. And a 138-foot Louisville Slugger–shaped smokestack, commonly called "The Big Bat," was added outside the Stadium near the home-plate entrance. This landmark became a popular pregame meeting spot for fans.

The renovated Stadium also reduced the great distances a player had to hit the ball for a home run. The fence in left-center-field, called Death Valley in the old Stadium, was reduced from 457 feet to 430 feet, and straightaway center field was brought in from 463 feet to 417 feet. Alterations in 1985 and 1988 would bring these fences in even more.

The remodeled Yankee Stadium was christened on April 15, 1976, with an 11–4 rout of the Minnesota Twins. Just as they had in 1923, the Yankees opened their new stadium in grand style by reaching the World Series, though it would be another year before they captured the championship trophy. In all, the Yankees won 10 American League pennants and six World Series titles in the remodeled Yankee Stadium (1977, 1978, 1996, 1998, 1999, and 2000).

In 2006, a groundbreaking ceremony was held for a new Yankee Stadium to be ready for the 2009 season. The remodeled original Yankee Stadium took its final bow during the 2008 season, hosting that year's All-Star Game, won by the American League 4–3 in 15 innings. The building hosted its final home game on September 21. Gates opened early to allow fans to visit Monument Park and walk around the ballpark. With a national television audience watching, the Yankees starters took their position in the field alongside all-time Yankees greats. Babe Ruth's daughter, Julia Ruth Stevens, threw out the ceremonial first pitch.

In the bottom of the seventh inning, longtime public address announcer Bob Sheppard appeared on the scoreboard's video screen. He recited a poem he had written just for the occasion: "Farewell, old Yankee Stadium, farewell. What a wonderful story you can tell. DiMaggio, Mantle, Gehrig and Ruth, a baseball cathedral in truth."

Fittingly, the Yankees won the game 7–3 over the Baltimore Orioles. After the final out, the players gathered near the pitcher's mound as captain Derek Jeter took the microphone and thanked the fans for their years of support, while reminding everyone of the new memories soon to be made.

"For all of us up here, it's a huge honor to put this uniform on every day and come out here and play," said Jeter. "And every member of this organization, past and present, has been calling this place home for 85 years. There's a lot of tradition, a lot of history, and a lot of memories.

"Now, the great thing about memories is you're able to pass it along from generation to generation. And although things are going to change next year, we're going to move across the street, there are a few things with the New York Yankees that never change—its pride, its tradition, and most of all we have the greatest fans in the world.

"And we are relying on you to take the memories from this stadium, add them to the new memories that come at the new Yankee Stadium, and continue to pass them on from generation to generation. So on behalf of the entire organization, we just want to take this moment to salute you, the greatest fans in the world."

Then the players walked around the warning track, waving to fans, and saying good-bye to the stadium.

31 Experience Déjà Vu Like David Cone

An early arriving crowd of 41,930 marched eagerly into Yankee Stadium on July 18, 1999, before a game between the Yankees and the Montreal Expos. They had come to the Bronx for Yogi Berra Day and to welcome a returning hero. Having been fired as manager in 1985, and then vowing never to enter Yankee Stadium while George Steinbrenner owned the team, Berra had settled his differences with The Boss. After 14 years of self-imposed exile, the franchise's most beloved catcher was finally coming back to the stadium for a long-overdue tribute.

The day was supposed to belong to Berra, who as a player had helped the Yankees win 10 World Series championships. Several old-timers including Whitey Ford, Phil Rizzuto, Gil McDougald and Bobby Richardson had ventured to the venerable ballpark to honor him in a 30-minute pregame ceremony. Then Don Larsen threw out the ceremonial first pitch to Berra, who had been Larsen's battery mate in the only World Series perfect game at Yankee Stadium in 1956.

Pitching for the Yankees that day was David Cone, a right-hander with more deliveries than FedEx. After Larsen completed his toss, he and Cone shook hands near the mound. Cone jokingly asked if Larsen was going to jump into Yogi's arms like he did in 1956. According to Cone, Larsen said, "Kid, you got it wrong. It was Yogi who jumped into my arms."

If Cone made another mistake that afternoon, the Expos batters would have swung and missed. He retired the side in order in the first and second innings. After a 33-minute rain delay, he struck out the side in the third inning and whizzed through a 1-2-3 fourth. By the sixth inning, the fans at Yankee Stadium were reveling in every pitch, and when Rondell White struck out to end the seventh, the crowd's roar lingered long after Cone had disappeared into the dugout.

The fans in Yankee Stadium were buzzing. Only six outs to go and Cone would accomplish the unthinkable—upstaging Yogi Berra on Yogi Berra Day—by pitching a perfect game. Brad Fullmer whiffed for out No. 24. Three outs away. In the ninth, when Orlando Cabrera popped to third baseman Scott Brosius for the final out, Cone dropped to his knees and grabbed his head in disbelief as Bjorn Borg did after winning Wimbledon. After being carried off the field by his teammates, Cone told reporters, "I probably have a better chance of winning the lottery than this happening today. It makes you stop and think about the Yankees magic and the mystique of this ballpark."

He retired all 27 Montreal batters he faced as the Yankees defeated the Expos 6–0. It was only the 14th perfect game in modern baseball history, and yet the third at Yankee Stadium. (It came only one season after David Wells accomplished the feat.) Of the previous 13 perfect games, Cone's was perhaps the most efficient. He threw only 88 pitches—an average of less than 10 pitches per inning—and didn't go to a three-ball count on a single batter. Working in stifling 95-degree heat, Cone was coolly in command, using a wicked slider to strike out 10 while inducing 13 fly outs and four grounders. His premier performance was all the more remarkable because of his age—at 36 he became the oldest pitcher to throw a perfect game since Cy Young in 1904—and the career-threatening surgery he endured three seasons earlier. Doctors discovered an aneurysm in Cone's pitching arm in 1996. In his first game back from surgery he flirted with a no-hitter for seven innings against the Oakland Athletics before being relieved to protect the surgically repaired shoulder.

Cone, who pitched three career one-hitters, said he wondered if he'd ever get a chance at a no-hitter again. "Going into the latter innings today, running through my mind [was] how many times I've been close and how this might be the last chance I get," he said. "My heart was pumping. I could feel it through my uniform."

One man in the stands could identify with what Cone was feeling. "I was just thinking about my day," said Larsen. "I'm sure David will think about this every day of his life."

As Yogi would say, it's déjà vu all over again.

32 Mattingly's Home Run Hot Streak

It was a hot summer night in Arlington, Texas, on July 18, 1987, when Don Mattingly, a hard-hitting doubles machine not known for his home run stroke, put his name in the Major League Baseball record books by belting a home run in an eighth consecutive game. Mattingly equaled a 31-year-old record many said would never be broken.

The sellout crowd of 41,871 Texas fans—the majority there to see if Mattingly would make history—was abuzz when Mattingly came to bat in the first inning at Arlington Stadium. Mattingly's amazing home run streak started July 8 against Mike Smithson of the Minnesota Twins. Then the Yankees first baseman also went deep off Minnesota's Juan Berenguer; Chicago's Richard Dotson, Joel McKeon, Jose DeLeon, and Jim Winn; and Texas' Charlie Hough, Mitch Williams, and Paul Kilgus.

That set the stage for Mattingly to try to equal the record against Texas right-hander Jose Guzman. Only one major leaguer, Pittsburgh first baseman Dale Long, had hit homers in eight straight games, back in 1956. (Seattle's Ken Griffey Jr. duplicated the record in 1993.) In the fourth inning, Mattingly let Guzman's

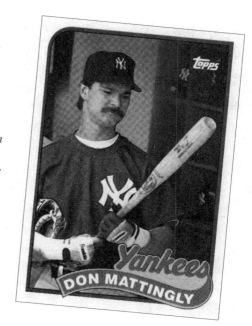

Though not known as a power hitter, first baseman Don Mattingly homered in eight consecutive games in 1987 to tie a major league record.

first two pitches go by for balls. Then on the third pitch he took a mighty swing and deposited the ball over the left-field fence, just past the outstretched glove of outfielder Pete Incaviglia. The roaring fans erupted to give Mattingly a standing ovation as he rounded the bases. The home run was his record 10th during the eight-game span, and his simultaneous streak of 10 games with at least one extra-base hit surpassed the American League record set by Babe Ruth in 1921.

The next night, on July 20, Mattingly was held homerless, but in that game he tied the major league record of 22 putouts by a first baseman in a game. During his remarkable 1987 season, Mattingly also hit six grand slam home runs to set a new single-season mark. The record-setting sixth grand slam was hit off Boston's Bruce Hurst on September 29, 1987. (Cleveland's Travis Hafner tied the mark in 2006.)

During his 14 seasons in the Bronx, Mattingly became one of the most popular and well-respected Yankees in team history. He

Homer Heroics

Don Mattingly may not make it to the Hall of Fame like Babe Ruth, Lou Gehrig, Joe DiMaggio, and Mickey Mantle have, but during the 1987 season, by hitting 10 home runs in eight games, he accomplished home run heroics that overshadow even those Yankees legends.

showed promise from the start, winning the batting title with a .343 average in his first full season in 1984. He was the American League Most Valuable Player in 1985, when he hit .324 with 35 home runs and 145 runs batted in. The Indiana native with the flowing long hair and rock-star mustache kept getting better. In 1986, he set Yankees records for doubles (53) and hits (238), becoming the first Yankee since Lou Gehrig to collect at least 200 hits for three seasons in a row.

Mattingly matched his hitting with outstanding defense, and won nine Gold Glove awards for his fielding excellence at first base. "Donnie Baseball" put up Hall of Fame caliber numbers at the plate when healthy. He had a lifetime batting average of .307 with 222 home runs and 1,099 RBIs in a career hampered by a painful back. In 1991, the Yankees appointed Mattingly as the 10th captain in team history. When the aching back was more than he could bear, Mattingly retired after the 1995 playoff series loss to Seattle, a rare Yankees legend to have never reached the World Series. In 1997, his jersey uniform No. 23 was retired and a bronze plaque unveiled. The last line reads: "A Yankee forever."

1996 Yankees: Return to Greatness

The Yankees won the 1996 American League East and then defeated the Texas Rangers in four games in the divisional playoff round. Texas slugger Juan Gonzalez became the first player to homer in each of his first four postseason games, but the Yankees bullpen recorded wins in Games 2, 3, and 4, allowing just one earned run in 20 innings over the series.

With the Yankees trailing 4–3 in the eighth inning of Game 1 of the American League Championship Series against Baltimore, Jeffrey Maier, a 12-year-old fan, reached over the right-field wall and deflected a Derek Jeter fly ball into the stands. The umpires ruled it a home run that tied the score. The Yankees went on to win 5–4 when Bernie Williams smacked a walk-off homer off Randy Myers in the 11th inning.

Williams hit .474 and was the series MVP, but it was Darryl Strawberry who had the best postseason series of his career. In the Yankees' five-game triumph over the Orioles, Strawberry hit .417 (5-for-12) with three home runs. Two of those homers came in Game 4, an 8–4 Yankees victory that put them on the brink of their first AL championship in 15 years.

Strawberry's second homer, a two-run shot in the eighth inning off Armando Benitez, provided the Yankees with important insurance runs before John Wetteland closed it out in the ninth. The next day, Strawberry showed that he was not finished, and hit a home run to help the Yankees close out the series with a 6–4 victory.

The Yankees were returning to the Fall Classic for the first time since losing to the Los Angeles Dodgers in 1981. It had been 18 years since the Yankees had won a World Series. Their longest previous dry spell since winning their first title in 1923 had been from 1962 to 1977. And it looked for a while like the 1996 title would go to the defending champion Atlanta Braves, a team with the most imposing pitching staff in baseball. John Smoltz was an easy 12–1 winner over Andy Pettitte in the opener at Yankee Stadium. Adding insult to embarrassment for the Yankees, the Braves' 19-year-old Andruw Jones broke Mickey Mantle's record by becoming the youngest player ever to hit a World Series home run. In fact, he hit two in the game.

Greg Maddux, the four-time Cy Young award winner, was masterful in Game 2, blanking the Yankees on six hits over eight innings. In World Series history, only two teams had ever come back to win after dropping the first two games at home. "I don't know any words of wisdom when you go down 0–2 against the defending world champions," said David Cone, New York's Game 3 starter. The Yankees did not need wisdom—they needed some clutch hits and good pitching, and they got both in Cone's 5–2 win. The Yankees, trailing 2–1 in the World Series and 6–0 after five innings in Game 4, rallied to stun the Braves 8–6 in 10 innings at Atlanta. After three runs in the sixth, the Bombers tied it on Jim Leyritz's three-run homer in the eighth, and won it on Wade Boggs' bases-loaded, two-out walk.

After the dramatic Game 4 win, Pettitte kept the Yankees momentum going by outdueling Smoltz the next night, pitching a four-hit, 1–0 shutout against the Braves going into the ninth inning. After Pettitte allowed a leadoff double to Chipper Jones and retired Fred McGriff on a grounder to first, manager Joe Torre brought relief ace John Wetteland in to preserve the victory. With Braves on first and third and two outs, Luis Polonia stood in the batter's box at Fulton County Stadium and fouled off six Wetteland fastballs before connecting and sending a searing line drive into right-center field. Right fielder Paul O'Neill, playing despite a painful left hamstring, ran with a hobbled gait toward the ball that looked like it was going to win the game for the Braves. But at the last instant O'Neill lunged and snared the ball for the final out.

"I'm glad I had enough to get to the ball," he said.

So were a lot of Yankees fans. Two nights later catcher Joe Girardi's triple in the third inning of Game 6 drove in a run, and he later scored from third. The Yankees' three-run rally that inning was all Jimmy Key needed to defeat Maddux 3–2 in the title-clinching game. "[The Braves] said they could beat the '27 Yankees. But they forgot about the '96 Yankees," said Girardi.

The Yanks were champs for the first time since 1978. The triumph started a run of four Yankees titles in five years. John Wetteland saved each of the Yankees' victories, earning the Series MVP honors. Third baseman Boggs celebrated by trotting around Yankee Stadium on a policeman's horse. During the regular season, Boggs had hit over .300 for the 14th time in his Hall of Fame career.

34 Fear Murderers' Row

It's easy to start an argument among baseball fans. All you need do, for example, is tell a Yankees follower that Leo Durocher was a far better manager than Casey Stengel. Or that Willie Mays could run rings around Mickey Mantle. You can get some mighty sharp retorts, too, when trying to name the greatest team of all time, although you would be hard-pressed to top the New York Yankees of 1927. This was a team that had everything—speed, crushing power, and a marvelous defense.

The 1927 Yankees started the season in first place—and finished in first place. The winning margin? Nineteen games.

The number of victories? One hundred and ten, at that time an American League record. To climax their historic season, the Yankees swept the Pittsburgh Pirates in the World Series. As Casey would say, "You could look it up."

Certainly, teams have won more regular season games. The 1906 Chicago Cubs and the 2001 Seattle Mariners both won 116. Neither of those teams won the World Series, though. The 1998 Yankees won 114 games and, like their pinstriped predecessors, swept the Series. Still, there was something so dominant about the 1927 Yankees that even now it is just about impossible to rank any other team above it.

Start with Babe Ruth, who, batting third in the lineup, broke his own home run record by blasting 60 homers—the first man to reach that total (his record stood until Roger Maris hit 61 in 1961). Batting fourth was Lou Gehrig, who hit 47 home runs, the most any player not named Ruth had ever whacked in one season. Gehrig also had a record-setting 175 runs batted in. Who knows how many more RBIs Gehrig might have had if Ruth hadn't homered so often right before him in the lineup?

But Ruth and Gehrig didn't do all the hitting for the Yankees. Four players drove in more than 100 runs. The team batting average was .307 and no regular player batted under .269. Gehrig batted .373. Ruth and center fielder Earle Combs hit .356, and Combs

Yankees 100-Win Seasons

The Yankees have won 100 or more games in a season 19 times during their history. They won 114 games in 1998 to capture the division title by 22 games over the next-closest opponent, their largest margin ever in the standings. In 1927, they won 110 games for a franchise-best .714 winning pace.

The Yankees won 109 games in 1961, 107 games in 1932, and 106 games in 1939, winning a World Series championship in each of those seasons. They won 104 games in 1963 but lost in the Series to the Dodgers.

Three members of the famous Murderers' Row—Tony Lazzeri, Babe Ruth, and Lou Gehrig—pose at Yankee Stadium in 1927.

led the league in singles. Second baseman Tony Lazzeri batted .309 and pounded out 18 homers, the third-best in the league behind Ruth and Gehrig. All four would one day enter the Hall of Fame. The team slugging percentage—.498—is an all-time record.

So fearsome was the hitting of this group that it became known as "Murderers' Row." Only one pitcher, Lefty Grove of the Philadelphia Athletics, was able to hold the Yankees scoreless in 1927. In a tingling ballgame, the A's won 1–0.

Baseball teams do not win pennants without good pitching. The Yankees of 1927 certainly had their share of it, with four pitchers winning 18 or more games. Waite Hoyt won 22 games, and Herb Pennock won another 19. Much of the credit for the performance of the mound staff, however, went to a relief pitcher—Wilcy

"Cy" Moore. Moore appeared in 50 games as a reliever and won 19 times. Urban Shocker added 18 victories.

The numbers are numbing, but how better to display this team's outrageous power? Well, legend has it that the Pirates were so intimidated watching the Yankees take batting practice before Game 1 of the World Series that playing the games was merely a formality. Indeed, it's hard to believe there was ever a better baseball team than the Yankees of 1927.

35 Bill Dickey

Bill Dickey was one of the best all-around catchers in Major League Baseball history. He was known as a great handler of pitchers, and as a durable iron-man who played a key role on dominant title teams. As a player, Dickey's New York Yankees went to the World Series eight times and won seven championships. Legendary sportswriter Dan Daniels once wrote of Dickey: "He isn't just a catcher, he's a ballclub. He isn't just a player, he's an influence."

Dickey was the foundation of a Yankees dynasty. His playing career extended from 1928 to 1946, bridging the Babe Ruth and Lou Gehrig era to the Joe DiMaggio era. As Gehrig's roommate, Dickey was the first Yankee to find out about Gehrig's illness. Dickey also managed the Yankees in 1946, and mentored a young catcher named Yogi Berra. He completed his connection to the dynasty as a coach with the team throughout the 1950s in the Mickey Mantle era.

As a rookie in 1928, Dickey tried to impress manager Miller Huggins with his home run swing. Huggins explained to him that a team with power hitters such as Ruth and Gehrig didn't need another home run threat. What Huggins wanted was for Dickey to be consistent behind the plate and in the batter's box. And consistency is exactly what the young catcher would provide.

One of the finest hitting catchers of all time, Dickey batted .300 or better in 11 different seasons. His best seasons were in 1936, when he hit .362 and drove in 107 runs in just 112 games; and in 1937, when he hit .332 with 29 homers and 133 RBIs in 140 games. An excellent judge of the strike zone, Dickey struck out only 289 times in 6,300 at-bats, including the 1935 season when he struck out just 11 times. No player has ever hit a higher percentage of home runs at his home ballpark than Dickey, who hit 135 of his 202 career homers (66.8 percent) at Yankee Stadium.

Defensively, he set a record by catching at least 100 games for 13 seasons in a row, a mark that wasn't equaled until Johnny Bench accomplished it in the 1970s. Dickey led AL catchers in assists three times and putouts six times. In 1931, he became the first catcher to play an entire season without allowing a passed ball. He was the American League's starting catcher in six of the first nine All-Star Games, and was selected as an All-Star 11 times.

"Dickey was the heart of the team defensively and commanded tremendous respect from the Yankee pitchers," said teammate Billy Werber. "Once the game started, he ran the show."

No catcher has caught more World Series games than Bill Dickey (38), and he caught every inning of those games he played in. Dickey wasn't just along for the ride, of course. He hit .438 in the 1932 World Series, went 4-for-4 in Game 1 of the 1938 Series, and drove in at least one run in each game of the 1939 Series. But his biggest October moment came in the fifth game of the 1943 World Series—with the Yankees minus the great DiMaggio, who was away on military duty—when Dickey broke a scoreless battle in the sixth inning with a two-run home run against the St. Louis Cardinals that spurred the Yankees to another title, Dickey's last as a player.

He spent the 1944 and 1945 seasons in the U.S. Navy. Midway through the 1946 season Dickey took over as manager of the Yankees, but didn't return the following season. He returned as a Yankees coach under manager Casey Stengel and helped teach Yogi Berra to be a great catcher. Dickey handed the task of catching for a Yankees dynasty over to Berra, and Berra carried the torch into the 1960s before he followed Dickey into the Hall of Fame.

Dickey was inducted into the Hall of Fame in 1954 and Berra in 1972, the year the Yankees retired uniform No. 8 for both men. Ironically, Dickey didn't wear that number at the start or the end of his career. When Dickey was a rookie, Benny Bengough wore No. 8. When he came back to coach, Yogi Berra was wearing it. On August 21, 1988, the Yankees honored both catchers with plaques in Yankee Stadium's Monument Park.

36 Ron Guidry

Ron Guidry's 170 victories rank fifth on the Yankees' all-time win list. He's also third-best in strikeouts, with 18 of those 1,778 occurring one otherwordly night against the California Angels in 1978. Guidry was dominant that year, with a 25–3 record and 1.74 earned-run average rating among the best seasons any pitcher has ever had.

Guidry burst on the scene as a fill-in starting pitcher in 1977. He pitched well and never left the rotation. He ended the year with a 16–7 record with five shutouts and a 2.82 earned-run average. Then he won a playoff game and a World Series game.

Guidry won his first 13 decisions of the 1978 season, including an 18-strikeout performance against the California Angels on June

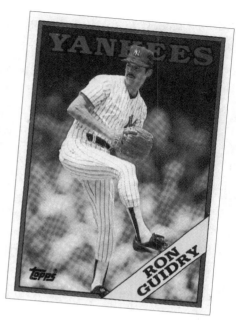

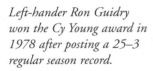

Left-hander Ron Guidry won the Cy Young award in 1978 after posting a 25–3 regular season record.

17. He would win his 20th game of the season on September 4 in typically dominant fashion. He went the distance for a 9–1 victory over the Detroit Tigers. He struck out eight, walked three, and allowed only five hits. With the win, Guidry extended his record to 20–2, a start bettered only by Roger Clemens, who began 20–1 in 2001. But Guidry was far from done. He won five more games in the season's final month to win 25, the fourth-highest total in Yankees history.

That season his 1.74 earned-run average was the lowest in the majors for a left-hander since Sandy Koufax was in his prime, and the lowest for an American League lefty since 1914. His .893 winning percentage set a major league record for 20-game winners. He set a team record with nine shutouts, the most by an American League left-hander since 1916, when Babe Ruth had nine. He pitched 16 complete games, 12 of them five-hitters or better. And his 248 strikeouts broke Jack Chesbro's 74-year-old team record. Guidry was the unanimous choice for the Cy Young award and he finished second to Boston's Jim Rice in the Most Valuable Player voting.

It was Guidry who single-handedly kept the Yankees close to the first-place Red Sox during the regular season. When the two teams ended the 1978 season in a first-place tie, Guidry won the tie-breaking game on just three days' rest at Fenway Park in Boston, when Bucky Dent hit his famous three-run home run off Mike Torrez, propelling the Yankees into the playoffs and highlighting one of the great team comebacks in baseball history. For an encore, Guidry won two games in the postseason, including a complete-game victory over future Hall of Famer Don Sutton in Game 3, as the Yankees won their second consecutive World Series title.

During this time, Guidry developed a strong relationship with Thurman Munson, who caught Guidry regularly until Munson's death in a plane crash in 1979.

"What was so great about Munson to me was that I never had to think about pitching," said Guidry. "All he ever said to me was, 'Whenever you see me give you a [sign], just give me your best pitch. Don't worry about where the glove is—just throw it.' If Munson asked for a fastball away, it didn't mean he wanted it exactly where his glove was. It meant that he wanted your best fast-ball from the middle of the plate away. Munson was very easy to pitch to, and I didn't have to think about many things as a pitcher, other than to trust what he was doing."

In 1979, Guidry posted the lowest earned-run average by an American League pitcher, earning his second ERA title, and was selected to his second All-Star Game. He won 21 games in 1983 and 22 games in 1985. Cat-like quick off the mound and a natural athlete, Guidry won five Gold Glove awards in a row for fielding excellence at his position from 1982 to 1986.

Guidry was a Yankees co-captain from 1986 to 1988, when he called it a career after 14 years wearing pinstripes. His jersey No. 49 was retired in 2003.

37 Dynasty Years 1936 to 1939: The Bronx Bombers

Babe Ruth had ruled as the king of baseball in the Roaring Twenties, but by 1935, he had retired. Not to worry, for the Yankees were reloading and building a new dynasty to dominate the end of the decade. Ammunition arrived in 1936 in the form of Joe DiMaggio. The shy, soft-spoken center fielder hit .323 his rookie season, with 29 home runs and 125 runs batted in. First baseman Lou Gehrig, a holdover from the great Yankees teams of the 1920s, batted a sparkling .354, drove in 152 runs, and hit an American League–leading 49 homers. The Yankees bludgeoned their opponents, winning 102 regular season games, and sprinted past the other teams in the standings as if they were standing still, winning the American League pennant by 19.5 games over their next-closest rival. In the first Subway Series since 1923 and the Yankees' first Fall Classic without the Babe, the Bronx Bombers whipped the New York Giants in six games. DiMaggio banged out nine hits, including three doubles, and drove in three runs. It was the start of a record-setting winning streak.

The Yankees used 1936 as a springboard to an unprecedented four consecutive World Series victories. A lineup that included Gehrig, DiMaggio, second baseman Tony Lazzeri, shortstop Frank Crosetti, third baseman Red Rolfe, catcher Bill Dickey, and outfielders George Selkirk and Jake Powell fronted a pitching staff that featured Red Ruffing, Lefty Gomez, and Monte Pearson. Outfielders Tommy Henrich and Charlie Keller arrived in 1937 and 1939, respectively. Joe Gordon replaced Lazzeri in 1938.

The Yankees were good enough in 1937 to win 102 regular season games for the second straight season, this time romping to a 13-game bulge in the pennant chase. The Yankees again made short work of the Giants in the World Series, this time needing only five games to defeat their crosstown rivals. Gehrig enjoyed his last productive season, batting .351 with 37 homers and 159 RBIs. DiMaggio enjoyed a monster season, batting .346 with a league-leading 46 homers to go with 167 RBIs. Dickey finished at .332 and smacked 29 homers and 133 RBIs. The Yankees also had the American League's only two 20-game winners in lefty Gomez and righty Ruffing, and a standout relief pitcher in Johnny Murphy, who recorded 12 victories coming out of the bullpen.

Gehrig would drop off to .295 in 1938, but the Yankees were still good enough to reach 99 wins and reach the World Series again. This time, led by pitchers Ruffing, Gomez, Pearson, and Spud Chandler, the two-time defending world champion Yankees swept their opponent, the Chicago Cubs, in four games, in the process becoming the first team to win three straight World Series.

In 1939, Gehrig would fall victim to amyotrophic lateral sclerosis, a crippling, incurable disease that would force him out of the Yankees lineup after 2,130 consecutive games and take his life two years later. Yankees fans hoped that DiMaggio would be "another Gehrig." But DiMaggio was his own man, and in the years that followed he showed that he was a superstar in his own way.

For the Yankees, 1939 was business as usual; they won 106 games and the pennant by 17 games. DiMaggio batted .381 to lead the American League, and captured the first of his three Most Valuable Player awards. The Yankees won their fourth consecutive World Series by sweeping the Cincinnati Reds. The Yankees had won 12 of their last 13 Series games and 28 of their last 31 Series games.

Without Gehrig, the mantle of leadership fell on DiMaggio's shoulders, and he wore it well in 1940, again pacing the team and leading the American League with a .352 batting average. This time, however, the Bronx Bombers fell short. In a tight three-team race, it was the Detroit Tigers who beat the Cleveland Indians (by a game) and the Yankees (by two games) to take the pennant.

While manager Joe McCarthy was fortunate enough to have a great collection of stars in pinstripes in the late 1930s, he ran his ballclub as a unit. Some say he developed a machine that operated so efficiently he only had to push a button to win a ballgame. If one looks at the record, it certainly did seem that the Yankees had a machine-like quality. They won four consecutive World Series between 1936 through 1939, and they didn't lose a game in the 1938 and 1939 Series. Four world championship titles in a row—and only three losses in 19 World Series games played.

But Joe McCarthy was not a "push-button manager," for it takes great skill to handle a large group of talented ballplayers. It isn't easy to keep them happy and to keep them winning. As for the players, they need more than mechanical ability to win consistently. It takes spirit, unselfishness, and courage. The team captain, Lou Gehrig, above all others personified those qualities.

38 Phil Rizzuto

Phil Rizzuto took over for Frank Crosetti as the Yankees shortstop in 1941 and played his entire career in the Bronx, spanning the years of the Yankees' greatest dynasty. He overcame his diminutive size—he is generously listed as 5'6" and 160 pounds—to anchor Yankees teams that won eight World Series titles, including an unprecedented five in a row from 1949 to 1953.

Born in Brooklyn, the son of a trolley car conductor, Philip Francis Rizzuto was affectionately known as "Scooter." To fans of an earlier time lucky enough to see him glide after a ball in the third-base hole or flash up the middle to snare a grounder, the

An eight-time World Series champion and five-time All-Star, shortstop Phil Rizzuto was an anchor of the Yankees during the 1940s and early 1950s.

PHIL RIZZUTO
Champion Base Ball Fielder

moniker was a perfect fit. For 13 seasons Scooter wore the pin-stripes with flair—and a wad of gum on the button of his cap.

He played with a youthful exuberance, but he was dead serious about winning. Unfazed by pressure, Rizzuto performed at his best in October. In fact, he played in 52 World Series games—the most of any shortstop—and made just five errors. He played in 21 consecutive Series games without an error. So reliably did he make the routine play that pitcher Vic Raschi once told a reporter, "My best pitch is anything the batter grounds, lines, or pops up in the direction of Rizzuto."

Stellar defense made Rizzuto a difference maker, but he was also a catalyst at the top of the batting order. He peaked offensively in 1950, reaching career highs with a .324 batting average and 125 runs scored. He won the American League's Most Valuable Player award that year, and the next year was MVP of the World Series. Following his retirement in 1956, Rizzuto moved right into the Bombers' broadcasting booth and manned the microphone as the voice of the Yankees for another 40 years. Rizzuto spoke a unique language of malapropisms and non sequiturs, and he was a shameless homer. His distinctive cry of "Holy cow!" was the rallying call of Yankees fans for two generations.

The Yankees retired Rizzuto's jersey No. 10 at Yankee Stadium on August 4, 1985. Several members of the superb Yankees teams of the late 1940s and early 1950s were brought together for the occasion. They gathered around Rizzuto near home plate, listening

Holy Cow! It's Scooter's Big Day!

Holy cow! There was a Phil Rizzuto Day at Yankee Stadium on August 4, 1985. A celebration to retire Rizzuto's uniform jersey No. 10 was held during a pregame ceremony before the Yankees took on the Chicago White Sox. Most of the crowd of 54,032 filing excitedly into Yankee Stadium on that sunny Sunday afternoon in the Bronx had come out to honor Rizzuto, the legendary shortstop and loveable broadcaster. But some had come out to witness another New York icon, Tom Seaver, now pitching for Chicago, try for his 300th career victory.

It turned out to be a terrific day.

Returning to the city where he won his first game back in 1967 as a 22-year-old Mets phenom, Seaver, now 40, pitched a six-hit, complete-game victory. When Don Baylor hit a high fly to left field on Seaver's 145th pitch for the final out of the 4–1 win, the crowd roared its appreciation for the pitcher who turned New York's National League team, the Mets, from loveable losers into world champions.

Seaver became only the 17th pitcher in major league history to reach 300 wins—and the first ever to achieve the feat at Yankee Stadium.

While it is understandable why Yankees fans would want to witness Seaver make history, the game played on Phil Rizzuto Day may have been the only time Yankees fans ever rooted against their team at Yankee Stadium.

with approval as the master of ceremonies on the field spoke in glowing terms of their celebrated former teammate.

Among many of the gifts given to Rizzuto as part of the pregame festivities, the Yankees brought on to the field a cow wearing a halo—a real, live, holy cow. The bovine, named Huckleberry, accidentally stepped on Rizzuto's foot, knocking the elegant 67-year-old honoree to the ground. Holy cow, indeed! Hushed thousands watched and waited for Rizzuto to regain his feet (and his dignity). He did so gracefully, waving to the row upon row of relieved, smiling faces that walled the stadium. Then the crowd, along with former Yankees greats Joe DiMaggio, Mickey Mantle, Whitey Ford, Hank Bauer, and Tommy Heinrich, proudly watched as Rizzuto's jersey No. 10 was retired, and a plaque dedicated in Monument Park commemorating the career of a lifelong Yankee.

Suddenly, the microphone was thrust at Rizzuto, and when he said simply that having his number retired by the Yankees meant more to him than making the Hall of Fame, the ecstatic crowd erupted into a prolonged ovation. To Rizzuto, it must have felt like a group hug from a loving family.

As time passed, Hall of Fame voters annually underestimated Rizzuto's deserving credentials. Slick fielding and intelligent leadership, to be sure, are assets not easily quantified, so Rizzuto's vote total for induction always seemed to come up short. Throughout the years of being passed over for the Hall, he had said he would accept entrance any way into Cooperstown—"If they want a batboy, I'll go in as a batboy."

In 1994, after a 38-year wait, Scooter finally did get the call telling him that he was voted into the Hall of Fame.

Those huckleberries are still looking for a batboy.

39 Terry's Redemption

Ralph Terry's name is synonymous with one of the most famous home runs in baseball history. In the 1960 World Series, the Yankees and Pittsburgh Pirates were deadlocked at three games apiece and the score was tied 9–9 in the deciding seventh game. Pittsburgh second baseman Bill Mazeroski was the leadoff batter in the bottom of the ninth inning against Terry. The right-hander threw one ball and, on Terry's second pitch, Mazeroski swung and blasted a high fly ball that cleared the Forbes Field left-field wall for a home run to win the Series for the Pirates. The home run was the most dramatic conclusion to a Game 7 in World Series history.

Afterward in the Yankees clubhouse, the press hounded Terry, the losing pitcher. When asked if he had thrown Mazeroski a fastball or curve, a dejected Terry said, "I don't know what the pitch was. All I know is it was the wrong one."

Two years later, Ralph Terry was standing nervously on the mound at San Francisco's Candlestick Park in the bottom of the ninth inning of Game 7 of the 1962 World Series. The Yankees were clinging to a 1–0 lead, but Matty Alou stood on third base as the tying run for the Giants, and Willie Mays was on second representing the winning run. The imposing figure coming up to bat was the left-handed slugging Willie McCovey, who had already blasted a tape-measure home run off Terry in Game 2 of the Series, and in his previous at-bat had hit a booming triple over the center fielder's head.

Yankees manager Ralph Houk went to the mound to speak to his pitching ace. Terry was the American League's winningest and most durable pitcher in 1962 with 23 wins and 299 innings pitched. He also surrendered a league-high 40 home runs, the most ever given up by a Yankees pitcher in a season. Traditional strategy in such a tight spot says to intentionally walk McCovey, creating a force at any base, and pitching to the next batter, the right-handed hitting Orlando Cepeda, also no slouch. Houk asked his pitcher what he wanted to do.

"I'd just as soon get it over now," Terry replied.

At this tense moment Terry could only be thinking that he had been in this situation before. Terry was facing another confrontation that would end with him being a Series hero or goat. In baseball, the difference often is measured in inches.

Terry anxiously made his crucial decision to pitch to the 6'4", 225-pound McCovey. If Terry could get McCovey out, it would be his Fall Classic redemption. With two outs and the World Series on the line, Terry let fly a fastball. McCovey nailed it, smashing a blistering line drive that was heading toward right field like a bullet. But Yankees second baseman Bobby Richardson speared the ball in his mitt for the final out.

"I really didn't have time to think about it," Richardson recalled. "It was just hit too hard."

The Yankees were champions for the second straight season and had captured the World Series flag for the 20th time in their history. Terry, who was named the Series Most Valuable Player, had atoned for losing the seventh game against Pittsburgh in 1960 by shutting out the Giants on four hits in a nerve-wracking Game 7 that clinched the 1962 Series for New York.

McCovey's near-Series-winning hit was immortalized by *Peanuts* cartoonist and anguished Giants fan Charles M. Schulz, in a strip in which a glum Charlie Brown laments: "Why couldn't McCovey have hit the ball just three feet higher?"

40 Ron Blomberg

Ron Blomberg was the first overall pick in the 1967 amateur draft and he made his New York Yankees debut on September 10, 1969. But he made baseball history when he stepped into the batter's box on Opening Day in 1973. The Yankees were playing the Boston Red Sox in Fenway Park, and the American League was unveiling its new designated hitter rule. The "designated pinch hitter" is a player used as an extra batter who usually hits in the pitcher's spot in the batting order. In the first inning, Blomberg became the first DH to bat in a major league game.

Nearly four decades have passed since Blomberg's momentous at-bat, and his claim to fame—as well as the DH rule—is here to stay.

"It's incredible," said Blomberg of his notoriety. "I was an answer in Trivial Pursuit. I was a question on *Jeopardy*. And it all happened because I pulled a hamstring in spring training 20 years ago."

Indeed, it was a twist of fate that made Blomberg the first designated hitter. Yankees manager Ralph Houk had not once tried Blomberg, a first baseman, as the DH during spring training, opting instead for Felipe Alou or Johnny Callison. But days before the season started, Blomberg suffered a slight pull in his right hamstring.

"Ralph told me that if it was cold in Boston on Opening Day, he might put me in the lineup as the DH to keep me from really hurting myself," said Blomberg.

On April 6, 1973, the temperature in Boston was in the low 40s, but 25-mph wind gusts made it feel much colder. When the Yankees lineup card was posted, Blomberg was listed as the designated hitter. Immediately, the sportswriters flocked around him to ask how he liked being the DH. "I don't know," Blomberg answered, "I've never done it before."

At game time, the wind played a key role in Blomberg's destiny. After Red Sox starting pitcher Luis Tiant retired the first two Yankees batters, Matty Alou hit what should have been a routine, inning-ending fly ball. But the wind currents played havoc with the baseball, and it dropped in front of center fielder Reggie Smith for a double. Tiant then walked Bobby Murcer and Graig Nettles to load the bases, setting the stage for Blomberg.

He approached the plate and dug in. "Why are you the designated hitter?" Red Sox catcher Carlton Fisk asked Blomberg. "I thought the DH is supposed to be some guy 60 years old."

"Sometimes," joked Blomberg, "my body does feel 60."

Tiant still had trouble finding his control, and he walked Blomberg, forcing in a Yankees run. The first major league appearance by a designated hitter was not an official at-bat, although Blomberg was credited with a run batted in. The DH rule wasted no time adding offense to the game.

"When I got to first base, I looked at the umpire and I didn't know what to do," explained Blomberg, who was unsure about his status as a DH once on base. "He told me to just do what I always do."

The Yankees scored twice more in the inning to take a 3–0 lead. When the side was retired, Blomberg instinctively remained on the base paths, waiting for a teammate to bring him his glove. It never arrived.

"Our pitcher [Mel Stottlemyre] was already warming up and [first baseman] Felipe Alou was throwing grounders for infield practice when I hustled off the field. [Coach] Elston Howard told me to sit down next to him on the bench."

The Yankees' 3–0 lead was short-lived, and they eventually lost 15–5. The batting star was Fisk, who hit two home runs, including a grand slam, and drove in six runs. Ironically, the only Red Sox regular who didn't get a hit was their DH, Orlando Cepeda.

For the record, Blomberg went 1-for-3 on the day. He walked, got a broken-bat single, lined out, and flied out. Still, he was the media's focal point in the clubhouse when the game ended.

"We lose 15–5, and what seemed like 100 reporters were asking me questions about being the first DH," said Blomberg. "That's when I realized that I was a part of history."

Yankees public relations director Marty Appel never doubted that history was in the making. He grabbed Blomberg's bat and shipped it to the Hall of Fame, where the Louisville Slugger is still prominently displayed. The wood Blomberg used to get his broken-bat single ended up in the garbage heap.

If Blomberg had not hurt his leg, and if the weather had not been cold, and if a windblown fly ball had not fallen safely, Cepeda, not the Boomer, might have been the first DH to bat.

"People might have forgotten about me if I wasn't the first DH," said Blomberg. "There aren't too many firsts in baseball, and I'm a first. The first DH. I went into the Hall of Fame through the back door. Who ever thought that one at-bat could be so important?"

By early July of 1973, Blomberg was batting over .400 when *Sports Illustrated* featured him and teammate Murcer on the magazine's cover with the billing "Pride of the Yankees." Blomberg finished his best season ever batting .329 in 301 at-bats with 12 homers and 57 runs batted in.

Blomberg served as the Yankees DH in 56 games in 1973, and he projected the proper attitude about his role, "If Ralph [Houk] thinks I can help most by being the DH, then it's all right with me," he said. "I love to play, but I know that I'm a better hitter than anything else."

In the three years that followed, knee and shoulder injuries limited the Boomer's playing time, and he missed the 1977 season entirely. He attempted a comeback in 1978 with the Chicago White Sox, but his stroke had disappeared.

Blomberg hit with little power and his .231 average dropped his lifetime batting average from .302 to .293. At age 30, the Boomer's career was over.

"I'm happy I gave it one last shot," said Blomberg, "but it did cost me my .300 lifetime average. Maybe then I'd be remembered for something else besides being the first DH. But at least I have that."

41 Chant Roll Call with the Bleacher Creatures

The Bleacher Creatures are a fanatical group of Yankees rooters who are known for their imaginative use of chants and songs. The most popular chant is the roll call that starts each game, in which the Creatures chant the name of each starting position player ("DER-ek JE-ter!" clap-clap-clapclapclap) until each one responds with a wave, a tip of the hat, or something more inventive.

The Bleacher Creatures occupied Section 39 in the right-field bleachers of the original Yankee Stadium. In 2009, they were relocated and currently sit in Section 203 of the right-field bleachers in the new Yankee Stadium.

"You should know what you're getting into when you sit with the Creatures," said Filip Bondy, author of *Bleeding Pinstripes: A Season with the Bleacher Creatures at Yankee Stadium*. "If you want a nice, comfortable seat where you never have to stand up and nobody ever curses, the Creatures are not for you. But if you want to be among passionate people and you don't mind standing half the game, it's a fun place to be."

Yankee Stadium's Bleacher Creatures have become an integral part of the New York game-day experience.

The roll call tradition started during a game in the early 1990s, when longtime fan Ali Ramirez organized the fans in his section of the bleachers to chant the name of popular Yankees first baseman Tino Martinez, who responded with a wave of his glove, delighting the cheering fans. Roll call has been one of the trademarks of Yankee Stadium ever since.

Ramirez, known as "the original Bleacher Creature" because he rang a cowbell to inspire the fans to cheer, died in 1996. That year, the Yankees paid tribute to Ramirez before a game against the Seattle Mariners by installing a gold plaque where he sat, in Section 39, Row A, Seat 29, which reads, "This seat is taken. In memory of Ali Ramirez, 'The Original Bleacher Creature.'" Fittingly, Yankees pitcher Dwight Gooden threw a no-hitter to cap off the day. The plaque was moved to the new stadium and is now located in Section 203, Row 7, Seat 25. Before every game a Creature polishes the plaque.

Since 1999, the job of starting roll call has belonged to "Bald" Vinny Milano, who joined the group of Bleacher Creatures in the late 1990s. The Creatures' roll call occurs in the top of the first inning, when the Yankees are on the field, right after the starting pitcher throws the game's first pitch. Everyone in the section stands

Sing and Dance to "YMCA"

The Village People was one of the most successful disco groups from the late 1970s. The group's big hit, "YMCA," released in 1978, reached No. 2 on the pop charts. The song has remained a favorite for 40 years and is still a very popular song at sporting events, especially baseball games where it is often played between innings.

The song plays at Yankee Stadium after the fifth inning while the grounds crew is dragging the infield base paths. When the song reaches its chorus, the groundskeepers drop what they're doing to lead the crowd in the "YMCA" dance. The wildly popular "YMCA" dance craze involves the dancers moving their arms to form the letters Y-M-C-A as they are sung in the chorus:

Y - Arms outstretched and raised
M - Made by bending the elbows from the "Y" pose so the fingertips meet atop one's head
C - Arms extended to the left, forming a "C"
A - Hands held together above head, forming a triangle

The tradition began at the original Yankee Stadium when the Yankees opened at home against the Kansas City Royals on April 9, 1996. With a driving snowstorm battering players and fans alike, five Yankee Stadium groundskeepers began their customary walk to clean the infield after the fifth inning. Then, from the loudspeakers, a familiar horn riff and disco beat kicked in. Soon, the groundskeepers began to dance, strut, and gyrate around second base while they dragged the field. The capacity crowd roared with approving laughter, and a tradition was born. The grounds crew performed the song in the ticker tape parade that celebrated the Yankees' 1996 World Series win. And in July of 2008, the Village People performed "YMCA" with the Yankees grounds crew at the last MLB All-Star Game held at the original Yankee Stadium.

and begins clapping their hands. After the first pitch is thrown, Bald Vinny shouts out the name of center fielder Jacoby Ellsbury ("Ells-bur-ry!"). The rest of the group then chants the player's name until there is a response, usually a perfunctory wave of the glove. Some Yankees, however, respond with extra enthusiasm, such as left fielder Brett Gardner, who typically flexes his muscles in what is called his "gun show," and right fielder Aaron Judge, who turns to face the Creatures, points to them, and taps his glove two times.

The Creatures move through the defensive alignment, going from the center fielder to the left fielder, right fielder, first baseman, second baseman, shortstop, and third baseman, in that order. (With the exception of a few rare instances, the pitcher and the catcher are not a part of the roll call. The only pitcher included in the roll call every time he pitched was David Wells.) While most players respond immediately to their name during roll call, former Yankees third baseman Scott Brosius was known for teasing the Creatures by waiting as long as a minute to acknowledge them. In Hideki Matsui's first game at the stadium in 2003, the chant of "Mat-Su-I" continued for nearly two minutes, because the Japanese star had no idea how to react when faced with this form of culture shock.

Over the years, the Creatures have had a love-hate relationship with the Yankees organization. The Creatures' antics toward opposing fans, which sometimes bordered on vitriolic, are one reason beer sales were banned in the old stadium's bleachers for several years. But the Creatures also credit the team's front office with helping them migrate from the old stadium to the new place and for making sure they got a large bloc of season tickets together.

As to whether or not the Creatures' enthusiasm contributes to the Yankees' success, there's no scientific answer. But one thing is an absolute: Yankee Stadium is regarded by many opponents as one of the most intimidating venues in pro sports. Not surprisingly, Bald Vinny believes the Creatures have something to do with the menacing atmosphere. "We like to create the energy. If we're loud and the players know we've got their back, they get amped up," he declares.

The players agree, especially former right-fielder Nick Swisher, whose position in right field is closest to the Creatures' hangout. "The Bleacher Creatures are the best. They're the essence of the stadium's vibe. To have that honor to play right field in front of them every day has been great. I think I've developed a great relationship with them. They're my peeps."

After leaving the Yankees in 2009, Jason Giambi went even further in his praise. "The biggest thing I miss is [the Bleacher Creatures'] roll call. There's no doubt about it, it's the best thing in baseball."

That made all Bleacher Creatures proud. "I mean, of all the things to miss about the city of New York, he's going to miss me and my yokel friends! That's unreal," said Bald Vinny.

42 A-Rod Makes History

Alex Rodriguez proved to be a one-man wrecking crew when the Yankees demolished the Angels in a 12–4 rout at Yankee Stadium on April 26, 2005. Rodriguez hit three home runs in his first three at-bats and became only the 11th major league player with 10 or more RBIs in a game. It was surely his greatest game in pinstripes.

All three blasts were hit off Bartolo Colon, who would win the Cy Young award that season. Alex's first home run was a three-run moon shot high over the left-center-field wall. His second homer was a two-run blast lined into the same area. His third homer, a grand slam, was a towering drive that crashed into the center-field bleachers some 475 feet away. In his first three at-bats, Rodriguez had three home runs and nine runs batted in—but he wasn't done. He added a run-scoring single in the sixth inning and finished with 10 runs batted in, falling one short of the American League record of 11, set by the Yankees' Tony Lazzeri in 1936. The major league single-game record of 12 RBIs is shared by the St. Louis Cardinals' Jim Bottomley (1924) and Mark Whiten (1993).

"When I got to first base after that last hit, I was on top of a cloud," said Rodriguez. "You definitely don't want a moment like that to end. Tonight was one of those magical nights. You want it to last forever. This is definitely a night I'll never forget."

Later that year, he slugged his 400th career home run on June 8, 2005—making him the youngest ever to reach that mark. Rodriguez was 29 years and 316 days old; Ken Griffey Jr., the previous record holder, reached 400 home runs at 30 years, 141 days. Rodriguez also is the youngest ever to hit 500 and 600 homers. He hit his 500th career home run against Kansas City Royals pitcher Kyle Davies at Yankee Stadium on August 4, 2007, just eight days after his 32nd birthday. On the three-year anniversary of hitting his 500th home run, he hit No. 600 at Yankee Stadium against Shaun Marcum of the Toronto Blue Jays. Fittingly, the ball landed on the netting atop Monument Park in center field. At 35 years and eight days old, he was again the youngest to reach the milestone.

Rodriguez is without question one of the greatest players in all of baseball history. He was a complete player. He could run, throw, field, and hit with the best. His powerful bat produced eye-popping statistics. During his first 15 full seasons in the major leagues, he batted .300 or better nine times, hit 30 or more home runs 14 times, won five home run titles, and three Most Valuable Player awards.

Rodriguez had surgery to repair a torn labrum in his right hip prior to the 2009 season. He returned to the team on May 8 in Baltimore at Camden Yards and hit a three-run home run on the first pitch he saw from Orioles starter Jeremy Guthrie in the Yankees' 4–0 victory. The team struggled early in the season without Rodriguez, but after his return, the Yankees caught fire, winning the division and posting the best record in baseball.

On the final day of the 2009 season against the Tampa Bay Rays at Tropicana Field, Alex hit a grand slam and a three-run home run in the sixth inning, becoming the first American League player ever to drive in seven runs in an inning. (The major league record is eight and was set by Fernando Tatis of the St. Louis Cardinals, who hit two grand slams in one inning on April 23, 1999.) With those blasts Rodriguez also set a major league record, becoming the first player to have 13 seasons with at least 30 home runs and 100 runs batted in.

"It's magical," said Yankees hitting coach Kevin Long. "He comes in his first game in Baltimore and hits a home run, and then this last game he hits a grand slam. You just shake your head at the things he's able to do."

But despite his formidable gifts, Alex has never won the deep or lasting affection of fans, likely because of his huge contract, good looks, and his reputation for struggling in the postseason. That changed when Rodriguez shined during the 2009 playoffs. He hit a game-tying home run off Minnesota's Joe Nathan in the bottom of the ninth of Game 2 of the AL Division Series and in the ALCS against the Angels, he hit .429 with three homers and six RBIs. During a torrid seven-game stretch he hit five homers, drove in 11 runs, and scored nine times. Rodriguez then won his first World Series when the Yankees defeated the Philadelphia Phillies in six games. A-Rod got a clutch hit in Game 4, driving in the go-ahead run with two outs in the ninth inning off closer Brad Lidge.

"It's wonderful to see," Reggie Jackson said of Rodriguez's postseason success. "I'm diggin' it. It's like watching a star in a movie. We all knew he had it in him. And when you see it come out like this, there's a real joy in it."

Chesbro's 1904 Season

Jack Chesbro pitched the very first game in the history of the New York Yankees, then known as the Highlanders, on April 22, 1903. The Yankees lost the game 3–1 in Washington, D.C., that day, but did very little losing when Chesbro pitched thereafter. By the end of the following season, Chesbro was the winningest pitcher in the game. Using his masterful spitball to great effect, Chesbro threw a four-hit complete game to beat the Boston Red Sox (then known as the Americans) 3–2 on October 7, 1904. It was a respectable effort for the 30-year-old right-hander; what made it extraordinary was that it was Chesbro's 41st win of the season, a major league record that still stands.

Chesbro produced eye-popping pitching statistics in 1904, but is best remembered for his final pitch of that ill-fated season. The Yankees were in a neck-and-neck battle with the Red Sox. On October 10, the last day of the season, the teams met in a double-header at Hilltop Park in New York. Boston was in first place, one game ahead of the New Yorkers. To win the pennant, the Yankees needed to win both games of the doubleheader. With Chesbro on the mound for the first game, their chances looked promising.

But Chesbro had his hands full, dueling Boston's Bill Dinneen through eight innings. When Chesbro strode from the dugout to start the top of the ninth inning, the score was tied at 2–2. Boston catcher Lou Criger opened with a single. A sacrifice bunt put him on second base. An infield out moved him to third. Chesbro needed only one out to get out of the inning. The 30,000 New York fans were confident Chesbro would work out of the jam when the count on the batter reached one ball and two strikes. Then Chesbro uncorked a spitball that sailed over the catcher's head to the backstop, allowing the go-ahead run to score. When New York failed to score in the bottom of the ninth, the pennant was clinched for Boston. The Highlanders had lost on Chesbro's wild pitch. For years fans said it was the costliest wild pitch ever thrown.

Chesbro had been enjoying a dream season in 1904. He won 41 games—six by shutout— and lost only 12, with a miniscule 1.82 earned-run average. He completed 48 of 51 starts—including his first 30 starts in a row—and pitched four games in relief. He pitched 454⅔ innings, and allowed just 338 hits. During a particularly dominant stretch he won 14 consecutive games. He led the American League in wins, winning percentage, games started, complete games, and innings pitched. It had been a magical season for Chesbro—until the wild pitch.

"Happy" Jack Chesbro won 19 games in 1905 and 23 in 1906 before retiring in 1909 with 198 career victories. He was forever haunted by the wild pitch until his death in 1931. Friends are said to have lobbied the commissioner's office to change the official scorer's decision to a passed ball, but without success. Chesbro was elected to the Hall of Fame in 1946. His plaque incorrectly credits him with only 192 victories. It says nothing about the wild pitch.

44 Joe DiMaggio: The Yankee Clipper

Someone once asked Joe DiMaggio why he played so hard day in and day out. He replied, "There might be someone in the park who's never seen me play before."

DiMaggio was among the game's greatest natural right-handed hitters. He could hit for average and hit for power. He had a lifetime batting average of .325 and hit 361 home runs. DiMaggio had a great batting eye for a power hitter, as the numbers suggest: in his 13-year career, he struck out only 369 times. He was the picture of grace in the outfield—not flashy, but he always knew where he should be and got there in plenty of time to make the catch. His manager, Joe McCarthy, called him the best base runner he had ever seen.

DiMaggio couldn't hit a ball as far as his Yankees predecessor, Babe Ruth, and DiMaggio did not relish the spotlight off the field either, despite his marriage to movie star Marilyn Monroe. He was quiet and kept to himself most of the time. But there was no question that he was the Yankees' leader.

Raised in San Francisco, the son of a fisherman, DiMaggio preceded two brothers, Vince and Dom, in the big leagues. Dom was a noted player for the Boston Red Sox in his own right. But it was Joe who inspired songs and poems and married America's sexiest movie star in 1954. And it's Joe who has come to symbolize the beauty and grace of sports in a purer time.

The Yankee Clipper was perhaps the most elegant player the game has known. He had a style and presence that both teammates and fans recognized and appreciated. And while his reserved, private nature might today be viewed as aloofness, in the 1940s DiMaggio was considered the epitome of class. It didn't hurt that he played for the dominant team of the era, in the country's biggest media market.

DiMaggio first attracted attention when he joined the Yankees in 1936, setting American League rookie records for runs (132) and hitting .323 with 29 home runs and 125 RBIs. Yankees fans knew they had found their next star. DiMaggio was voted the AL MVP three times, in 1939, 1941, and 1947. He won two batting crowns, hitting .381 in 1939 and .352 in 1940. In 1941 he beat Ted Williams for the MVP award despite the fact that Williams hit .406 for the season. DiMaggio did something even more incredible that year: he hit safely in 56 consecutive games, setting a major league record that may never be broken.

After the 1942 season DiMaggio, along with many other great stars of the game, went into military service during World War II. He missed three years (1943–45) at the height of his career. He returned to the Yankees in 1946 and picked up where he had left off, leading the league in home runs (39) and RBIs (155) in 1948.

DiMaggio was a champion. In his 13 seasons with the Yankees, the team won 10 AL pennants and an incredible nine World Series. Four of those titles—1947, 1949, 1950, and 1951—came after DiMaggio's return from military service.

When fans welcomed him back on Joe DiMaggio Day, the Yankee Clipper addressed the crowd from home plate. He apologized to the people in the bleachers because the microphones made

Joe and Marilyn

When Joe DiMaggio and Marilyn Monroe began their courtship in 1952, the public was captivated. It was a storybook romance between a legendary baseball hero and the biggest, most alluring star on the screen. On January 14, 1954, the two were married in a civil ceremony in San Francisco, DiMaggio's hometown. Only one of his former teammates, Lefty O'Doul, attended.

The marriage never had a chance, though. DiMaggio, who retired after the 1951 season, was a quiet and reserved man, and preferred to remain out of the public eye. He wanted a family. Monroe attracted attention wherever she went. She wanted a career. Less than nine months after their marriage, she filed for divorce, and the marriage ended in October of 1955.

It was apparent from the start that the two were not suited as husband and wife. While they were on their honeymoon in Japan, Monroe was asked to detour to Korea to entertain the American troops. DiMaggio didn't like the idea, but Monroe went. When she returned, she was ecstatic. "Joe, you've never heard such cheering," she said.

To which DiMaggio, who had been adored by tens of thousands of fans every time he stepped to the plate at Yankee Stadium, replied, "Yes, I have."

him turn his back to them. In his speech, DiMaggio said, "When I was in San Francisco, Lefty O'Doul told me: 'Joe, don't let the big city scare you. New York is the friendliest town in the world.' This day proves it. I want to thank my fans, my friends, my manager Casey Stengel, my teammates, the gamest, fightingest bunch of guys that ever lived. And I want to thank the good Lord for making me a Yankee."

But he was never the same after the war. Injuries followed DiMaggio throughout his career after he returned from duty. In 1947, a bone spur was removed from his left heel. The next year, he developed one in his right heel, but he played through the pain, telling a teammate it was "like having a nail in your heel." By 1949 his career seemed to be over. He couldn't stand on the heel without pain, and he missed the first 65 games of the season. But on June 28 the pain suddenly went away just in time for a three-game series in Boston. In one of the greatest comebacks in baseball history, DiMaggio hit four home runs, had nine runs batted in, and made 13 catches in the outfield in the series. The Yankees won all three games. DiMaggio, playing in only 76 games, finished the season with 67 runs batted in. The Yankees went on to win the world championship against the Brooklyn Dodgers in five games.

Physical problems dogged DiMaggio into the new decade, and after batting only .263 in 1951, DiMaggio, the Yankees center fielder since 1936 and perhaps the most graceful player ever to play the game, decided to retire, at the age of 37, rather than play with diminishing skills. "When baseball is no longer fun, it's no longer a game," he said. "And so, I've played my last game of ball."

In 1951 he retired the way he had begun in 1936, as a member of the world champion New York Yankees. He was named "The Greatest Living Player" in 1969, and held the title for 30 years until his death in 1999 at the age of 84.

45 Dave Winfield

With more than 3,000 hits, 450 home runs, and 200 stolen bases, Dave Winfield was one of baseball's greatest all-around outfielders for more than 20 seasons on a total of six teams. He also won seven Gold Gloves for fielding excellence.

Winfield was a star pitcher at the University of Minnesota. In 1973, he won 13 of 14 decisions, posted a .400 batting average, and was named the MVP of the College World Series. He was drafted by professional teams in baseball, basketball, and football. He chose baseball and went right from college to the major leagues with the San Diego Padres, hitting safely in his first six games. By 1979, Winfield was the star of a mediocre Padres team. That season, he hit 34 home runs and drove in 118 runs. After an eight-year career in San Diego, he signed a 10-year free-agent contract worth a reported $15 million with the Bombers on December 15, 1980, making him the highest-paid player in team sports history at the time.

In his first season in the Bronx in 1981, Winfield helped the Yankees reach the World Series, finishing the strike-shortened season with a .294 batting average, 13 homers, and 68 runs batted in. He had an awful 1-for-22 performance in the World Series loss to the Los Angeles Dodgers. But Winfield came back strong the next season to hit a career-high 37 homers. He also drove in over 100 runs, and would become the first Yankee to drive in at least 100 runs in a season for five consecutive seasons (1982–86) since Joe DiMaggio accomplished that feat over seven straight years (1936–42).

The infamous "Seagull Incident" occurred on August 4, 1983. Winfield was playing catch with a ballboy while warming up before the bottom of the fifth inning at Toronto's Exposition Stadium. A flock of seagulls had landed on the artificial turf. One of Winfield's

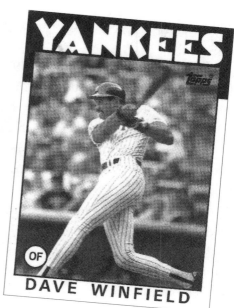

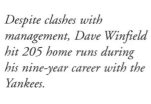

Despite clashes with management, Dave Winfield hit 205 home runs during his nine-year career with the Yankees.

tosses struck and killed a low-flying gull. "They say he hit the gull on purpose," said Yankees manager Billy Martin with tongue firmly in cheek. "They wouldn't say that if they'd seen the throws he'd been making. First time he hit the cutoff man all year."

But this was no laughing matter to Toronto police, who arrested Winfield in the Yankees locker room on a charge of animal cruelty. Winfield posted $500 bail and was released 90 minutes later. Charges were later dropped, as no criminal intent could be proven. "It's quite unfortunate that a fowl of Canada is no longer with us," said Winfield.

In 1984, Winfield and teammate Don Mattingly staged an exciting race for the season's best batting average. The battle came down to the final game of the season. Winfield led Mattingly by two points (.341 to .339) entering the last game against Detroit. Winfield went 1-for-4 and his average dropped to .340, but Mattingly went 4-for-5 and pushed past Winfield with a .343 average to capture the batting title. In a display of mutual respect and good sportsmanship, the two players later walked off the field arm-in-arm.

Winfield missed the entire 1989 season with a herniated disc in his back and was traded to the Angels during the 1990 season before his contract expired. He joined the Toronto Blue Jays for the 1992 season and helped them reach the World Series. In Game 6 of the Series, Winfield's two-out, two-run double in the 11th inning gave Toronto a 4–2 lead and, ultimately, the championship, over the Atlanta Braves. He went into the Hall of Fame in 2001 wearing a Padres cap, and was honored with a day at Yankee Stadium on August 18, 2001.

"I knew when I put on these pinstripes for the first time, it's a moment I'll never forget, and it's a moment that changed my life," Winfield said. "I put my heart and soul on this field every day. I'm truly proud to be remembered as a member of the Yankee family."

46 Root for a Subway Series

The New York Yankees reached the World Series in 1921 and 1922, each time facing the rival New York Giants in a Polo Grounds World Series. The Yankees were then playing their home games in the Giants' ballpark, and the teams exchanged dugouts between games. The Giants won the Series both years.

In 1923, each team again won their respective pennants, setting up a Yankees-Giants World Series for a third straight season. But this matchup had a plot twist. The 1923 World Series was the first Subway Series. The subway had become the main form of public transportation in the city and was a convenient way to travel between ballparks. The Yankees, in their first year in the new

Yankee Stadium, gained a measure of revenge by clinching their first-ever championship in a Game 6 win on the very Polo Grounds field from which they'd been evicted.

Nobody knew it at the time, but the Giants were a team in decline. The Yankees, on the other hand, would become the toast of the town against a new opponent. By 1941, the Brooklyn Dodgers had become the National League's elite team. In the 16 seasons from 1941 to 1956, the Yankees and the Dodgers met in the World Series seven times, with the Yankees coming out on top six times. "Wait 'til next year," fans of the Brooklyn Dodgers were fond of saying after their team repeatedly came tantalizingly close to a World Series title. In 1955, "next year" finally arrived when Dem Bums defeated the Damn Yankees.

The Yankees played in eight World Series in the 1950s, winning six of them. The great Yankees pitcher Whitey Ford once said, "You kind of took it for granted around the Yankees that there was always going to be baseball in October." Even when the Yankees didn't win the World Series, it was still a New York story. From the National League, the New York Giants won in 1954 and the Brooklyn Dodgers in 1955. Baseball fans living in the Big Apple had only to board a subway to see every game in the World Series in five different seasons of the 1950s. After the 1957 season, the Dodgers moved to Los Angeles and the Giants moved to San Francisco. The West Coast edition of the Dodgers and Giants faced the Yankees five more times in the World Series, the Yankees winning in 1962, 1977, and 1978, and losing in 1963 and 1981.

The 2000 World Series was New York's first Subway Series in 44 years—and the first between the Yankees and Mets. The Yankees beat the Mets in five games for their third straight Series crown. In the clincher at Shea Stadium, in the top of the ninth with the score tied 2–2, Luis Sojo hit an RBI single off Mets starter Al Leiter, leading to a 4–2 win and the Yankees' 26th world title. The magic of New York baseball was back.

Yankees in the Subway Series

1923—Yankees 4, Giants 2
Casey Stengel hit two home runs to win two games for the Giants, but Babe Ruth swatted three solo home runs and Herb Pennock won two games to help the Yankees open Yankee Stadium in grand style with the first of their 27 world championships.

1936—Yankees 4, Giants 2
The Yankees offense exploded, scoring 18 runs in Game 2 and 13 runs in the clinching Game 6. Lou Gehrig hit two home runs and drove in seven runs, rookie Joe DiMaggio hit .346, and Red Rolfe and Jake Powell each had 10 hits.

1937—Yankees 4, Giants 1
The Yankees took the first two games by identical 8–1 scores. Lefty Gomez won two games and drove in the go-ahead run in Game 5 to win the clincher for a second straight year.

1941—Yankees 4, Dodgers 1
Tiny Bonham, Red Ruffing, and Marius Russo each pitched complete games, and Mickey Owen's dropped third strike on Tommy Henrich in Game 4 doomed the Dodgers.

1947—Yankees 4, Dodgers 3
The Yankees won a memorable Series despite Cookie Lavagetto spoiling Bill Bevens' no-hit bid in the ninth inning of Game 4 and Al Gionfriddo's homer-robbing catch of Joe DiMaggio's long drive in Game 6.

1949—Yankees 4, Dodgers 1
On the final day of the season, Tommy Henrich's leadoff eighth-inning home run gave the Yankees a 2–0 lead and propelled the Bombers to a 5–3 win over the Red Sox in front of 68,055 roaring fans at the Stadium. The win gave the Yanks the American League pennant by one game over Boston and first-year manager Casey Stengel the first of his 10 pennants. Henrich continued his hot hitting in the World Series against the Dodgers; his Game 1 home run was all Allie Reynolds needed in a 1–0 Yankees victory.

1951—Yankees 4, Giants 2

In the Game 6 clincher, Hank Bauer's bases-loaded triple with two outs in the sixth inning cleared the bases to give the Yankees a 4–1 lead. Then, in the ninth inning, after the Giants closed the deficit to 4–3 and with the tying run in scoring position, a racing Bauer made a sensational catch on a low line drive to end the game.

1952—Yankees 4, Dodgers 3

Brooklyn, still in search of its first championship, had a 3–2 series lead, but couldn't put the Yankees away in the sixth game. In Game 7, Billy Martin made a game-saving catch of Jackie Robinson's bases-loaded infield pop-up. The Dodgers lost in the World Series for the sixth time in six tries.

1953—Yankees 4, Dodgers 2

The Yankees added to the Dodgers' frustration by winning the World Series again from their Brooklyn neighbors. New York's six-game victory was its record fifth championship in a row. Billy Martin won the series for the Yankees in Game 6 with a run-scoring single in the ninth inning.

1955—Dodgers 4, Yankees 3

Jackie Robinson stole home in the eighth inning of the Series opener. Sandy Amoros made a game-saving running catch of Yogi Berra's fly ball near the left-field foul pole as Johnny Podres blanked the Yankees 2–0 in Game 7.

1956—Yankees 4, Dodgers 3

In Game 5, Don Larsen pitched the only perfect game and no-hitter in Series history. Johnny Kucks clinched it with a shutout in Game 7.

2000—Yankees 4, Mets 1

Jose Vizcaino singled home the winning run in the 12th inning to take Game 1; Roger Clemens hurled a broken bat at Mike Piazza in Game 2; Series MVP Derek Jeter homered to lead off Game 4 at Shea Stadium; and a two-out ninth inning single by Luis Sojo brought in the clinching run in Game 5.

47 Yankees Rookies of the Year

When Aaron Judge was named the 2017 Rookie of the Year in November 2017, he became the ninth New York Yankees player honored since the award was established in 1947. Only the Dodgers, with 18, have more. (Cody Bellinger was the 18th Dodgers rookie to be honored in 2017.) The Rookie of the Year is voted on by the Baseball Writers Association of America (BBWAA). The winner receives the Jackie Robinson Award, officially named in 1987 for the great Dodgers player who 40 years earlier in 1947 became the first African American player in the major leagues in the 20th century. Only one award was given out for both leagues in 1947 and 1948. Since then, the American and National leagues have both had a player recognized as Rookie of the Year.

Gil McDougald became the first Yankees player to win the award in 1951 when he hit .306 with 14 homers. Three years later, Bob Grim became the second Yankee to claim the award after posting a 20–6 record with a 3.26 earned-run average. Grim played in two World Series for the Yankees—in 1955 against Brooklyn and in 1957 against Milwaukee—and was on the losing end both times. In Game 4 of the 1957 World Series against the Braves, he relieved Tommy Byrne in the bottom of the 10th inning with a 5–4 lead after Byrne had hit Milwaukee's Nippy Jones with a pitch. Umpire Augie Donatelli had originally called Byrne's pitch to Jones a ball, but Jones insisted he had been struck on the foot—and he set out to prove his point. Jones retrieved the baseball, showed Donatelli a smudge of shoe polish on the ball, and was awarded first base. The hit-batsman ruling proved crucial as it set off a series of unfortunate events for the Yankees and Grim. After a sacrifice, Grim surrendered a double that tied the game, and then gave up a two-run home run to Eddie Mathews as the Yanks lost the game 7–5, and then the Series in seven games.

Twenty-year-old shortstop Tony Kubek earned Rookie of the Year honors after hitting .297 to help the Yankees win the American League pennant in 1957. In the World Series against the Braves, Kubek crushed two home runs in Game 3 to make a triumphant return to his hometown of Milwaukee. For the eight seasons from 1958 to 1965, Kubek and second baseman Bobby Richardson formed one of baseball's most reliable double-play combinations. Unfortunately, the play for which Kubek is most remembered was a double play that wasn't. It happened in Game 7 of the 1960 World Series. With the Yanks winning 7–4 in the bottom of the eighth, Pittsburgh's Gino Cimoli was on first base when Pirates outfielder Bill Virdon slapped an apparently tailor-made double-play groundball at Kubek. The ball took a bad hop off the Forbes Field infield, skipped up, and struck Kubek in the throat, prolonging a five-run Pittsburgh rally that set the stage for Bill Mazeroski's Series-winning home run in the bottom of the ninth.

Tom Tresh was the AL's top rookie in 1962 when the switch-hitting shortstop hit a career-high .286 with 20 home runs and 93 runs batted in. Tresh's powerful stroke from either side of the plate led him to be unfairly heralded as the next Mickey Mantle. Tresh tried his best to live up to the billing. His three-run home run broke an eighth inning tie and was the deciding blow in Game 5 of the 1962 World Series. In Game 1 of the 1963 World Series he hit a two-run homer off Sandy Koufax. In three World Series with the Yankees, Tresh hit .277 with four homers and 13 runs batted in.

In 1968, pitcher Stan Bahnsen received rookie honors with a 17–12 record and an impressive 2.05 ERA. Two years later, Thurman Munson won the award when he hit .302 with six homers and 53 RBIs. Not until 1981, when pitcher Dave Righetti came up for the Yankees, did the team have another winner. Righetti won the award after going 8–4 with a 2.05 ERA. Derek

Jeter was the next Yankee to win the Rookie of the Year award. The shortstop claimed the honor after the 1996 season by receiving all 28 first-place votes. Jeter hit .314 and emerged as a team leader with maturity far beyond his 22 years.

48 Joe Torre

The New York Yankees were already the 20th century's most successful baseball team, capturing 22 world championships from 1923 to 1978, but the Bronx Bombers suffered through a slump from 1979 to 1995. That drought ended with the unpredictable 1996 World Series.

After winning back-to-back championships in 1977 and 1978, the Yankees returned to the Fall Classic following the strike-shortened 1981 season, but lost to the Los Angeles Dodgers in six games. Then came a string of futility from 1982 to 1994, during which New York failed to win the American League East (they were atop the division in 1994 before the strike ended the season) and changed managers a dozen times. They finally returned to the postseason in 1995, as the AL's first wild-card entry, only to lose in the opening round to the Seattle Mariners in a thrilling finish.

Principal owner George Steinbrenner made yet another managerial switch before the 1996 season, naming Joe Torre as the 14th skipper of the ballclub since Steinbrenner took the reins in 1973. A 10-time All-Star player from 1960 to 1977, and the NL MVP in 1971, Torre had previously managed the New York Mets, Atlanta Braves, and St. Louis Cardinals, though with only modest success. His hiring was ridiculed by the New York tabloid press with the headline "Clueless Joe."

But the Brooklyn native proved to be a perfect fit in the Bronx. In 1996, Torre's first year, the Yankees finished the regular season in first place with a 92–70 record and met the Texas Rangers in the best-of-five AL Division Series. After losing Game 1 at Yankee Stadium, New York won the next three to advance to the ALCS against the Baltimore Orioles. With a little help from a 12-year-old boy who leaned over the outfield wall to catch a fly ball that was incorrectly ruled a game-tying home run, the Yankees took Game 1 and went on to wrap up the best-of-seven series in five games.

The Yankees faced the Atlanta Braves in the World Series, and the Braves stunned the Yankees 12–1 in Game 1 at Yankee Stadium, sparked by 19-year-old Andruw Jones, who hit home runs in his first two at-bats. When Atlanta shut out the Yankees 4–0 in Game 2—behind an 82-pitch, eight-inning gem from Greg Maddux—many wondered if New York was plainly outmatched. Not quite, as the Yankees won three straight games in Atlanta. The Series took a dramatic turn in Game 4 when New York battled back from a 6–0 deficit; the decisive moment was a three-run homer by Jim Leyritz in the eighth inning to tie the score. The Yanks prevailed 8–6 in 10 innings.

Game 6 finally produced a win for the home team, with the Yankees winning their first Series title in 18 years. Torre, perhaps sensing a measure of job security, said after the deciding contest, "Second place is not an option with George Steinbrenner, which is fine by me."

After a stunning, heart-wrenching first-round loss to the Cleveland Indians in 1997, Torre's Bombers came back strong, posting a team-record 114 wins in 1998, World Series sweeps over the San Diego Padres in 1998 and Atlanta Braves in 1999, a monumental Subway Series beating of the Mets in 2000, an astonishing 11 consecutive playoff series triumphs, and a 14-game World Series winning streak. The team came a broken-bat single away from making it four world championships in a row, but lost to the Arizona Diamondbacks in the 2001 Fall Classic. The Yankees under Torre also reached the World Series in 2003, falling to the Florida Marlins in six games.

Torre served as the Yankees skipper from 1996 to 2007, the longest tenure of any manager under owner George Steinbrenner. Torre's calming presence and hands-off manner was a perfect fit for a team comprised of veteran players. During Torre's 12-year reign, the Yankees reached the postseason each year and won 10 American League East Division titles, six American League pennants, and four World Series titles. He managed the Yankees to a won-loss record of 1,173–767, for a .605 winning percentage. With an overall total of 2,326 wins, he is currently ranked fifth on the all-time list of managerial wins.

49 Count the Yankees Plaques in Cooperstown

A total of 56 members of the National Baseball Hall of Fame have been associated with the New York Yankees at one time or another as a player, manager, or front office executive—the highest representation of any other team.

The Yankees' first inductee was Babe Ruth. In 1936, the year following Ruth's retirement, he was one of five players elected in the first National Baseball Hall of Fame balloting, along with Honus Wagner, Christy Mathewson, Walter Johnson, and Ty Cobb. Ruth's plaque calls him simply the "greatest drawing card in [the] history of baseball." The plaque makes no mention of Ruth's career pitching mark of 94–46 (for a .671 winning percentage), or his 2.28 earned-run average. In World Series competition, he had a record of 3–0, with a 0.87 ERA, allowing only 19 hits in 31 innings.

On June 12, 1939, to coincide with baseball's 100th anniversary, the National Baseball Hall of Fame and Museum was officially dedicated in colorful ceremonies in Cooperstown, New York. All 11 living Hall of Famers and 15,000 fans gathered to honor the greatest of the great. All major league games were canceled that day, and the ceremonies were broadcast on radio. Connie Mack, manager of the Philadelphia Athletics, spoke first. Following Mack to the podium came a parade of baseball legends—Tris Speaker, Cy Young, Walter Johnson, George Sisler, and Grover Cleveland Alexander. Finally, it was Babe Ruth's turn to speak. "They started something here," he said, "and the kids are keeping the ball rolling. I hope some of you kids will be in the Hall of Fame. I'm very glad that in my day I was able to earn my place. And I hope the youngsters of today have the same opportunity to experience such a feeling."

Following Ruth's statement, commissioner Kenesaw Mountain Landis took the microphone and said, "I now declare the National Baseball Museum and Hall of Fame in Cooperstown, New York— home of baseball—open!"

Today, visitors entering the first floor of the museum are greeted by a life-size statue of the Babe (and Ted Williams). The incredibly realistic statues are carved from wood and painted to give the effect of real skin and uniform cloth. Exhibits include a large collection of equipment, uniforms, baseballs, photographs, trophies, and other items chronicling the history of the game. There's a bat Mickey Mantle used to hit his 565-foot homer, believed to be the longest homer ever hit. There's a warm-up jacket worn by Lou Gehrig, over here is Joe DiMaggio's locker, and there is a jersey Derek Jeter wore. There is a large collection of plaques at the center of the museum, each one representing a member of the Hall, as well as an entire room devoted just to Babe Ruth.

Many of the artifacts on display at the National Baseball Hall of Fame and Museum are tied to memorable moments in baseball—and hence, Yankees—history. Some of the most famous are:

- The bat used by Babe Ruth to hit his record-setting 60th home run of the season on September 30, 1927, a mark that stood for 34 years
- The bat used by Roger Maris to hit his 61st home run of the season on October 1, 1961, breaking Babe Ruth's single-season record
- The glove used by Yogi Berra to catch Don Larsen's World Series perfect game for the Yankees against the Dodgers on October 8, 1956

Cooperstown is located in upstate New York, 70 miles west of Albany. The National Baseball Hall of Fame and Museum is open seven days a week all year, except Thanksgiving, Christmas, and New Year's Day.

50 1961 Yankees: The M&M Boys

Babe Ruth was still making headlines in 1961, as home runs were on everyone's mind. The New York Yankees won 109 games and, fueled by "M&M Boys" Mickey Mantle and Roger Maris, hit an earth-shaking 240 home runs, a team record that stood for 35 years. The top sluggers were Maris with a record 61, Mantle with 54, Bill Skowron with 28, Yogi Berra with 22, and Elston Howard and backup catcher and pinch hitter Johnny Blanchard with 21.

That year, Maris and Mantle both made a run at Ruth's single-season home run record of 60, established in 1927. Mantle started out red-hot, but injuries forced him to drop out of the race in

Run-Scoring Machine

The Yankees hit a franchise-record 245 home runs in 2012, surpassing the mark set by the 2009 team. But a scoring record set by the 1932 Bronx Bombers can never be broken. That season, the Yankees scored at least one run in every game played, becoming the only team in major league history to avoid being shut out over an entire season. They were held to one run in 11 games, and won three of those. The Yankees led baseball with 1,002 runs scored and 107 wins in 1932. Incredibly, their only player to lead the American League in a major offensive category was Ben Chapman with 38 stolen bases.

The Bombers scored at least one run in 308 straight games from August 3, 1931 to August 2, 1933—the big league record for consecutive games without being shut out. The Yankees were not silenced in the final 55 games of the 1931 season after August 1 and did not get blanked again until August 3, 1933, when their streak ended at 308 games. The streak was broken by a 7–0 shutout pitched by future Hall of Fame left-hander Lefty Grove of the Philadelphia Athletics.

mid-September with 54 homers. Maris pulled ahead and claimed the record with his 61st four-bagger on the last day of the season.

"People always talk about the home run battle as the thing that made us such a great team," said rookie manager Ralph Houk. "It wasn't that. It was our pitching and defense."

Leading the way was Whitey Ford, who had a 25–4 record and received the Cy Young award for best pitcher at a time when pitchers in both leagues competed for only one award. Behind Ford were Ralph Terry (16 wins), Bill Stafford (14 wins), left-handed reliever Luis Arroyo (15 wins, 29 saves), and right-hander Jim Coates (11 wins).

After Maris surpassed the Babe's season record for home runs, Ford would knock the Great Bambino out of the World Series record book, too. As a Boston Red Sox pitcher, the Babe pitched 29 consecutive scoreless innings in the 1916 and 1918 World Series. After twice shutting out the Pittsburgh Pirates in 1960, Ford continued his mastery against the Cincinnati Reds in the 1961 World Series. The Reds, National League pennant-winners for the first time in 21 years, were no match for the mighty Yanks, who won easily in five games.

Ford started Game 1 at Yankee Stadium and pitched a two-hit shutout. The Reds' only victory came in Game 2 in support of pitcher Joey Jay, the first Little Leaguer to reach the big leagues. In Game 3 at Cincinnati's Crosley Field, a Roger Maris home run broke a 2–2 tie in the top of the ninth inning, and relief ace Luis Arroyo slithered out of a jam in the bottom of the ninth to preserve the victory. Maris' homer was "the most damaging blow of the Series," said Reds manager Fred Hutchinson. "After that we couldn't bounce back."

The Yankees put a stranglehold on the series in Game 4 as Ford and Jim Coates combined on a 7–0 shutout. The Yanks cruised to a 13–5 runaway in the clinching game and celebrated as champions again. Role players took center stage in the series. Second baseman Bobby Richardson had nine hits, a record for a five-game Series; backup catcher Johnny Blanchard hit two home runs; and Hector Lopez, in place of the ailing Mantle, drove in seven runs.

Ford, the Series MVP, won two games and pitched 14 shutout innings to extend his World Series streak to 32 consecutive scoreless innings, breaking the old record held by Ruth. As the historian Robert Creamer wryly noted, "It was a bad year for the Babe."

It was a good year for Ralph Houk, the former backup catcher and coach who took over as manager after the Yankees dismissed Casey Stengel following the 1960 World Series. Houk guided the Yankees to a pair of World Series titles and three American League pennants in his three seasons at the helm. The Major became the only manager to win World Series championships in his first two seasons as a major league skipper. He led the Yankees to World Series wins in 1961 over the Cincinnati Reds and 1962 over the San Francisco Giants.

51 Red Ruffing

Charles "Red" Ruffing overcame a childhood mining accident in which he lost four toes on his left foot to become a Hall of Fame pitching great for the New York Yankees. Although a coal mining injury dashed his hopes of becoming an outfielder, Ruffing took the mound and won 273 major league games for the Boston Red Sox and New York Yankees. His 231 wins as a Yankee ranks second on the team's all-time list. "The foot bothered me [during] my career," said Ruffing. "I had to land on the side of my left foot in my follow-through."

Ruffing joined the Red Sox at the age of 19 and struggled for last-place Boston clubs from 1924 to 1930, putting together a 39–96 record. During one horrid stretch in 1929, he lost 12 games in a row and then was traded to New York in 1930. He was still just 26 years old. Ruffing's turnaround was immediate. He went 15–5 in his first season with the Yankees. In the next 14 seasons, the Yankees won seven pennants and six World Series. Ruffing went 231–124, including four straight 20-win seasons from 1936 to 1939, helping the Yankees win four straight championships during those years.

"If I were asked to choose the best pitcher I've ever caught," said Hall of Fame catcher Bill Dickey, "I would have to say Ruffing."

In World Series play, Ruffing was 7–2 with a 2.63 earned-run average. The highlight of his World Series career was his stretch from 1937 to 1941: five World Series games, five wins, five complete games. He allowed just six earned runs in 45 innings. He nearly achieved pitching immortality against the St. Louis Cardinals in Game 1 of the 1942 World Series, coming four outs away from hurling the first no-hitter in Series history.

Ruffing was one of the best hitting pitchers ever to play the game. He put together a .269 lifetime batting average, driving in more runs (273) than any pitcher in major league history, and his 36 lifetime home runs (34 as a pitcher) rank fourth among pitchers. He batted over .300 eight times, including .364 in 1930. On September 18 of that season he hit two home runs in one game, a feat he would repeat on June 17, 1936. He was a 20-game winner in 1939 and batted better than .300, becoming one of the few pitchers in major league history to accomplish both feats in the same season.

In spite of his severely damaged left foot, Ruffing was drafted into military service after a 14–7 record in 1942. "The last doctor I saw was an Army doctor," said Ruffing. "He would have drafted any ballplayer." Following three years in the Army, Ruffing returned to baseball but was plagued by injuries. He was 3–5 for the Chicago White Sox in 1947 before retiring at age 42.

After managing in the minors and working as a scout, he became the New York Mets' first pitching coach in 1962. He told his young pitchers: "There are two important things to remember. Keep in shape and know where each pitch is going. It pays off. I knew where my pitches were going because I worked on control continuously. I never had a curveball. If I threw a curve at a batter he'd laugh. But by being able to pitch the ball hard and where I wanted, I became successful. Ask [Hall of Famer] Hank Greenberg, I struck him out a few times."

52 Listen to Mel Allen

Mel Allen was the voice of the Yankees dynasty from 1939 to 1964. He had one of the most recognizable voices in broadcasting, and his style and approach to calling the games inspires baseball announcers to this day.

Born in Birmingham, Alabama, as Melvin Allen Israel, and educated as a lawyer at the University of Alabama, he began his career as a sportswriter before turning to sports announcing. His first broadcast was not a baseball game but a football game, between Tulane University and the University of Alabama. In 1937, Allen joined the CBS Radio Network as an announcer, lending his voice to introduce game shows such as *Truth or Consequences*.

In 1939, he was hired to call Yankees and Giants home games on radio. After the war, when he legally changed his name, Allen began doing Yankees games exclusively, both at home and on the road, later adding television to his radio duties. Among Allen's many catchphrases were "Hello there, everybody!" to start a game and "Three and two, what'll he do?" His trademark home run call of "Going, going, gone" and his signature call out "How about that?" to punctuate a clutch hit by the Yankees was a rallying cry for two generations of fans. And he is credited as the first person to call DiMaggio, "Joltin' Joe."

Allen delivered the play-by-play for the Yankees for 25 years at the height of the team's success. Beginning in 1947, the Yankees appeared in the World Series 15 of 18 years. In those days, broadcasters from the two league champions always handled the national network coverage of the Series. Before long, the soundtrack of the Fall Classic would be narrated by Mel Allen. In all, he called 22 World Series, including 18 in a row between 1946 and 1963. He

John Sterling

Following the final out of a Yankees victory, John Sterling exclaims, "Ballgame over! Yankees win! Theeeeeee Yankees win!"

No statement is as synonymous with the current Yankees run of success as John Sterling's winning call. As the radio play-by-play voice of the Yankees since 1989, Sterling has called 162 games a year without missing a single one. He has worked more than 4,600 regular season and postseason games for the Yankees, making him the dean of New York baseball announcers.

Sterling began his broadcasting career in Baltimore as the play-by-play announcer for the Washington Bullets (now Wizards) during the 1970–71 NBA season. He came to New York in 1971 to host a call-in sports radio talk show, and from 1975 to 1980, he served as the radio voice for the NHL's New York Islanders and the ABA's New York Nets during Julius Erving's heyday. He then spent nine years in Atlanta, Georgia, covering the Braves (1982–87) and Hawks (1981–89).

In 1989, Sterling returned to New York to broadcast the games for the Yankees on radio. One of his signature radio remarks is his home run call "It is high, it is far, it is gone!" On back-to-back home runs hit by players who bat from opposite sides of the plate, he says, "It's a back to back! And a belly to belly!"

For fans, Sterling's personalized home run calls are a subject of much amusement. Whether making-up a word for Nick Swisher ("Swishalicious"), rhyming for Russell Martin ("Russell has muscle!"), or making reference to Babe Ruth's nickname whenever a home run was hit by Jason Giambi ("The Giambino") and Tino Martinez ("The Bam-Tino"), Sterling's home run calls are memorable and unique.

Sterling's love of music is evident in home run calls for Bernie Williams ("Bern, baby, Bern!") in reference to lyrics from the song "Disco Inferno"; Eric Hinske ("Hinske with your best shot!") in reference to the song "Hit Me With Your Best Shot" by Pat Benatar; and Curtis Granderson ("Oh Curtis, you're something sort of Grandish!") in reference to a lyric from the musical Finian's Rainbow. Sterling also sings "The Grandy-man can!" in reference to the song "The Candy Man."

Some of our favorite home run calls from the past include tributes to Hideki Matsui ("A thrilla by Godzilla!"), Melky Cabrera ("The Melkman delivers!"), Bernie Williams ("Bernie goes boom!"), and Johnny Damon ("It's a Johnny rocket! Positively Damonic!"). Other recent favorites are for Robinson Cano ("Robbie Cano, dont'cha know?"), Alex Rodriguez ("An A-bomb from A-Rod!"), Jorge Posada ("Jorgie juiced one!"), and Mark Teixeira ("You're on the mark, Teixeira!" and "He sends a Tex-message to the seats in right!").

Mel Allen was the voice of the franchise for generations of Yankees fans until his passing in 1996.

was such an authoritative voice for Major League Baseball that even when the Yankees didn't play in the Series, he was hired as the play-by-play announcer anyway.

It was undoubtedly Allen's intimate knowledge of the game and his Southern charm that accounted for his popularity. In addition to chronicling the Yankees dynasty, Allen was hired by the networks as the play-by-play announcer for 24 All-Star Games. He was also the nation's top college football announcer during the 1950s and early 1960s, broadcasting 14 Army-Navy contests and 12 Rose Bowl games. He was the play-by-play announcer of Giants football games on CBS Radio in 1960, and was behind the microphone when Philadelphia Eagles linebacker Chuck Bednarik made a ferocious tackle against the Giants' Frank Gifford that clinched the Eastern Conference title for the Eagles at Yankee Stadium on November 20, 1960. The legal hit forced Gifford to miss the next season.

But Allen is best known for his work with the Yankees. He stayed with the team until 1964, when he was fired without any public explanation. Eventually, he was invited back to Yankee Stadium as master of ceremonies for Old Timers' Day games and to serve as Voice of the Yankees. In 1978, Allen, along with Red Barber, became the first broadcasters to win the Hall of Fame's Ford C. Frick award for broadcasting excellence. Allen was inducted into the Radio Hall of Fame in 1988.

In 1976, team owner George Steinbrenner brought Allen back to call 40 Yankees games a season on cable telecasts. During this second tour of broadcast duty, Allen called such memorable Yankees moments as Reggie Jackson's 400th career home run on August 11, 1980, and Dave Righetti's no-hitter against the Red Sox on July 4, 1983.

In his later years, Allen hosted the syndicated program *This Week in Baseball*. Just before the show was to start its 20th season, Allen died of a heart attack at his home in Connecticut on June 16, 1996. He was 83 years old.

"Mel Allen meant as much to Yankee tradition as legends like Ruth, Gehrig, DiMaggio, and Mantle," Steinbrenner said. "He was the voice of the Yankees."

On July 25, 1998, the Yankees dedicated a plaque in his memory for Monument Park at Yankee Stadium. The plaque calls him "A Yankee institution, a national treasure" and includes his much-spoken line, "How about that?"

53 Appreciate Derek Jeter

Derek Jeter grew up wanting to be the shortstop for the New York Yankees, and his wish came true. "All I ever wanted to be was a Yankee," he is fond of saying. "When I was a kid I was always hoping there'd be a jersey left for me to wear with a single digit." Born in New Jersey but raised in Kalamazoo, Michigan, where a poster of Dave Winfield hung on his bedroom wall, Jeter had a great high school career, and was drafted by the Yankees with the sixth pick in the 1992 amateur draft.

When Jeter joined the Yankees' Class A rookie team in Greensboro, North Carolina, later that summer, the skinny kid made nine errors in his first 11 games. Still, a teammate on that team, pitcher Andy Pettitte, saw something extraordinary in the raw rookie. "You knew that he was special," said Pettitte. "You knew that he carried himself a little bit different than a lot of other guys. A lot of class, a lot of charisma, a lot of confidence for as young as he was."

Jeter reached the major leagues to stay at age 21 in 1996, batting .314, winning the American League Rookie of the Year award, and leading the Yankees to their first World Series championship in 19 years. Between 1998 and 2000, Jeter was the biggest star on Yankees teams that won three straight World Series titles. In 1998, he led the AL in runs scored (127) and in 1999 he led in hits (219). That season, he achieved career highs with 24 homers, 102 runs batted in, and a .349 batting average. In 2000, he became the first and only player to be named All-Star Game Most Valuable Player and World Series Most Valuable Player in the same season.

Jeter has played in 14 All-Star Games, won five Gold Gloves, and earned a reputation as a clutch player who has made some of the most famous plays in recent memory. When the New York Yankees need a big defensive play, there is Jeter to dive into the stands, face-first, emerging with a bloody chin, as he did to catch a foul pop-up against the Boston Red Sox, the team's most fierce rival, during the heated pennant race of 2004. When the team needs a clutch hit, there is Jeter to slap the ball the other way, slashing it to the opposite field with that inside-out swing of his. Need a stolen base? No problem; he has more than 300 steals, and is the club's all-time leader in that category, too.

Jeter only plays the game one way: hard. He pushes himself in the field, on the bases, and at bat. Long before Jeter was named captain in 2003, he had earned the respect of his peers. "Derek Jeter is the kind of player who one day I will get to say, 'I played with him,'" said teammate Paul O'Neill.

While an active player, Jeter played in more winning games than any other player during those years. He reached the postseason 16 of 20 years. He holds the career postseason records for most hits, runs scored, and total bases. In 2009, Jeter helped lead the Yankees to their 27th World Series title, the fifth for the shortstop since he broke into the majors in 1996. Jeter hit .407 in the World Series, part of a postseason in which he batted .344. More importantly for him, he was named the winner of that year's Roberto Clemente Award for his charitable work away from the field with his Turn 2 Foundation.

"From the first day I met Derek, he has not only impressed me as a great athlete but more importantly a person who has always tried to make other people's lives better," said former manager Joe Girardi. "He has dedicated his life to being a champion on the field and off the field."

No. 2 has set a new standard for the Yankees, and fans everywhere are grateful.

54 1947 World Series: One Out Away from Immortality

The 1947 World Series featured baseball's most popular player, the New York Yankees' Joe DiMaggio, and its man of the hour, the Brooklyn Dodgers' Jackie Robinson. This was the year when the Dodgers introduced Robinson as the first African American player in modern-day major league history. But this wild, six-game Fall Classic wound up being dominated by virtual no-names.

These Yankees were no Bronx Bombers, as no player knocked in 100 runs and only one, DiMaggio, belted 20 home runs. The 1947 Yanks won with great pitching from Allie Reynolds, Spud Chandler, rookie Spec Shea, and reliever Joe Page. Yet in the World Series, the Yankees came out swinging, winning the first two games by scores of 5–3 and 10–3. In the opener, Dodgers starter Ralph Branca pitched four perfect innings before the Yankees exploded to score all five runs in the fifth inning. The rookie Shea was credited with the win but needed four innings of relief help from Page. The Yankees banged out 15 hits in the second game as Reynolds coasted to a complete-game victory.

Back at home in Ebbets Field for Game 3, the Dodgers, desperately in need of a victory, took control early, scoring six runs in the second inning. New York staged a valiant comeback attempt, but the Brooklynites held on to win 9–8, though a young Yankees catcher named Yogi Berra smashed the first pinch-hit home run in Series history.

The next game was the one that left fans in disbelief. Yankees starter Floyd "Bill" Bevens had a fastball like lightning, but his accuracy was always a question. He had labored to a 7–13 record in 1947. In Game 4 of the Series, he was at his unpredictable best and worst. After eight innings on a cold afternoon at Ebbets Field in Brooklyn, Bevens had surrendered eight walks. He was also three outs away from becoming the first pitcher to throw a no-hitter in a World Series game. The Dodgers had scored once in the fifth inning (on two walks, a bunt, and an infield out), but trailed 2–1 as they came to the plate for their last at-bat in the bottom of the ninth.

Bevens retired the first batter, catcher Bruce Edwards, on a long fly ball, and then walked Carl Furillo. After a foul-out by Spider Jorgensen, pinch runner Al Gionfriddo stole second base. When pinch hitter Pete Reiser came up, Bucky Harris, in his first season as Yankees manager, ordered Reiser walked intentionally. It was Bevens' 10th walk, and put the winning run on base.

Dodgers manager Burt Shotton then turned to Harry "Cookie" Lavagetto to pinch-hit. The veteran had only 69 at-bats in 1947. With the count no balls and one strike, Lavagetto drilled the ball past right fielder Tommy Henrich. Gionfriddo scored, and so did pinch runner Eddie Miksis. Bevens lost the game, the no-hitter, and the Series lead on one pitch.

Now the Series was tied, and more excitement was still to come. The Yankees responded to the devastating loss by winning the next game 2–1, as DiMaggio homered and Shea pitched a four-hitter and helped his cause by driving home a run. The American Leaguers looked to clinch the title in Game 6 at Yankee Stadium, but the National Leaguers had other ideas. Brooklyn jumped out of the gate strong by scoring four early runs, but by the fourth inning the Yankees had gained the lead 5–4. In the sixth inning, the Dodgers went back ahead with a four-run rally, capped by Pee Wee Reese's two-run single.

The Yankees made a bid to tie the score in the bottom of the sixth inning against Dodgers starter Joe Hatten, a 17-game winner that season. Joe DiMaggio strolled to the plate to face the left-hander. The Yankees trailed 8–5 with two outs and two runners on base. DiMaggio smashed the ball 415 feet toward the left-center-field bullpen at Yankee Stadium, but Al Gionfriddo—a defensive replacement just inserted into the game by Dodgers manager Burt Shotton—made a spectacular, game-saving catch at the wall. A frustrated DiMaggio, in a rare public display of emotion, kicked at the dirt over his disappointment, correctly sensing this dramatic blow would be the Yanks' last hurrah of the day. As it turned out, Brooklyn held on for an 8–6 victory to even the series at 3–3.

The momentum seemed to stay with the Dodgers in the deciding seventh game as Shotton's troops took a 2–0 lead and knocked out Shea in the second inning. But the Yankees fought back to take the lead in the fourth inning, and bolstered by impressive relief pitching from Joe Page—who shut down the Dodgers over the final five innings—the Yankees held on for a 5–2 victory and another world championship triumph.

The strangest twist to this wacky Series was that the three most memorable performers—Bevens, Lavagetto, and Gionfriddo—were all playing their last major league games.

55. Sit in "The Judge's Chambers"

The verdict is in: the Yankees are officially marketing Aaron Judge as the star attraction in the Bronx after the rookie's hot start to the 2017 season. In May 2017, the Yankees unveiled "The Judge's Chambers," a specific cheering section for their towering outfielder in the right field stands directly behind the real estate where Judge plays. This cheering section draws huge crowds of fans who show up in long white cotton wigs and wearing black judges' robes emblazoned with the Yankees logo.

The three-row, 18-seat area near Section 104 in the lower level in right field features faux wood paneling around the front and back rows to resemble a courtroom's jury box, plus THE JUDGE'S CHAMBERS clearly written in capital letters along the back of the paneling. It also includes some judge's props, such as foam gavels, for anyone sitting in the section.

There's a catch: you can't buy tickets to sit there. Instead, the team will choose specific fans and their families to sit in the seats. "It's pretty cool," said Judge of the new seating area. "When you come to a game, it's supposed to be fun for the players and fans. I feel like it might be something that's fun for the fans out there."

He didn't know about it beforehand. "They just brought it up to me and said, 'Hey, this is what we're going to do.' I think it turned out great." Judge was surprised to already have a permanent spot in the stadium: "It's pretty unreal. I never would have thought so soon. But the fans like it, so I'm glad they're having fun."

For a player whose mounting popularity enabled him to receive more All-Star votes than any American Leaguer, who graced the cover of *Sports Illustrated*, and who earlier in the 2017 season manager Joe Girardi likened to Derek Jeter in the way he handles himself, the creation of "The Judge's Chambers" section is the latest form of praise heaped on the 25-year-old outfielder. Hall of Famers Babe Ruth and Reggie Jackson patrolled right field for the Bombers, and although Mr. October had a candy bar that bore his name, neither the Bambino nor Jackson ever had an entire seating section named after them. That's pretty good for someone who was playing his first full season in the majors.

And what a rookie season it was. Judge received the most votes for the American League All-Star team, collecting 4,488,702—and for good reason. "He's must-watch TV," said Washington Nationals right fielder Bryce Harper. But first, Judge was the head-liner at the Home Run Derby. The New York Yankees' breakout star rose to the occasion. In a prolific power display, he hit 47 total homers during the derby that traveled 3.9 miles worth of distance—including four that traveled more than 500 feet. Judge was the first rookie ever to win the home run derby outright. He was also the fourth Yankees player to win the competition, joining Robinson Cano (2011), Jason Giambi (2002), and Tino Martinez (1997).

But Judge was just getting started. He became the first rookie to hit 50 home runs in a season, breaking Mark McGwire's 1987 rookie record of 49 with Oakland. Judge joined Babe Ruth, Mickey Mantle, Roger Maris, and Alex Rodriguez as the only Yankees to reach 50 home runs or more in a season. Judge finished the season with 52 and surpassed Ruth's franchise record of 32 homers at home, a mark set in 1921.

The emergence of Aaron Judge catapulted the Yankees into the postseason in 2017. He finished the year with a .284 batting average and led the American League in home runs (52), runs scored (128), walks (127), and strikeouts (208), and was second in runs batted in (114) and slugging percentage (.627). He put together one of the most memorable rookie seasons in history, setting records for most home runs and most walks by a first-year player. His numbers were staggering, leading many experts to predict that Judge could join Fred Lynn in 1975 and Ichiro Suzuki in 2001 as the only players to win the Rookie of the Year and Most Valuable Player Awards in the same season. As it turned out, Judge won Rookie of the Year but finished second in the MVP voting.

56 Miller Huggins

Though very short and small (5'6", 140 pounds), manager Miller Huggins was the big man in the Yankees clubhouse from 1918 to 1929. A no-nonsense and feisty type, Huggins was known as "Mighty Mite." He led the Yankees to the World Series six times between 1921 and 1928, winning the world championship trophy three times. Huggins' 1927 team is considered by many to be the finest in baseball history.

Best known for his success as a Yankees manager, Huggins was also a top-notch second baseman for the Cincinnati Reds and St. Louis Cardinals. At one time or another, he led the National League in putouts, assists, fielding percentage, and double plays. An ideal leadoff hitter, Huggins walked more than 1,000 times in his career—four times leading the league—and averaged 25 stolen bases per season.

Huggins was known for his baseball acumen. In 1910, the Cardinals picked up Huggins from the Reds, and by 1913, Huggins was the Cardinals' player-manager. This arrangement lasted until 1917, when Rogers Hornsby arrived in St. Louis, and Huggins wisely turned over his second base spot to the future Hall of Famer and became a full-time manager.

A shrewd businessman, Huggins made a bid to buy the Cardinals, but it fell through. Bitter over his failed deal, he resigned as Cardinals manager. Seeing an opportunity, the Yankees hired Huggins as manager in 1918 in hopes of turning around the franchise. Prior to Huggins being named the team's manager, the Yankees had been an awful baseball team, with only three second-place finishes since 1903 to show for their futile efforts. Huggins led the Yankees to fourth- and third-place finishes in his first two years at the helm.

Then, following the 1919 season, Huggins persuaded the Yankees front office to purchase Babe Ruth from the Boston Red Sox. Ruth was a stellar left-handed starting pitcher and part-time outfielder who hit the occasional home run. Ruth wanted to come to bat in every game. But the Red Sox were fearful of moving a successful pitcher to the outfield on a permanent basis. This upset Ruth, and so Boston looked to ship an unhappy player out of town. The Yankees acquired Ruth for $125,000, and baseball changed forever. Huggins developed the slugging power teams that ended baseball's dead-ball era and ushered in the beginning of the first great Yankees dynasty.

The Yankees won the American League pennant in 1921 and 1922, but lost in the World Series to the rival New York Giants both times. They again faced the Giants in the 1923 World Series, but this time playing in their new stadium, the Yankees defeated the Giants and won the first of their 27 world titles.

Huggins was a taskmaster. He feuded openly with pitchers Carl Mays and Joe Bush, and he publicly suggested that Ruth's hard-partying ways were exacting a toll on his body and causing his baseball skills to prematurely diminish. Huggins tried to keep Ruth in line by setting training rules. But Ruth's fondness for good times went beyond his loyalties to following the team's training rules. Ruth fought frequently with his manager. Among Babe's many feuds with Huggins was one that developed over a 1925 "stomach ache" that caused Ruth to miss the season's first 41 games and hit only .290 with 25 homers. On April 5, Ruth, whose weight had ballooned to over 250 pounds, collapsed in a train station in Asheville, North Carolina, and was rushed to the hospital in an ambulance. Rumors of his death flew around the world. He was diagnosed with an ulcer that required an operation. The six-week hospital stay was referred to as the "Bellyache Heard 'Round the World."

He returned weak, having lost 30 pounds, and unable to swing the bat with his usual force. Pitchers were not afraid of him and hardly ever walked him anymore. Adding insult to injury, Huggins fined him $5,000 that year—10 percent of his salary—and publicly called Ruth "out of shape" and "wasting talent." The two developed a strong mutual dislike. The Yankees finished seventh in 1925, the only bad season they had during the Ruth era.

In 1926, shortstop Mark Koenig and second baseman Tony Lazzeri joined the team, giving the Yankees a strong defense up the middle of the diamond. That year the Yankees began a three-year domination of baseball. They won pennants every year and the World Series in 1927 and 1928 without losing a game. In 1929, the Yankees failed to make the World Series for the first time in three years. Near the end of that season, Huggins died suddenly at age 51 from a disease that causes swelling under the skin. Babe Ruth was now 35, and he was hoping to be named the Yankees' new manager. But former pitcher Bob Shawkey was chosen instead, much to Ruth's dismay.

Huggins finished his managerial career with 1,413 victories and a .555 winning percentage. Only five managers have won more pennants than the six won by Huggins. In 1932, a monument in honor of Miller Huggins was placed in center field in Yankee Stadium, and in 1964, he was elected into the Hall of Fame.

57 Match the Yankee to His Retired Number

At the end of the 1939 season, the Yankees retired Lou Gehrig's No. 4, making his the first retired number in baseball. (Since then, more than 120 numbers have been retired.) To this day, Gehrig is the only Yankees player to have ever worn the number. Since Lou Gehrig's No. 4 was retired in 1939, the Yankees have retired

21 uniform numbers to honor 23 players and managers. No other team has more retired numbers, or does so with as much pomp and circumstance.

On June 13, 1948, a crowd of 49,641 turned out at Yankee Stadium to celebrate the 25th anniversary of the opening of the House That Ruth Built. The day was also significant for the sentimental ceremonies honoring Babe Ruth. His famed uniform No. 3 was permanently retired by the Yankees and his uniform formally presented to officials from the baseball shrine at Cooperstown, where it would be hung in a special Babe Ruth Room in the National Baseball Hall of Fame and Museum.

Now in the late stages of his cancer, Ruth was no longer the hulking, domineering figure he once was. In a touching scene and using a bat to support his fragile frame, Ruth walked slowly to the microphone and spoke in a soft, raspy voice. Babe Ruth knew he was dying. He told the fans how happy he was to have hit the first home run at the Stadium, and he bid them farewell. It was the Babe's final appearance at Yankee Stadium, the house that he frequently filled.

The following are the players and managers who have been recognized over the years by the Yankees organization by having their uniform numbers retired:

- Lou Gehrig—wore No. 4 and played for the Yankees from 1925 to 1939. Known as The Iron Horse, he played in an astonishing 2,130 games in a row. Number retired in 1939.
- Babe Ruth—wore No. 3 and played for the Yankees from 1920 to 1934. Hit a total of 714 home runs and led the league in homers 12 times. Number retired in 1948.
- Joe DiMaggio—wore No. 5 and played for the Yankees from 1936 to 1942 and from 1946 to 1951. His 56-game hitting streak is considered the top baseball feat of all time. Number retired in 1952.

- Mickey Mantle—wore No. 7 and played for the Yankees from 1951 to 1968. The most feared switch-hitter in baseball history, he powered the Yankees to 12 World Series appearances and seven world championships. He also owns most important World Series batting records. Number retired in 1969.
- Casey Stengel—wore No. 37 and managed the Yankees from 1949 to 1960. In 12 seasons at the helm, he guided the Yankees to 10 pennants and seven World Series titles. Number retired in 1970.
- Yogi Berra—wore No. 8 and played for the Yankees from 1946 to 1963. He played on 10 World Series championship teams, more than anyone in history. Though he never led the league in any major offensive category, he was a three-time Most Valuable Player award winner. Number retired in 1972.
- Bill Dickey—wore No. 8 and played for the Yankees from 1928 to 1943 and in 1946. Hailed as one of the greatest catchers of all time, he handled pitching staffs on seven World Series winners. Number retired in 1972.
- Whitey Ford—wore No. 16 and played for the Yankees in 1950 and from 1953 to 1967. The ace pitcher won 236 games, the most of any Yankee, and holds most important World Series pitching records. Number retired in 1974.
- Thurman Munson—wore No. 15 and played for the Yankees from 1969 to 1979. He won both the Rookie of the Year (1970) and Most Valuable Player (1976) awards while leading the team to consecutive World Series titles in 1977 and 1978. He died tragically in a plane crash on August 2, 1979. Number retired in 1979.
- Roger Maris—wore No. 9 and played for the Yankees from 1960 to 1966. His 61 home runs in 1961 is still the American League record. Number retired in 1984.
- Elston Howard—wore No. 32 and played for the Yankees from 1955 to 1967. The first African American player in Yankees

history, Howard retired in 1968 and was a Yankees coach until his death in 1980. Number retired in 1984.

- Phil Rizzuto—wore No. 10 and played for the Yankees in 1941 and 1942, and from 1946 to 1956. He also spent 40 years as a Yankees broadcaster from 1957 to 1996. Number retired in 1985.
- Billy Martin—wore No. 1 and played for the Yankees from 1950 to 1953 and from 1955 to 1957. Was a member of five World Series winners as a player and also managed the Yankees to a world title in 1977. Number retired in 1986.
- Reggie Jackson—wore No. 44 and played for the Yankees from 1977 to 1981. In Game 6 of the 1977 World Series he hit three home runs, each on the first pitch, as the Yankees clinched the club's first world title since 1962. Number retired in 1993.
- Don Mattingly—wore No. 23 and played for the Yankees from 1982 to 1995. The slick-fielding first baseman was a nine-time Gold Glove winner. Number retired in 1997.
- Ron Guidry—wore No. 49 and played for the Yankees from 1975 to 1988. The power pitcher ranks among the team's all-time leaders in wins, strikeouts, innings pitched, and shutouts. Number retired in 2003.
- Mariano Rivera—wore No. 42 and played for the Yankees from 1995 to 2013. The closer with the cut fastball was a crucial part of five World Series teams and holds the all-time saves record. Number retired in 2013. (Major League Baseball retired No. 42 to honor Jackie Robinson in 1997.)
- Joe Torre—wore No. 6 and managed the Yankees from 1996 to 2007. His teams went to the postseason 12 consecutive seasons, winning 10 division titles, six American League pennants, and four World Series championships. Number retired in 2014.
- Bernie Williams—wore No. 51 and played for the Yankees from 1991 to 2006. The centerfielder played on four World Series winners, was a five-time All-Star selection, won four Gold

Gloves, and drove in a record 80 postseason runs. Number retired in 2015.

- Jorge Posada—wore No. 20 and played for the Yankees from 1995 to 2011. The switch-hitting catcher played on five World Series winners and was also a five-time All-Star and five-time Silver Slugger winner. Number retired in 2015.
- Andy Pettitte—wore No. 46 and played for the Yankees from 1995 to 2003, 2007 to 2010, and 2012 to 2013. The left-handed pitcher is the team leader in strikeouts and is third in wins. The five-time World Series champion totaled 19 postseason wins, the most in MLB history. Number retired in 2015.
- Derek Jeter—wore No. 2 and played for the Yankees from 1995 to 2014. The shortstop won Rookie of the Year in 1996 while helping the Yankees win their first World Series since 1978. He led the Yankees to three more titles in the next four years and won a fifth in 2009. "The Captain" was a 14-time All-Star and the franchise all-time hits leader. Number retired in 2017.

58 Dave Righetti

Dave Righetti set the major league single-season saves record with 46 in 1986. The mark has since been surpassed, but it remained the most saves ever by an American League left-hander until 2009.

Acquired from the Texas Rangers as part of the Sparky Lyle trade after the 1978 season, Righetti began his Yankees career as a starter and was the 1981 AL Rookie of the Year with an 8–4 record and 2.05 earned-run average. In the postseason, he won two games against the Milwaukee Brewers in the AL Division Series and one game against the Oakland Athletics in the ALCS. Though he

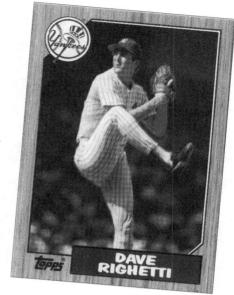

A onetime Rookie of the Year, left-hander Dave Righetti set the major league saves record with 46 in 1986.

pitched in 14 more big league seasons, Righetti's rookie year would be his only postseason appearance.

Righetti struggled to find the strike zone early in the 1982 season, and the Yankees sent him back to the minor leagues to regain his control. He returned to the Bronx with newfound command and finished strong with 11 wins. The following season, boasting a rising fastball to complement a hard-breaking curve, he won 14 games, including a no-hitter against the Boston Red Sox on July 4 at Yankee Stadium.

"It wasn't a full house that day, but the Yankees were playing the Red Sox…and it was hot," the pitcher remembers, adding, "I had a decent fastball and a lot of luck."

He also was the recipient of a few excellent defensive plays. Shortstop Roy Smalley made two diving plays—the first in the third inning on a ground ball into the third-base hole to throw out Jerry Remy and another to grab Glenn Hoffman's blooper behind second base. Right fielder Steve Kemp also reached into the stands to snare a foul ball off the bat of Dwight Evans.

How to Lose a No-Hitter

New York Yankees pitcher Andy Hawkins didn't give up a hit, but he still lost a game 4–0 to the Chicago White Sox at Comiskey Park, on July 1, 1990. Hawkins was the victim of some brutal fielding by the Yankees, allowing the White Sox to score four runs with two outs in the eighth inning thanks to two walks and three errors.

Hawkins' eighth inning was nothing short of a nightmare. It started with two out when third baseman Mike Blowers mishandled Sammy Sosa's ground ball. The right-hander followed by walking Ozzie Guillen and Lance Johnson, loading the bases. But Chicago third baseman Robin Ventura lifted a harmless-looking fly ball to left field, an apparent rally killer.

Not so. Rookie Jim Leyritz, fighting a swirling wind, dropped the ball as three runners raced home. Ivan Calderon followed with another harmless-looking fly ball to right that Jesse Barfield dropped, allowing Ventura to score. Dan Pasqua popped out to end the inning and the Yankees, held to four hits by three Chicago pitchers, were retired in the top of the ninth, sealing the final verdict.

Though the complete-game no-hitter loss put Hawkins in select company, his postgame feeling was not jubilation. Only Ken Johnson of the Houston Colt .45s in 1964 had previously suffered such an indignity, losing a 1–0 decision to Cincinnati on a ninth-inning throwing error. Johnson didn't give up a hit, either.

In 1991, a committee on statistical accuracy appointed by commissioner Fay Vincent made clear the definition of a no-hitter as a complete game in which the pitcher must throw a minimum of nine full innings. Since Hawks pitched for the visiting Yankees and the home team never batted in the bottom of the ninth inning, Hawkins lost credit for a no-hitter.

And only one other pitcher since, Matt Young of the Boston Red Sox, has been credited with a complete-game loss and not allowed a hit. Young lost his eight-inning gem 2–1 to the Cleveland Indians in 1992.

Righetti struck out nine batters and walked four in the 4–0 shutout. The last out of the game was a strikeout of future Yankee Wade Boggs, who was batting .361 coming into the game, and rarely struck out. It was the first no-hitter thrown by a Yankee since Don Larsen's perfect game in the 1956 World Series.

"Going out for the ninth inning the fans were cheering long before I hit the mound, so I was definitely thinking about it when I was warming up," Righetti recalled. "It actually gave me a little bit of a boost because I was fatiguing in my legs. But I was gonna give it everything I had. The one thing I regret is that I never got to go into the clubhouse with my teammates. The press grabbed me on the field to take pictures and I was interviewed in the dugout for television, so I never got to go inside and soak it in with my teammates."

Nobody knew it at the time, but the no-hitter was Righetti's last hurrah as a starting pitcher. Moved to the bullpen the next year to replace Rich Gossage as the team's closer, Rags made a smooth transition to relief pitching, and went on to average 32 saves over the next seven seasons. In the record-setting season of 1986, Righetti converted 29 of his final 30 save chances, including saving both ends of a season-ending doubleheader against the Boston Red Sox at Fenway Park, to break the record of 45 held by Dan Quisenberry and Bruce Sutter. The record would stand until Bobby Thigpen saved 57 games for the Chicago White Sox in 1990.

A two-time All-Star, Righetti has 224 career saves as a Yankee. He also pitched for the San Francisco Giants, Oakland Athletics, Toronto Blue Jays, and Chicago White Sox before retiring in 1995. He has served as the Giants pitching coach since 2000, and was a member of the coaching staff in 2010, 2012, and 2014 when the Giants won the World Series.

59 Unleash the "Kraken"

In December 2015, general manager Brian Cashman was asked about the Yankees' top minor league catching prospect, Gary Sanchez. That's when Cashman dubbed Sanchez the "Kraken," the sea monster from the 1981 film *Clash of the Titans*. "I'd like to unleash the Kraken, which is Gary Sanchez, on our roster in 2016 if I can."

Sanchez arrived in the big leagues to stay as a 23-year-old in August 2016. Soon after, he was named the American League Player of the Week in consecutive weeks, and he became the first rookie in MLB history to accomplish that feat. He won the award the first time by batting .524 (11-for-21) with four home runs and six RBIs. He followed that with a nearly identical week, batting .522 (12-for-23) with five homers and nine RBIs, including a stretch in which he homered in three straight games. His 11 home runs in his first 23 games are also a feat never accomplished by anyone before.

"It feels great to win the award, but the reality is that the focus is to keep winning games right now," Sanchez said through a translator.

Aside from the honor of being named the player of the week, Sanchez received a watch from MLB in recognition of the award. Asked what he would do with two watches, Sanchez said, "I don't know. I haven't even gotten the first one yet." One month into his pro career, Major League Baseball could not keep up with Gary Sanchez's spectacular accomplishments.

By earning back-to-back AL Player of the Week honors, Sanchez was an easy choice for voters of the AL Player of the Month award. Sanchez hit .389 with 11 home runs, 21 RBIs, nine doubles, and 20 runs scored in 24 games during the month of August. Sanchez, who also earned AL Rookie of the Month honors, is the first Yankees catcher ever to win either award. He's the first Yankee to win Player of the Month since Curtis Granderson in August 2011 and the first to win Rookie of the Month since Robinson Cano in September 2005.

"Pretty impressive considering what he's done," manager Joe Girardi said. "Coming up at an important time and facing good teams, it's really impressive."

Since the promotion of Sanchez from Triple-A on August 3, 2016, the Yankees began playing much better baseball and even climbed back into wild-card contention. "I think it's hard not to look at Gary Sanchez and be in awe of what he's done," said Girardi, who installed Sanchez as his everyday catcher and No. 3 hitter.

"It's been amazing what he's been able to do," said pitcher C.C. Sabathia. "He's brought energy to the team."

Sanchez became a first-time All-Star in 2017. He was also selected to participate in the Home Run Derby festivities the day before, to take place at Miami's Marlins Park, on July 10. Sanchez, the No. 8 seed, would take on defending champion and No. 1 seed Giancarlo Stanton in Round 1. Against the hometown favorite, Sanchez unleashed the biggest upset of the tournament, knocking out Stanton 17–16. It was a sign of amazing home run feats to come.

Sanchez blasted two home runs during the Yankees' 13–4 pounding of the Detroit Tigers at Comerica Park on August 22, one a mammoth shot estimated at 493 feet, the second longest homer of the 2017 season. "I think I've still got him by two feet," said teammate Aaron Judge with a grin, still the reigning 2017 home run distance leader with a 495-foot blast against Baltimore in June. The scorching Sanchez now had hit 11 home runs over his last 24 games, dating to July 27. By early September, Sanchez would hit his 31st home run of the season, a record for a Yankees catcher.

Sanchez and Aaron Judge have catalyzed the Yankees' offense with their home run heroics, giving the Yankees a fearsome 1-2 punch that could rattle any postseason opponent. With these two Baby Bombers leading the way, New York's faster-than-anticipated youth movement helped catapult the club into the 2017 American League Championship Series. And now, after making a trade to acquire Giancarlo Stanton, the reigning National League home run king and league most valuable player, the Yankees are positioned for even more success in the coming seasons.

60 Dynasty Years 1998 to 2000: Bring Out the Brooms

The Yankees, though not quite perfect, came pretty darn close in 1998. With an ideal combination of outstanding pitching, timely hitting, solid defense, and unselfish team chemistry, the Yankees won an American League–record 114 games in the regular season (against just 48 losses). After sweeping the Texas Rangers in the best-of-five AL Division Series, the Yankees found themselves in trouble against the Cleveland Indians in the American League Championship Series. The Yankees won the opener 7–2, but lost Game 2 in 12 innings when Chuck Knoblauch failed to call time when arguing a play at first base. In the third game, Cleveland socked four homers and got a complete game from Bartolo Colon.

To avoid an early exit from the playoffs after compiling the best record in team history, the Yankees needed a big performance in Game 4 in Cleveland and got one from Orlando "El Duque" Hernandez. Hernandez delivered by striking out six batters in seven innings as he combined with Mike Stanton and Mariano Rivera on a four-hit shutout. The Yankees won again the next day and wrapped up the series in six games at Yankee Stadium. Saving their best for last, New York brought down its World Series opponents, the San Diego Padres, in a four-game sweep.

In 1999, after winning the American League East with 98 wins, the Yankees powered through two rounds of the playoffs to meet the Atlanta Braves again in the World Series. It was billed as a showdown to decide not just the best team of the year, but also the best team of the decade. Although the Braves had only captured one World Series since 1990 (defeating the Cleveland Indians in 1995), compared to two World Series titles for the Yankees (against Atlanta in 1996 and San Diego in 1998), the Braves had dominated the National League, winning eight division titles and five league championships.

It didn't turn out to be much of a battle. But for the lone defeat against eventual AL Cy Young winner Pedro Martinez of the Boston Red Sox in Game 3 of the ALCS, the Yankees went undefeated in the postseason, winning 11 of 12 games. In sweeping the Braves in four straight games, the Yankees starting pitchers only gave up seven earned runs and held opposing batters to a paltry .200 average. New York relief pitcher and Series MVP Mariano Rivera pitched 4⅔ innings, earned two saves, and registered an unblemished earned-run average of 0.00.

After the Yankees limped to the finish line in 2000 with 87 victories, the club returned to its predictable postseason pattern. In the ALCS against the Seattle Mariners, David Justice helped get the Yankees to their third straight World Series with a three-run home run in Game 6 off lefty reliever Arthur Rhodes. The blast into the upper deck in right field put the Yankees up 6–4 and sent them on their way to a 9–7 clinching victory.

The Mets defeated the Cardinals in the National League Championship Series, so the 2000 World Series was New York's first Subway Series in 44 years—and the first between the Yankees and Mets. Todd Zeile's drive in the sixth inning of Game 1 at

Yankee Stadium bounced off the top of the wall. David Justice picked it up, fired it to Derek Jeter, and Jeter relayed the ball to Jorge Posada, who tagged Timo Perez to end the top of the sixth inning with the game still scoreless. The Yankees got two runs in the bottom of the inning, but the Mets took the lead in the top of the seventh. In the ninth, Paul O'Neill drew a hard-fought walk from Mets closer Armando Benitez and came around to score the tying run on a sacrifice fly. After the Yankees squandered golden opportunities to score in the 10th and 11th, former Met Jose Vizcaino finally ended the game with a bases-loaded single in the 12th.

The Yankees won again the next night, holding on in the ninth inning after brilliant pitching from Roger Clemens, who overshadowed his own performance by flinging a piece of a broken bat at

Curtis' Bat Says It All

In his only start of the 1999 World Series, Chad Curtis made an impact. He smashed two home runs to bring the Yankees back from a 5–1 deficit in Game 3, including the game-winner in the 10th inning for a dramatic 6–5 victory over Atlanta. The Yankees went on to sweep the Braves in four straight games.

Curtis' homer over the left-center-field fence off lefty relief specialist Mike Remlinger was the first walk-off World Series homer since Joe Carter's in Game 6 in 1993. It was also the first game-ending homer by a Yankee in the World Series since Mickey Mantle slugged one against the St. Louis Cardinals in Game 3 in 1964.

This might be the only time that Curtis, a journeyman outfielder with a .264 lifetime batting average over a 10-year career, is linked with one of the premier players in baseball history, but that is why it was such a memorable night.

"It was a rush," Curtis said. "I can't say I ever felt that before. Rounding the bases, I was kind of tingling. I've heard people talk about that, but I've never felt it before. I was tingling."

After the game, Curtis refused to answer a question posed by sportscaster Jim Gray. Curtis felt, as did most players, that Gray's interview of Pete Rose prior to Game 2 had been too aggressive.

Mets slugger Mike Piazza in the first inning. The 6–5 win marked the team's 14th consecutive victory in World Series play, breaking the 12-game record set by the 1927, 1928, and 1932 Yankees. In the Game 5 clincher at Shea Stadium, Andy Pettitte and the Mets' Al Leiter staged a marvelous pitching duel. With the score tied 2–2 in the ninth, Leiter finally ran out of steam when Luis Sojo, a Yankees reserve, clubbed the biggest single of his life to score the winning run. Piazza later lined out to Bernie Williams in the bottom of the inning to end it. The Yankees won their third consecutive world championship, 26th overall title, and became the first club to win three straight World Series since the 1972–74 Oakland Athletics.

61 Make Sense of the Peterson-Kekich Swap

The Yankees have been involved in many headline-grabbing trades during their history, but no deal compares to the weirdest, most unbelievable trade of all. It involved no other team, only two families.

Teammates and friends since 1969, Yankees left-handed pitchers Fritz Peterson and Mike Kekich created a scandal by swapping families before the 1973 season. Kekich moved in with Marilyn Peterson, and Peterson moved in with Susanne Kekich. They swapped wives, houses, cars, kids, and even pets.

"We didn't trade wives—we traded lives," said Kekich.

After the blockbuster trade was announced during spring training, team executive Lee MacPhail said, "We may have to call off Family Day this season."

When news of the "life swap" became public in March of 1973, baseball fans were stunned to learn what the two Yankees teammates had done. "It was a '70s-era thing," said Ron Swoboda, who played with both pitchers in 1971 and 1972. This was the year the American League had instituted the designated hitter, and as a result, for the first time since the AL was organized in 1901, the two big leagues would play under different rules. But in the ensuing media storm, the bizarre wife-swap scandal received far more publicity than the historic new DH rule.

"Nobody was for it," noted a spokesperson in commissioner Bowie Kuhn's office. "None of the letter writers or phone callers said, 'Good going, guys.'"

Jake Gibbs, a former Yankees catcher and battery mate to both Peterson and Kekich, remembers, "they were fun-loving guys. Fritz and Mike were good friends. They were really close, and their families were close. I guess we just didn't know how close."

"Of course," adds Gibbs, "they were both left-handers. You can never tell about lefties."

The trade worked out better for Peterson. Before long, Mike and Marilyn split, but Susanne and Fritz got married in 1974 and had four kids of their own. "We didn't do anything sneaky or lecherous," Susanne said at the time. "There isn't anything smutty about this."

Besides seeming to get the better of the deal, Peterson was also the more successful pitcher of the two. He had a modest career with the Yankees, going 109–106 with a 3.10 earned-run average from 1966 to 1974. He enjoyed his best success in 1970 when he went 20–11 with a 2.90 ERA and pitched in the All-Star Game. In 1969 and 1970, Peterson had the best strikeouts-to-walks ratio in the American League. He also led the league in fewest walks per nine innings for five seasons in a row from 1968 to 1972. The last pitcher before Peterson to accomplish that feat was Denton True "Cy" Young, after whom they named an award. The answer to a different sort of trivia question, Peterson was the starting pitcher for the Yankees in the last game ever played at the original Yankee Stadium, on the final day of the 1973 season, before it was renovated. He also has the all-time lowest earned-run average at Yankee Stadium, with a 2.52 ERA. Whitey Ford is second with a 2.58 ERA.

"Fritz had great stuff and super control," said Gibbs. "He had some great years. Kekich had good stuff, but he didn't always know where it was going."

The erratic Kekich was an inconsistent pitcher before the swap—a record of 10–9 for New York in 1971 and 10–13 in

Yankees left-handed pitchers Fritz Peterson and Mike Kekich switched wives—and lives—in 1973, one of the most bizarre incidents in baseball history.

1972—but after the swap his career fell apart. He pitched in five games for the Yankees after the swap became public and then was traded to the Indians. By the time Peterson was exiled to Cleveland in a trade with three other pitchers the following season, Kekich was no longer there. In 1974, Kekich played in Japan for the Nippon Ham Fighters. He returned to the big leagues with the Texas Rangers in 1975 and the Seattle Mariners in 1977 before his career was ended by a shoulder injury. He attempted a comeback by pitching in Mexico, but that was short-lived.

Peterson was never the same pitcher after the controversial family swap and the outcry that followed. He posted a 23–25 record during three years with Cleveland, and was traded to Texas in 1976. After winning one game for the Rangers he was released and signed a free-agent contract with the Chicago White Sox, but he never threw another pitch in the major leagues.

Although after their playing days the two men were never again close friends, in his 2009 book, *Mickey Mantle Is Going to Heaven*, Peterson revealed that he and Kekich do keep an email correspondence. "If I saw him at an Old-Timers' game," said Peterson, "we'd have some great laughs."

62 Mick's Tape-Measure Blasts

Mickey Mantle could hit a baseball as far as anyone. Legendary sluggers like Babe Ruth, Jimmie Foxx, and Hank Greenberg all hit the ball for great distances, yet the era of the tape-measure homer didn't arrive until Mantle did. The longest home run on record was a 565-foot clout hit at old Griffith Stadium on April 17, 1953. The switch-hitting Mantle was batting right-handed against left-handed pitcher Chuck Stobbs of the Washington Senators. Mantle hit a rising line drive that nicked the lower right-hand corner of a huge beer sign atop a football scoreboard behind the left-center-field bleachers. The ball left the stadium, carried across a street, and landed in the backyard of a nearby home.

This blow was responsible for the expression "tape-measure home run" because the Yankees publicity director, Red Patterson, immediately left the press box, found himself a tape measure, and paced off the distance to the spot where witnesses said the ball came down.

Mantle and perhaps others probably have hit longer home runs. That was certainly the view of Stobbs.

"He hit 'em pretty far against a lot of people," said Stobbs. "The only reason they remember this one is because they marked the spot on the beer sign where the ball left the park, but [Senators manager] Bucky Harris later made them take the marker down.... I got Mantle out pretty good later on. I think he was 2-for-25 off me one year, but nobody ever talks about that."

One of Mantle's 52 homers in 1956, his 19th of the season, blasted on May 30, carried special significance. It came within 18 inches of becoming the only fair ball ever hit out of Yankee Stadium. Hitting left-handed against Pedro Ramos of the Washington Senators with two men on base in the fifth inning, Mantle hit a mammoth drive to right field that struck just below the cornice high above the third deck. Ever since Yankee Stadium was built in 1923, nobody had ever come close to hitting that copper filigree, some 525 feet away from home plate. There is no telling how far the ball might have traveled had it managed those 18 inches to clear the façade, but the ball would likely have wound up nearly 600 feet away from its starting point.

Yankees fans had become accustomed to the Mick's power, but on May 22, 1963, Mantle nearly put a ball into orbit. The Yankees were hosting the lowly Kansas City Athletics, so fewer than 10,000 fans were on hand to witness the Bombers edge the A's in extra innings. With the score tied 7–7 in the bottom of the 11th inning, Mantle faced Kansas City right-hander Bill Fischer. Batting left-handed, Mantle laced a 2-2 pitch that hit the upper-deck façade in right field while still rising. The Yankees won, but all everyone could talk about was Mantle's shot, estimated at 535 feet. It was the Mick's fourth-longest homer, but Mantle himself said, "It's the hardest ball I ever hit left-handed."

Mantle's longest home run batting left-handed traveled 560 feet. He hit it off Paul Foytack of the Detroit Tigers on September 10, 1960; the blast cleared the right-field roof at Briggs Stadium and landed across Trumbull Avenue. Mantle liked to hit against the Tigers at Briggs Stadium. Four years earlier, on June 20, 1956, batting right-handed off Detroit's Billy Hoeft, he hit a towering fly ball that cleared the center-field fence at the 440-foot mark and landed 525 feet away. Two and a half months later, he belted a ball 550 feet batting right-handed off Billy Pierce of the Chicago White Sox, which cleared the left-field roof at Comiskey Park on September 18, 1956.

63 Age Gracefully Like Casey Stengel

When the New York Yankees finished in third place in 1948, the owners of the team fired manager Bucky Harris. The Yankees were used to finishing first, so no one was surprised that Harris was let go. But the appointment of Casey Stengel as the new manager was shocking.

Charles Dillon Stengel had acquired the nickname Casey because he was from Kansas City (or K.C.). Because Casey achieved such success as a Yankees manager, many people don't realize he had a 14-year playing career from 1912 to 1925. In his years as an outfielder with the Brooklyn Dodgers, Stengel learned to play the tricky caroms off the Ebbets Field outfield wall. Before the 1952 World Series between the Yankees and Dodgers, Stengel took Mickey Mantle into the Ebbets Field outfield to pass along some tips on playing the oddly angled concrete wall. The young center fielder was shocked to learn that Casey had roamed this very outfield as a player some 35 years earlier.

Casey had been a fair major league ballplayer. He collected four hits in his first game with the Brooklyn Dodgers in 1912. "The writers promptly declared they had seen the new Ty Cobb," said Stengel. "It took me only a few days to correct that impression." His most memorable moments on the field occurred while playing for the New York Giants in the 1923 World Series against the Yankees. Stengel won the opening game with an inside-the-park home run with two outs in the ninth inning, the first Series homer in new Yankee Stadium. Then he won Game 3 with a seventh-inning home run into the right-field stands at Yankee Stadium for a thrilling 1–0 victory. But he is most remembered for entertaining fans during games. He once kept a sparrow hidden under his cap and at just the right moment tipped his hat to the crowd so the bird could fly away.

When Yankees general manager George Weiss campaigned to bring Stengel on board as skipper, Stengel had years of experience managing—but all the teams he had managed in the majors had been losers. In fact, Stengel had only one winning season out of nine when he joined the Yankees in 1949. Casey was most famous as a clown, not as a winner. His coming to the Yankees was like a country bumpkin marrying a glamorous movie queen—the match seemed unlikely to last, let alone succeed.

Try Speakin' Stengelese

Nicknamed "The Ol' Perfesser," Stengel was one of the most colorful characters in baseball history. He had a funny way of expressing himself, and the media dubbed his variation on English as "Stengelese."

Stengel died in 1975, but his Stengelese will live forever. In 1958, Stengel testified before a Senate subcommittee that was discussing a bill to officially recognize baseball's antitrust exemption, which bound a player to a team for life. When Stengel was asked why baseball wanted this bill passed, he replied in classic Stengelese:

> I would say I would not know, but I would say the reason they want it passed is to keep baseball going as the highest-paid ball sport that has gone into baseball, and from the baseball angle—I am not going to speak of any other sport. I am not here to argue about these other sports. I am in the baseball business. It has been run cleaner than any other business that was ever put out in the 100 years at the present time.

Mickey Mantle testified next and was asked the same question. He replied, "My views are just about the same as Casey's."

"This is a big job, fellows," Stengel told reporters upon taking over the Yankees, "and I barely have had time to study it. In fact, I scarcely know where I am at."

But those who scoffed at Casey overlooked something. He had learned his baseball by playing for such astute managers as John McGraw and Wilbert Robinson. He knew more about the game than most people ever learn. And he knew how to get the most from the players he worked with. Casey was an innovator in the use of his bench, employing a platoon system that was designed to get the most out of every man on his team. He was also an early proponent of the five-man starting pitching rotation.

Once Casey took over in 1949, the Yankees went on to win the American League pennant in nine of the next 10 years. From 1949 to 1953, the Yankees won of an unmatched five World Series titles in a row, the most successful stretch in baseball history. Casey's Yankees would also win championships in 1956 and 1958. The unlikely marriage between Stengel and the Yanks turned out to be just about perfect. But it wasn't a perfect ending when the Yankees "retired" him following the 1960 World Series defeat, labeling him too old to manage. He was 70. "I'll never make the mistake of being 70 again," he said.

The expansion New York Mets hired him as their first manager in 1962, and the 1962 Mets, with a 40–120 record, were the worst team in baseball history. Stengel served as front man for a team of lovable losers he dubbed "the Amazin' Metsies" for three more woeful seasons before retiring in 1965. The next year, Stengel was elected to the Hall of Fame, and his No. 37 jersey is retired by both the Yankees and the Mets.

64 Experience Monument Park

Monument Park is an open-air Yankee Stadium museum located behind the center-field fence. It is a collection of monuments, plaques, and retired numbers that honor former Yankees greats. On game days, it opens with the main entrance gates and remains accessible to ticket holders until 45 minutes before game time.

There are six monuments in Monument Park honoring individuals and one for the victims and heroes of September 11, 2001. In all, there are also 36 plaques: 26 for Yankees players and managers, two for Yankees executives, two for Yankee Stadium personnel, three for papal visits, one for Nelson Mandela, one for Jackie Robinson, and one for the Yankees insignia.

Yankees fans of all ages can immerse themselves in the franchise's history by visiting Monument Park at Yankee Stadium.

The first monument was dedicated in 1932 for manager Miller Huggins, who died unexpectedly during the 1929 season. The first plaque was placed on the center-field wall in 1940 in tribute to former owner Jacob Ruppert. The Yankees dedicated a monument to Ruth on April 19, 1949, eight months after his death. The inscription is memorably brief for such an outsize man; three lines of gold-faced letters read, "A Great Ballplayer/A Great Man/A Great American." The 4,700-pound monument joined the tributes to Gehrig and Huggins already located within the field of play. Fans could see the large stone monuments, giving some youngsters the impression that the remains of the Yankee greats were buried under their tombstones.

In the original Yankee Stadium, the monuments were in fair territory and part of the playing field. The monuments and flag-pole were located in straight-away center field on the warning track approximately 10 feet in front of the wall. Sometimes long hits and fly balls forced fielders to go behind the monuments to retrieve the baseball.

Every Yankees fan knows the significance of those hallowed stones in Monument Park. Those honored have claimed it is a distinction more precious than even a Hall of Fame induction. The greatest names of this most storied franchise are represented. Below are the inscriptions of each honoree.

Miller James Huggins
Dedicated May 30, 1932
As a tribute to a splendid character who made priceless contribution to baseball and on this field brought glory to the New York club of the American League.

Henry Louis Gehrig
Dedicated July 4, 1941
A man, a gentleman and a great ballplayer whose amazing record of 2,130 consecutive games should stand for all time.

George Herman "Babe" Ruth
Dedicated April 19, 1949
A great ballplayer. A great man. A great American.

Mickey Mantle
Dedicated August 25, 1996
A magnificent Yankee who left a legacy of unequaled courage.

Joseph Paul DiMaggio
Dedicated April 25, 1999
A baseball legend and an American icon. He has passed but will never leave us.

September 11, 2001 Tribute
Dedicated September 11, 2002
In tribute to the eternal spirit of the innocent victims…and to the selfless courage shown by both public servants and private citizens.

George M. Steinbrenner III
Dedicated September 19, 2010
He was considered the most influential owner in all of sports. In 37 years as principal owner, the Yankees posted a major league–best .566 winning percentage, while winning 11 American League pennants and seven World Series titles, becoming the most recognizable sports brand in the world. A devoted sportsman, he was Vice President of the United States Olympic Committee, a member of the Baseball Hall of Fame's Board of Directors and a member of the NCAA Foundation Board of Trustees. A great philanthropist whose charitable efforts were mostly performed without fanfare, he followed a personal motto of the greatest form of charity is anonymity.

Monument Park Plaques
Jacob Ruppert
Dedicated April 1940
Through whose vision and courage this imposing edifice, destined to become the house of champions, was erected and dedicated to the American game of baseball.

Edward Grant Barrow
Dedicated April 15, 1954
Molder of a tradition of victory under whose guidance the Yankees won 14 American League pennants and 10 world championships and brought to this field some of the greatest baseball stars of all time.

Pope Paul VI
To commemorate Mass offered at the Stadium on October 4, 1965.

Joseph Vincent McCarthy
Dedicated April 21, 1976
One of baseball's most beloved and respected leaders.

Charles Dillon "Casey" Stengel
Dedicated July 30, 1976
Brightened baseball for over 50 years with spirit of eternal youth.

Pope John Paul II
To commemorate Mass offered at the Stadium on October 2, 1979.

Thurman Munson
Dedicated September 20, 1980
Our captain and leader has not left us—today, tomorrow, this year, next… Our endeavors will reflect our love and admiration for him.

Elston Gene Howard
Dedicated July 21, 1984
If indeed, humility is a trademark of many great men—Elston Howard was one of the truly great Yankees.

Roger Eugene Maris
Dedicated July 21, 1984
The Yankees salute him as a great player and as author of one of the most remarkable chapters in the history of Major League Baseball.

Philip Francis Rizzuto
Dedicated August 4, 1985
A man's size is measured by his heart.

Alfred Manuel "Billy" Martin
Dedicated August 10, 1986
A man who knew only one way to play—to win.

Edward "Whitey" Ford
Dedicated August 2, 1987
Led Yankees to 11 pennants and six world championships. Leads all Yankee pitchers in games, innings, wins, strikeouts, and shutouts.

Vernon "Lefty" Gomez
Dedicated August 2, 1987
Known for his excellent wit as he was fast with a quip and a pitch.

William Malcolm "Bill" Dickey
Dedicated August 21, 1988
First in the line of great Yankee catchers. The epitome of Yankee pride.

Lawrence Peter "Yogi" Berra
Dedicated August 21, 1988
Outstanding clutch hitter and World Series performer led Yankees to 14 pennants and 10 world championships. A legendary Yankee.

Allie Pierce Reynolds
Dedicated August 26, 1989
One of the Yankees' greatest right-handed pitchers. Five-time All-Star. .686 Yankee winning percentage.

Donald Arthur Mattingly
Dedicated August 31, 1997
A humble man of grace and dignity. A captain who led by example. Proud of the Pinstripe tradition and dedicated to the pursuit of excellence. A Yankee forever.

Mel Allen
Dedicated July 25, 1998
With is warm personality and signature greeting "Hello there, everybody," he shaped baseball broadcasting by charismatically bringing the excitement and drama of Yankees baseball to generations of fans.

Bob Sheppard
Dedicated May 7, 2000
His clear, concise and correct vocal style has announced the names of hundreds of players—both unfamiliar and legendary—with equal and divine reverence, making him as synonymous with Yankee Stadium as its copper façade and monument park.

Interlocking NY Insignia
2001
This insignia was originally struck on a medal of honor in 1877 by Tiffany & Co. It was issued to the first New York City police officer shot in the line of duty. The New York Yankees adopted this logo and it became part of the uniform in 1909.

Reggie Jackson
Dedicated July 6, 2002
One of the most colorful and exciting players of his era. A prolific power hitter who thrived in pressure situations.

Ron Guidry
Dedicated August 23, 2003
A dominating pitcher and a respected leader of the pitching staff for three American League pennants and two world championships. A true Yankee.

Charles Herbert "Red" Ruffing
Dedicated July 10, 2004
The Yankees' all-time leader in wins by a right-handed pitcher with 231. The only pitcher in franchise history to compile four consecutive 20-win seasons, from 1936–1939, when he led the Yankees to four straight world championships.

Pope Benedict XVI
To commemorate Mass offered at the Stadium on April 20, 2008.

Nelson Mandela
Dedicated April 15, 2014
Nobel Peace Prize winner and global leader whose tireless efforts dismantled apartheid in South Africa.

Constantino "Tino" Martinez
Dedicated June 21, 2014
Known for his powerful bat and superlative defense at first base.

Paul Andrew O'Neill
Dedicated August 9, 2014
An intense competitor and team leader, O'Neill was beloved for his relentless pursuit of perfection.

Joseph Paul Torre
Dedicated August 23, 2014
His calm approach and dignified manner provided the foundation for one of the most successful eras in franchise history.

Bernabe Williams Figueroa Jr.
Dedicated May 24, 2015
Williams retired as baseball's all-time leader with 80 postseason RBIs.

Willie Larry Randolph
Dedicated June 20, 2015
A consistent and patient hitter, especially with runners on base, Randolph was popular with fans and teammates alike.

Melvin Leon Stottlemyre Sr.
Dedicated June 20, 2015
An elite pitcher in his day, Stottlemyre played his entire career with the Yankees.

Jorge Rafael De Posada Villeta
Dedicated August 22, 2015
Posada was a homegrown Yankee, playing all 17 of his major league seasons in pinstripes. Continued the legacy of great Yankees catchers.

Andrew Eugene Pettitte
Dedicated August 23, 2015
A five-time world champion and three-time All-Star, Pettitte was a model of consistency in the Yankees rotation for 15 seasons.

Mariano Rivera
Dedicated August 14, 2016
His signature cut fastball made him a dominant force, especially in October.

Jackie Robinson
Dedicated April 17, 2017
Broke baseball's color barrier in 1947 with the Brooklyn Dodgers.

Derek Sanderson Jeter
Dedicated May 14, 2017
As the cornerstone of five world championship teams, Jeter was a leader on the field and in the clubhouse.

65 Be Inspired by Jim Abbott

Since St. Louis Brown Stockings right-hander George Bradley became the first major league pitcher to do it on July 15, 1876, pitching a no-hitter has remained a remarkable personal achievement. But as hard as it is to pitch a complete game without allowing a single hit, they're not all that uncommon. At least one no-hitter has been thrown in all but four major league seasons (1982, 1989, 2000, and 2005) since 1960. But the 2–0 no-hitter pitched on September 4, 1993, at Yankee Stadium by New York Yankees left-hander Jim Abbott is the only one of its kind.

It's not because Abbott struck out only three hitters. Or because he shut down an explosive Cleveland Indians lineup who just six days earlier in Cleveland had pounded Abbott for seven runs and knocked him out of the game in the fourth inning. It's because Jim Abbott has only one hand.

His entire life, Abbott has refused to accept pity or be treated differently because he was born without a right hand. And he wouldn't take no for an answer when challenged to prove he belonged on the pitcher's mound. At age 11, in his Little League pitching debut, he threw a no-hitter. He pitched the gold-medal-winning game for the United States against Japan in the 1988 Summer Olympic Games in Seoul, South Korea. And without a day in the minor leagues, he jumped directly from the University of Michigan—where he won the Golden Spikes award as the nation's most outstanding college baseball player—to the California Angels' starting rotation.

"I don't think I'm handicapped," said Abbott. "My hand hasn't kept me from doing anything I wanted to do. I believe you can do anything you want, if you put your mind to it."

Jim Abbott threw one of the most improbable no-hitters in baseball history against the Cleveland Indians in 1993.

Against the Indians, Abbott did not get off to a good start when he issued a leadoff walk to Kenny Lofton. But Felix Fermin grounded into a double play and then Abbott settled down. Though Abbott walked five batters, the Indians never advanced a runner past first base and hit only six balls out of the infield. While recording 17 outs by ground balls, Abbott was assisted by several fine defensive plays from his infielders, most notably by third baseman Wade Boggs, who in the seventh inning dove to his left to snare a bouncer and throw out Albert Belle.

Earlier in the season, Abbott had carried a no-hitter into the eighth inning against the Chicago White Sox, but it was broken up by Bo Jackson's single. This time, however, Abbott would make history. Said first baseman Don Mattingly, "The last couple of innings, I had these huge goose bumps on my forearms, and the hair on the back of my neck was standing up. Maybe that would have happened with someone else. Maybe I'd have the same feelings. But I think because it was Jim there was a little something extra."

Leading off the ninth inning was Lofton, who attempted to force the Yankees' one-handed pitcher to field a bunt, but fouled his attempt off and heard raucous boos from the Stadium crowd before grounding out. Then Fermin smashed a long drive to left-center-field, some 390 feet away, but the ball hung in the air long enough to allow center fielder Bernie Williams to run it down. Finally, Carlos Baerga, a switch-hitter, took the unorthodox approach of batting left-handed against the left-handed-throwing Abbott, in the hopes of neutralizing Abbott's cut fastball, but the ploy did not work. Baerga hit one last grounder to shortstop Randy Velarde. When Velarde's throw reached Mattingly's mitt, Abbott exulted. He threw open his arms and shouted, "How about that!" as jubilant teammates mobbed him near the mound. It was the first no-hitter at Yankee Stadium since Dave Righetti did it 10 years earlier.

Normally stoic Yankees manager Buck Showalter jumped off the bench in celebration and nearly banged his head on the dugout roof. The last out provided him with welcome relief. "No one wants to be blamed for doing anything to jinx a no-hitter," said Showalter. "I had to go to the bathroom for the last four innings, but I was afraid to go."

The next morning, the Yankee Stadium grounds crew, which had dug out the pitching rubber from the mound, presented Abbott with the slab, which all of his teammates had signed. The Hall of Fame called for his hat and the baseball.

"The pitching rubber [is] very heavy. It weighs about 25 pounds," said Abbott. "I have it right outside my office at home. It's a great piece of memorabilia."

Center Field Excellence

Is there a more prestigious title in all of sports than New York Yankees center fielder? No other position is afforded such esteem. Center field at Yankee Stadium is hallowed ground. The ground is so revered that until the remodeling in the early 1970s there were three monuments honoring team immortals on the actual field of play.

With a fence 461 feet away, center field at Yankee Stadium was too expansive for just any outfielder to cover. (Center field at the old Yankee Stadium was called Death Valley because that was where home runs went to die.) Earle Combs, a fly ball chaser extraordinaire in the 1920s, was the first of the Yankees' four Hall of Fame center fielders. Joe DiMaggio and Mickey Mantle are legendary figures in baseball history, and Rickey Henderson also made some history during his four-plus seasons in pinstripes from 1985 to 1989.

After DiMaggio passed the center-field torch to Mantle, by the late 1960s, everyone was looking at Bobby Murcer as Mantle's heir apparent. Both men were from Oklahoma, and both men were signed by the same scout, Tom Greenwade. Murcer was even given Mantle's old locker. Of course, Murcer did not become the next Mantle, but he was a fan favorite. His best season was in 1972 when he blasted a career-high 33 home runs and scored a league-best 102 runs. Murcer's signature moment as a Yankee came on June 24, 1970, in a doubleheader against Cleveland, when he hit home runs in four straight at-bats.

Another center fielder named Mickey—Mickey Rivers—patrolled the Bronx's glamorous turf for several seasons in the 1970s. This leadoff specialist known as "Mick the Quick" helped lead the Yankees to three American League pennants and two World Series titles.

Then it was Rickey Henderson and his self-described "snatch catch"—catching easy fly balls by swatting his glove from over his head to his side—appearing in the Bronx for four-plus seasons in the 1980s. Henderson's first two seasons with the Yankees were awesome. In 1985, even after missing the first 10 games of the season with a sprained ankle, he scored 146 runs, the most in baseball since Ted Williams scored 150 in 1949. Henderson hit .314 with 24 homers, 72 RBIs, and a league-leading 80 stolen bases, becoming the first AL player ever with at least 20 homers and 50 steals in a season, a feat he repeated in 1986. That season, he hit 28 homers, nine to lead off the game, scored 130 runs, and upped the Yankees' single-season stolen base record to 87. Injuries limited his playing time to just 95 games in 1987, but he came back strong in 1988, when he stole 93 bases to set the club record. In just four seasons, he had become the Yankees' career stolen bases leader (since surpassed by Derek Jeter).

Bernie Williams took over in center as a worthy successor in the 1990s. Williams epitomized the quiet superstar. While others soaked up the spotlight, the soft-spoken Williams produced solid numbers year after year to little fanfare. That's why even the most zealous fan of the Bronx Bombers may be surprised to see Williams ranked seventh on the club's all-time home run list, this despite never hitting more than 30 in a season and never finishing among the American League's top 10 in any season. In fact, Williams has a lofty place in Yankees history: he ranks in the top 10 in homers, hits, runs batted in, and runs scored. Said manager Joe Torre, "Bernie bores you with consistency."

The consistency shown by Williams was impressive. He kept his batting average over .300 for eight consecutive seasons. He knocked in at least 90 runs in a season seven times in a row. He was a member of the American League All-Star team five straight years, a Gold Glove–winning center fielder for four straight years, and a World Series champion three years in a row, and owner of four rings in all. In 1995, he became the first player to homer from both sides of the plate in a playoff game. In 1996, he won Game 1 of the ALCS with a home run. In 1998, he won the batting title. He is among the career leaders in postseason homers (second) and RBIs (first).

All these accolades probably aren't enough to earn Williams a Hall of Fame plaque in Cooperstown. However, he understands his select place in baseball history.

"As I have gotten older, I have learned to appreciate playing the same position for the same organization as some of the greatest players in history," said Williams. "It's an honor. I have no other words to describe it. It's something I don't take for granted."

Curtis Granderson was guardian of Yankee Stadium's center field from 2010 to 2013. Like DiMaggio and Mantle before him, Granderson represented the Yankees as the American League's starting center fielder at the 2011 All-Star Game. The latest in a long line of great center fielders, it took little time for Granderson to appreciate the icons who once occupied his position.

"People started mentioning to me about the ghosts, the ghosts," said Granderson. "I was like, 'The ghosts? What are you talking about?' But I know what they mean now."

By 2017, the Yankees were successfully rotating three center fielders—Aaron Hicks, Jacoby Ellsbury, and Brett Gardner. Ellsbury and Gardner are Gold Glove Award winners.

67 Rise to the Occasion Like Jim Leyritz

Jim Leyritz was known for his brash playing style, irritating opponents with his bat twirling at the plate and teammates with his cock-sure swagger, earning him the nickname "The King." But when the journeyman catcher was in the lineup, especially in the postseason, he always made the best of his opportunities, hitting home runs when it mattered most. In fact, eight of Leyritz's 13 postseason hits were home runs, and many of them were the turning points of those series.

Leyritz first made his mark in the 1995 AL Division Series against the Seattle Mariners. In Game 2 at Yankee Stadium, Leyritz hit a two-run home run in the rain off Seattle pitcher Tim Belcher into the right-center-field bleachers in the 15th inning to win the game 7–5. The Yankees, who hadn't won anything since 1981, took a commanding two-game lead in the best-of-five series. Unfortunately, New York lost the next three games in Seattle's Kingdome, and the Mariners, in the postseason for the first time in team history, earned a thrilling, extra-innings victory in Game 5 of the series.

The most famous of Leyritz's playoff heroics occurred in Game 4 of the 1996 World Series against the Braves at Fulton County Stadium in Atlanta. The Yankees had lost the first two games of the Series at home, and narrowly won Game 3 in Atlanta. The Braves had built a 6–0 lead through five innings and seem poised to take a 3–1 lead in the World Series. Leyritz entered the game as a defensive replacement for catcher Joe Girardi in the sixth inning after New York had rallied for three runs to cut the deficit to 6–3. In the eighth, Braves manager Bobby Cox brought in closer Mark Wohlers to finish the job for the Braves. Wohlers had saved 39 games for Atlanta during the regular season, and his fastball regularly hit 100 miles per hour on the radar gun. After two runners reached base, Leyritz stepped into the batter's box with one out. He worked the count to 2-2, fouling off two wicked fastballs. Then Wohlers threw a hanging slider and Leyritz jumped all over it, lacing a high-arcing fly ball that soared over the left-field fence for a three-run homer to tie the game and swing the momentum in the Yankees' favor.

"I'm not thinking home run right there," said Leyritz. "I'm thinking I've got an opportunity to drive in one run if I get a base hit."

The Yankees would go on to win 8–6 in 10 innings to tie the series at 2–2, and they won it in six games. Leyritz's dramatic home run remains the signature moment of that series and of his career. It was also the turning point of the franchise. With one swing of the bat, Leyritz ignited a new Yankees dynasty, starting a run of four titles in five years.

"You win that game or else it is 3–1," said Yankees manager Joe Torre. "Instead, you had the snowball effect and win that year and it makes you feel different and able to win after that, no question. Leyritz's homer was huge. You know, Jimmy blew his own horn on how many big hits he had, but, you know what, Jimmy had a lot of big hits."

Despite his big-game success, Leyritz was traded four times over the next two years. Playing with the San Diego Padres in the 1998 NL Division Series against Houston, he hit three homers, including a two-out, game-tying home run in the ninth inning of Game 2. For good measure, he added another homer in the NLCS victory over Atlanta, a team surely sick of seeing Leyritz step up to the plate in big spots.

Traded back to New York in 1999 just in time for the World Series, also against the Atlanta Braves, Leyritz made a pinch-hitting appearance in the eighth inning of Game 4 with the Yankees leading 3–1. Leyritz hammered a solo homer to extend the Yankees lead to 4–1. The Yankees won the game and swept the Series. Leyritz's shot turned out to be the last home run hit in the 20th century.

68 Bobby Richardson

Yankees second baseman Bobby Richardson is the only player from the losing team to win the World Series Most Valuable Player award. In the 1960 World Series won by the Pittsburgh Pirates in seven games, Richardson drove in a Series-record six runs in Game 3 on his way to a record 12 runs batted in for the Series. Despite having driven in just 26 runs for the season, Richardson flexed his muscles in this Series. He had 11 hits, including two triples, two doubles, a grand slam home run, and eight runs scored. His record of six RBIs in a World Series game stood alone in the record book for 49 years until another Yankees World Series MVP, Hideki Matsui, equaled the feat in the clinching Game 6 of the 2009 World Series.

Looking at the statistics, the 1960 World Series should have been won by the New York Yankees. The Bronx Bombers set a number of Series records—highest batting average (.338), most hits (91), most runs (55), and most runs batted in (54). But this October, the Yankees lost to the Pittsburgh Pirates thanks to one of the most dramatic endings in World Series history.

The first six games of the 1960 Series had taken on an unusual tone with the Pirates winning three games by close scores and the Yankees winning three games by a combined 35 runs. After the Pirates won the opener 6–4, the Yankees came back in Games 2 and 3 with a vengeance to pound the Pirates 16–3 and 10–0.

Pittsburgh tamed New York's bats in winning Games 4 and 5 by scores of 3–2 and 5–2. New York answered in Game 6 by routing the Pirates 12–0 behind Whitey Ford's second shutout of the Series. In the deciding seventh game, New York rolled to a 7–4 lead in the eighth inning. Just six outs separated the Yankees from their 19th title. "I thought that would do it," said Yogi Berra. "We had a lot of good pitchers to hold the lead."

But the Pirates stormed back in the bottom of the eighth inning, scoring five runs to take a 9–7 advantage. The key play was a ground ball to Tony Kubek that took a bad hop and hit the Yankees short-stop in the throat, allowing the Pittsburgh rally to continue. In the top of the ninth inning, with the Yankees on the verge of defeat, Mantle singled to score one run, and then made a sensational base running play to elude a tag, allowing the tying run to score.

That set the stage for Pittsburgh second baseman Bill Mazeroski, the leadoff batter in the bottom of the ninth. Ralph Terry, the fifth Yankees pitcher of the game, threw one ball and, on the second pitch, Mazeroski swung and blasted a high fly ball that cleared the left-field wall for a home run to win the Series for the Pirates. Mazeroski jumped up and down, waving his cap in the air like a child who had fulfilled his boyhood dream. There were so many people on the field blocking his way by the time he rounded third base that Mazeroski barely made it around to touch home plate. He did make it home, though, and the Pirates won 10–9. The home run brought a dramatic conclusion to an improbable Series in which the resourceful Pirates had been outhit 91–60 and outscored 55–27.

69 1941 World Series: The Missed Third Strike

The 1941 World Series was a matchup pitting one experienced World Series team against an upstart in the Fall Classic. For the American League, Joe McCarthy's Yankees were making their fifth appearance in six years. But the National Leaguers, Leo Durocher's Brooklyn Dodgers, hadn't been in the Series since 1920.

The subway rivals—Brooklyn is one of New York's five boroughs, as is the home borough of the Yankees, the Bronx—were evenly matched, and the first three October games were decided by one run each. The Yankees took the first game 3–2 on Red Ruffing's six-hitter and a home run by Joe Gordon. The Dodgers claimed Game 2 by the same score behind a complete-game effort from Whitlow Wyatt. New York caught a break in Game 3. Brooklyn's Freddie Fitzsimmons and New York's Marius Russo were locked in a scoreless tie when, with two outs in the seventh inning, Russo hit a line drive that struck Fitzsimmons on the knee. Shortstop Pee Wee Reese caught the deflected ball in the air for the third out, but the injured Fitzsimmons was replaced by Dodgers relief ace Hugh Casey. The Yankees scored twice in the eighth inning against Casey to win the third game 2–1.

Game 4, played in Ebbets Field, is one that lingers in the memory of New York sports fans. Through eight innings of another tense battle, Brooklyn clung to a 4–3 lead, thanks to pinch hitter Jimmy Wasdell's two-run double and Pete Reiser's two-run homer. Casey had taken the mound again, and the reliever had shut down the Yankees from the fifth inning through the eighth. Casey promptly retired Johnny Sturm and Red Rolfe on ground balls for the first two outs in the ninth inning. With three balls and two strikes on New York's Tommy Henrich, the crowd stood in anticipation of a victory by the hometown Dodgers, which would have tied the series at 2–2. Brooklyn catcher Mickey Owen signaled for a curveball. Of course, he wasn't sure if Casey would be throwing his sharp-breaking curve or his big looper. The pitch fooled the batter completely. Henrich, a New York outfielder, swung and missed, and umpire Larry Goetz signaled a strikeout.

Unfortunately, the pitch fooled Owen as well. The ball glanced off his mitt and shot back to the wall. If a pitch gets past the catcher on a third strike, the batter is allowed to run to first base—and that's just what Henrich did. The next man up, Joe DiMaggio, singled to left, and Charlie Keller put the Yankees ahead with a two-run double. Casey was coming undone. After a walk to Bill Dickey, he yielded another two-run double to Joe Gordon. The Yankees' Johnny Murphy then pitched two scoreless innings of relief and New York handed Brooklyn a devastating 7–4 defeat. The next day, Ernie Bonham put the Dodgers out of their misery by tossing a four-hitter, and helped by Henrich's homer, the Yankees trampled the Dodgers 3–1 in Game 5 to win the title.

"That was a tough break for poor Mickey to get," said Henrich. "I bet he feels like a nickel's worth of dog meat."

Owen's miscue had let a potential Series-tying victory get away and had given the Yankees new life. Owen couldn't forgive himself for opening the door. "Sure, it was my fault," Owen said after the game. "The ball was a low curve that broke down. It hit the edge of my glove and glanced off, but I should have had him out anyway.

"It was as good a curveball as Casey ever threw," he added. "I should have had it."

70 Allie Reynolds

Allie Reynolds, nicknamed "The Chief" because he was one-quarter Creek Indian, was known to be a big-game pitcher for the Yankees from 1947 to 1954. As the anchor of the pitching staff, he led New York to the World Series six times during his eight seasons wearing pinstripes. In World Series play, Reynolds was 7–2 with four saves and a 2.79 earned-run average.

Twice, Reynolds' baseball career took a positive turn because he listened to good advice. In college at the school which is now Oklahoma State, Reynolds was a running back on the football team and a pitcher on the baseball team. After receiving professional contract offers from both sports he was forced to make a choice. Reynolds asked his baseball coach, Hank Iba, for help in making the decision. Iba, who would later be enshrined in the basketball Hall of Fame, recommended Reynolds stick to pitching. "It was a fine suggestion," said Reynolds.

The burly right-hander signed with the Cleveland Indians and reached the majors in 1942. While he possessed a blazing fastball, Reynolds couldn't always control it, leading the league in strikeouts and bases on balls over the next four seasons. By the time he was 30 years old, Reynolds had managed only a 51–47 lifetime mark for the Indians. Prior to the 1947 season, the Yankees acquired Reynolds in a trade for second baseman Joe Gordon. During spring training, veteran Yankees pitcher Spud Chandler urged Reynolds to setup batters by changing speeds. Reynolds did just that.

In his first season with the Yankees, Reynolds went 19–8 and won his first World Series game. In 1949, he proved himself a great World Series pitcher in the opener, throwing a two-hit shutout and outlasting Don Newcombe 1–0. In the fourth game he retired all

10 Dodgers batters he faced to earn a save. Said manager Casey Stengel of Reynolds' dual ability to start and relieve, "He's two pitchers rolled into one."

Reynolds entered the record books in 1951, becoming the first American League pitcher to record two no-hitters in the same season. The first no-hitter was on July 12, 1951, in Cleveland against Bob Feller and the Indians. Gene Woodling hit a home run in the top of the seventh inning for the only run of the game. Then, on September 28 at Yankee Stadium, Reynolds was one out away from joining Johnny Vander Meer of the Cincinnati Reds as the only pitchers to that point to accomplish the feat twice in a season. That final out was Ted Williams of the Boston Red Sox—one of the best hitters of all time—and Reynolds had to get him out twice. Williams hit a foul pop-up that catcher Yogi Berra dropped. Unfazed, on the very next pitch, Reynolds got Williams to hit another foul pop-up, and this time Berra squeezed the ball in his mitt for the final out of an 8–0 win, clinching another American League pennant for the Yankees.

The Chief's only 20-win season occurred in 1952, his last great season for the Yankees. That year he was 20–8 with a league-best 2.06 earned-run average, 160 strikeouts, and six shutouts. He also saved six games. Over the next two seasons Reynolds went 26–11 with 20 saves, but an injured back forced him to retire after the 1954 season. Despite pitching only eight seasons for the Yankees, Reynolds still ranks in the team's all-time top 10 in wins (131), won-loss percentage (.686), and shutouts (27).

71 Attend a Spring Training Game in Tampa

Baseball prepares for the regular season during February and March in Florida's Grapefruit League and Arizona's Cactus League. No matter which team is your favorite, there's always an exciting feeling of hope during spring training because everyone believes, deep down, that this could be the year their team wins the World Series.

Spring training is a great way to get a close-up look at major league players. You sit close enough to see the players' faces and hear their voices. The smell of freshly cut grass permeates the grandstands and you can buy a hot dog and a soft drink at a nearby concession stand without missing much action. Florida baseball in March is a much more intimate experience than anything you'll find up north during the regular season.

George M. Steinbrenner Field in Tampa, Florida, is the place the Yankees call home for their Grapefruit League season, which begins annually in early March. (The Yankees' spring training site from 1962 to 1995 was in Fort Lauderdale, Florida.)

Steinbrenner Field is a terrific venue for watching the games. Opened in 1996 and known then as Legends Field, it was renamed to honor team owner George Steinbrenner in 2008. The stadium seats 11,076, making it the largest spring training facility in the Grapefruit League. Once the major league club breaks camp and begins the regular season, the complex also serves as the home of the minor league Single A Tampa Yankees of the Florida State League.

As fans enter the complex, the first thing they see is an exhibit displaying the Yankees' retired numbers, just like at Monument Park. Fans will also notice another link to the Bronx—the field's dimensions are an exact replica of Yankee Stadium, measuring 318 feet down the left-field line, 408 feet to center field, and 314 feet down the right-field line.

One of the great joys of spring training is the lower cost of tickets for the best seats in the house. Whether you've purchased an infield box seat behind the dugout or have simply moved down closer to the action (the ushers are less vigilant in spring training), you can hear the players talk to each other, hear the umpire call strike or ball, and hear the ball smack into the first baseman's glove on a throw from across the diamond. The perspective makes for an unforgettable sensory experience at the ballpark.

Arrive early and soak up the sun and the atmosphere. Hours before a game can be spent watching practices and drills. Players take infield practice, fielding ground ball after ground ball, with

Spring training provides the perfect opportunity for fans to get up close and personal with Yankees stars such as Curtis Granderson.

Turning Heads

The James P. Dawson Award is presented annually to the top rookie in the Yankees spring training camp. The award was established in honor of James P. Dawson (1896–1953), who began a 45-year career with *The New York Times* as a copy boy in 1908. Eight years later, he became boxing editor and covered boxing and baseball until his death during spring training in 1953.

Two winners of the award—Tony Kubek in 1957 and Tom Tresh in 1962—went on to win the American League Rookie of the Year award.

unbelievable speed and precision. And that coach you recognize hitting ground balls might be a former star. The Yankees have a unique bond with their former players, and each year in Tampa you can traditionally find the likes of Reggie Jackson, Ron Guidry, and a host of other Yankees greats serving as guest instructors and chatting with younger players between practice sessions.

Smaller stadiums and fine weather are a great combination. People in the stands relax in the warm sun as they peer curiously at prospects trying to impress the manager and look over the older players getting in shape and hoping they'll be hired for one more season.

Everyone seems to be a little more hospitable before a spring training game. If you come early enough, you can talk with some of the players and get autographs. Since the outcome of the games don't count, major league players may get only two at-bats, and the starting pitcher may be gone by the third inning, before the minor league's prized prospects get their chance to shine. But on the bright side, spring training games move at a crisp pace because batters take fewer pitches, looking to get in more hacks and hone their batting eyes.

72 Earle Combs

Earle Combs was the table-setter for the most potent lineup in baseball history. As the leadoff hitter for the Yankees of the 1920s and early 1930s, Combs was followed by the Yanks' famous Murderers' Row—Babe Ruth, Lou Gehrig, and Bob Meusel.

Nicknamed "The Kentucky Colonel," Combs was well-suited to set things up for the big guns. A lifetime .325 hitter, Combs averaged nearly 200 hits and 70 walks per season during his peak years. The 6'0", 185-pound speedster was an adept bunter, and his keen eye resulted in high totals for base on balls. His career on-base percentage was .397. Whenever the Yankees power hitters came up, Combs seemed to be on base. Often, that base was third.

Combs' great speed helped him lead the American League in triples three times, picking up 154 for his career, including three in one game in 1927. That speed also helped him cover a great deal of ground while playing center field in the roomy outfield at Yankee Stadium.

Combs never got as many headlines as his superstar teammates, but his consistent play—he hit better than .300 in eight of his 11 seasons—made him an essential part of the Yankees' success. For eight consecutive years, Combs scored more than 100 runs per season and hit more than 30 doubles each season, as well.

The Yankees won the American League pennant in 1921, 1922, and 1923. Then they added Combs and looked to be even stronger in 1924. That year, the rookie outfielder was hitting over .400 when he suffered a broken ankle and was lost for the rest of the season. The injury likely cost the Yankees the pennant. New York finished in second place, just two games behind the Washington Senators.

Combs came back strong in 1925, batting .342 with 203 hits and 117 runs scored. In 1927, Combs whacked 23 triples and batted .356 with an American League–leading 231 hits—a Yankees team record that stood until Don Mattingly broke it in 1986. Combs also scored the winning run in the World Series in New York's four-game sweep of Pittsburgh that year.

The championship Yankees team of 1927, boasting seven future Hall of Famers, is widely believed to be the best team in baseball history. Combs thought a key reason for the team's success was a talented group of players, all performing at the highest level of their abilities. "I always thought that's what made us so dominant that year," said Combs.

Always a popular figure because he gave maximum effort, the fans in Yankee Stadium took up a collection in 1928 and bought Combs a gold watch to show their appreciation. Three years later, famed sportswriter Fred Lieb wrote, "I believe if a vote were taken of the sportswriters on who is the most popular player in New York, I think the vote would go to Combs."

Combs was always at his best at World Series time. In 1926, he batted .357 and hit safely in all seven games in a losing effort against the St. Louis Cardinals. Due to a fractured wrist suffered late in the regular season, he was limited to one pinch-hitting appearance in New York's four-game sweep of St. Louis in 1928. In 1932, he hit .375 as the Yankees swept the Chicago Cubs in four games. Combs never made an error in the 16 World Series games in which he played.

Unfortunately, Combs' career came to a sudden end in 1934; before ballfields had warning tracks or padded walls, Combs crashed into the wall at Sportsman's Park in St. Louis while chasing down a fly ball. Combs fractured his skull. He attempted a comeback the following year, but while chasing a fly ball in a game against the Chicago White Sox, he collided with another player and broke his collarbone. Combs retired at the end of the 1935 season, saying, "I'm getting out of this game before it kills me."

In 1936, Combs took a job as a Yankees coach. When Joe DiMaggio arrived that season to begin his career as the next great Yankees superstar, Combs helped teach the young outfielder the finer points of playing center field at Yankee Stadium.

Combs remained in coaching with the Yankees and several other teams through 1954 and then retired to his Kentucky farm. He was elected to the Hall of Fame in 1970, six years before his death. Ever humble, Combs was surprised by the honor. "I thought the Hall of Fame was for superstars," he said modestly, "not for average players like I was."

73 1978 Yankees: The Comeback Kids

The atmosphere in the New York Yankees clubhouse in 1977 was known as the Bronx Zoo. That didn't change in 1978, and neither did the end result: a World Series championship for the Yankees in six games over the Los Angeles Dodgers. But this time, the Bombers overcame a 2–0 deficit by winning four straight games for the title. No team in Series history had ever done that before.

The 1978 Yankees were no strangers to comebacks. Trailing the division-leading Red Sox by 14 games on July 19, the Yankees decided to make a change at the top. Manager Billy Martin was fired on July 24, and Bob Lemon replaced him. After Lemon took over, the Yankees responded to their new manager's easygoing style, shaving 10 games off the Red Sox's lead in just over six weeks. But on September 6 the Yankees were still four games out with just 24 to go when they rolled into Fenway Park for an important four-game series.

The Yankees crushed the Red Sox by scores of 15–3, 13–2, 7–0, and 7–4. They had a seven-run inning, a six-run inning, and a five-run inning. The Yankees outscored the Red Sox 42–9, outhit them 67–21, and the Red Sox committed six errors to boot. Thurman Munson went 8-for-16. Ron Guidry threw a two-hitter in the third game. When they left after their Boston Massacre, the Yankees had evened the Red Sox in the standings with identical 86–56 records. The Bombers were rolling, and the Red Sox were reeling. Six days later at Yankee Stadium, Guidry fired another two-hit shutout over Boston and the Yankees rocketed 2.5 games in front of the staggering Red Sox.

That, however, was not the end of the Sox. Although the Yankees under Lemon would win 48 games and lose only 20, the Red Sox won 12 of their 14 final games and eight of them in a row. Winning their last game of the season while the Yankees were losing, the Red Sox forced a one-game playoff on Monday afternoon, October 2, at Fenway Park. It was the American League's first tie-breaker playoff game since 1948. Bucky Dent, the light-hitting shortstop, socked a startling three-run homer off Mike Torrez in the seventh. The Yankees won the game 5–4 and the division title.

In the postseason, the Yankees swatted away the pesky Kansas City Royals in the playoffs, but then lost the first two games of the World Series against the Los Angeles Dodgers before storming back to win four straight and the series.

The Dodgers won the first two Series games in Los Angeles, 11–5 and 4–3. The second game featured a nerve-wracking confrontation between rookie pitcher Bob Welch and star outfielder Reggie Jackson, who made a career hitting in clutch situations such as this. In the ninth inning, with two runners on base and two outs, Jackson battled Welch over nine pitches, fouling off pitch after pitch, before fanning to end the game. "It was a great at-bat," said Jackson. "I enjoyed every pitch except the last."

The New Yorkers came home to the Bronx and won Game 3 behind the gutsy pitching of Guidry and the glove work of third baseman Graig Nettles. The Yankees needed 10 innings to win Game 4 on Lou Piniella's game-winning hit. Jackson, ever in the middle of it all for the Yankees, impacted this game with his guile in the sixth inning, breaking up a double play by getting in the way of Bill Russell's throw to first. The ball hit Jackson in the thigh and caromed into right field, allowing a pivotal run to score. Dodgers manager Tommy Lasorda protested that Jackson intentionally stuck out his hip and interfered with the ball, but umpires weren't buying it. "I didn't do anything but stand there," said Jackson.

New York blasted Los Angeles 12–2 in Game 5, as rookie Jim Beattie pitched a complete game and Thurman Munson led the way with five runs batted in as part of an 18-hit barrage. In the decisive sixth game at Dodger Stadium, Catfish Hunter pitched seven innings and Rich Gossage shut the door on the Dodgers for a relatively easy 7–2 Yankees win and a second consecutive World Series championship. The big blow of the game was Jackson's 430-foot home run off Welch. Jackson hit .391 with two homers and eight RBIs in the Series, but the Yankees won the trophy on the hitting of two men at the bottom of the order: Brian Doyle, substituting at second base for the injured Willie Randolph, batted .438; and shortstop Bucky Dent, the series MVP, batted .417 with seven runs batted in.

74 Snag a Souvenir Ball at Yankee Stadium

Most baseball fans go to a major league game hoping to catch a ball that is hit into the stands. A baseball makes a great souvenir, yet most fans believe the odds are against them. But it's not as hard as it seems. Zack Hample has snagged more than 10,000 baseballs at 53 different major league stadiums across North America since 1990, including Alex Rodriguez's 3,000th hit. He is also the author of *How to Snag Major League Baseballs*. With his help, here's how you can walk away from the ballpark with a souvenir baseball in your pocket.

- Go to batting practice. This is your best chance to snag a baseball. "There are fewer fans, and security isn't as strict," said Hample.

- Make sure to bring your glove to the game. When a ball is coming at you at 90 miles per hour, you're going to want to protect yourself. Also, most balls are twisting and spinning coming off the bat. Catching a ball with so much spin barehanded is nearly impossible. So put your glove on.

- Teams begin warming up on the field about two hours before game time, so arrive at the ballpark early, when fewer people are competing against you. When teams are warming up, they often toss balls to their fans in the stands. "Be loud and always say please," said Hample, who can say "Please throw me a ball" in several different languages, and once even used sign language with a deaf player.

- Most batters are right-handed and will pull the ball during batting practice. By placing yourself in left field, you increase your chances of snagging a ball. And make sure you stand on the aisle. "Don't get trapped in the middle of a long row. You need to be able to jump up and move," Hample said.

- Snagging a ball during the game is much more difficult than during pregame drills. The ideal place to be is on the aisle next to the field, about three-quarters of the way from third base to the foul pole. It's easy to reach over and field ground foul balls—but only if the wall separating the stands from the field is low enough to reach over, like it is at Yankee Stadium. "It's important to know the stadium, so do your research," said Hample. If the walls are high, your chances might be better if you go a little further back to catch a foul pop-up.

- With ground balls that roll near the wall, make sure it's a foul ball before you reach over and grab it. If you touch a ball in play or reach out onto the field and interfere with a live ball, you likely will be ejected from the stadium. "Don't get in the way of the players," said Hample.

- Snagging a ball during the game takes more strategy than trying to snag one during batting practice, so plan ahead and play the percentages. Check out the pitching matchups ahead of time so you know how many right- and left-handed batters are likely to be in the starting lineup. Most right-handed batters will hit foul balls to the first-base side; left-handed batters to the third-base side. According to Hample, 99 percent of foul balls are sliced the opposite way, so select a seat in the stadium accordingly. "For a right-hander, I draw an imaginary line from the left fielder through home plate," said Hample. "That's the perfect place to sit."

75 Elston Howard

In 1955, Rosa Parks, an African American woman in Montgomery, Alabama, refused to give up her seat to a white man on a city bus, sparking a civil rights movement that led to sweeping social changes.

While Major League Baseball had been integrated for nearly a decade by the 1950s, African American players still often took a backseat to their white counterparts. By the middle of the decade, four big league teams—most notably, the New York Yankees—still were not integrated.

The Yankees finally called up their first African American player to the parent club in 1955. Elston Howard, a burly catcher who bided his time in the outfield and at first base while Yogi Berra was in the prime of his career, made his debut in pinstripes on April 14, 1955. He singled in his first at-bat during New York's 8–4 loss to the Boston Red Sox.

Continuing to hit well for power and average, Howard's batting average topped .300 three times, with a career-best .348 average in 1961. By then, he was the catcher and Berra had been moved to left field. Howard proved to be an excellent receiver. A two-time Gold Glove catcher, his career fielding average of .993 ranks among the highest ever for a catcher. A baseball pioneer, Howard was one of the first catchers to use a hinged catcher's mitt, which eventually led to the modern one-handed catching technique popularized by Cincinnati's Johnny Bench in the early 1970s. Howard also popularized the use of the batting donut, a donut-shaped weight that slips over the bat and allows the on-deck batter to swing a heavier bat, so it will feel lighter when he's at the plate. In the past, waiting batters had swung several bats at the same time.

Howard batted .274 and slugged 167 home runs during his 14-year career. His best season was in 1963, when he won the American League MVP award—the first African American to win the award in the AL (African American players had won it in the National League 11 times). That season, Howard hit .287 with 28 home runs and 85 runs batted in to lead New York to a first-place finish for a fourth consecutive season.

"The Most Valuable Player isn't me," Howard told reporters after getting 248 of 280 votes to win the award. "He wasn't playing. If Mickey Mantle had been in there, he'd have won it."

Howard was selling himself short, for he may have been the only person in 1963 who did not believe he was deserving of the award. Thanks to Howard's leadership, the Yankees incredibly overcame injuries that would have decimated most other teams. Mantle hit 15 home runs in 65 games before being sidelined with a broken foot and torn knee cartilage. Roger Maris played in only 90 games that season, but the Yanks persevered and even prospered. With Howard behind the plate, flawlessly handling the pitching staff and driving in a bushel of clutch runs, New York won the American League pennant by 10.5 games. The only sour note in

Al Downing

In 1963, Al Downing became the first African American starting pitcher in Yankees history. The left-hander went 13–5 with a 2.56 earned-run average. In 1964, he won 13 games and led the league with 217 strikeouts, the last Yankees pitcher to do so.

Al Downing holds the distinction of being the only active player in uniform when Roger Maris and Hank Aaron broke Babe Ruth's two most famous home run records. Downing was a rookie pitcher for the Yankees on October 1, 1961, and watched from the bullpen as Maris hit his 61st home run of the season. Downing had a better view of Aaron's record-breaking 715th homer as the pitcher who served it up as a member of the Los Angeles Dodgers on April 8, 1974.

the season was their staggering loss to the Los Angeles Dodgers in the World Series in four straight games.

Howard played more than 1,400 games with the Yankees and was an American League All-Star nine consecutive years from 1956 to 1965. He was also a member of pennant-winning Yankees teams in nine of his first 10 seasons. Ironically, Howard finished his career with the Red Sox in 1968. Only nine years earlier, Boston had become the last major league team to integrate. The Yankees traded Howard to the Red Sox in August of 1967, and he helped spark their amazing run to the World Series, only to lose to the St. Louis Cardinals in seven games. It was the sixth time Howard had played on a World Series loser, a record he shares with Pee Wee Reese of the Brooklyn Dodgers. Howard was a member of four World Series winners with the Yankees.

Always a respected clubhouse leader, after Howard retired he became a Yankees coach until his death in 1980. His uniform No. 32 was retired in 1984; his plaque in Monument Park reads, "A man of great gentleness and dignity…one of the truly great Yankees."

76 Jim "Catfish" Hunter

It certainly was a Happy New Year for Yankees fans. Dangling the first multimillion dollar contract as bait, New York Yankees owner George M. Steinbrenner III landed the most celebrated catch in free-agent history, signing Oakland Athletics pitching ace Jim "Catfish" Hunter on December 31, 1974.

After leading the Athletics to a third straight World Series title and winning the Cy Young award following the 1974 season,

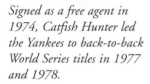

Signed as a free agent in 1974, Catfish Hunter led the Yankees to back-to-back World Series titles in 1977 and 1978.

a financial dispute with Oakland owner Charles O. Finley led Hunter to declare himself a free agent—two years before the beginning of official free agency. The dispute stemmed from a contract issue regarding deferred payments. The previous winter, Hunter and Finley agreed on a two-year contract for $100,000 a year, but each year only $50,000 was to be paid to Hunter as straight salary; the remaining $50,000 was to be paid to a life insurance fund. The straight-salary part was paid routinely, but the insurance payments were not made because it would involve unfavorable tax consequences for Finley. Hunter contended Finley did not honor the agreement and therefore voided the contract. Finley said there was no contract violation, just disagreement over interpretation. Undeterred, Hunter filed for free agency when Finley refused to pay. An arbitrator, Peter Seitz, ruled in Hunter's favor at a hearing on December 15, 1974, and declared Hunter a free agent.

The 28-year-old pitcher was a prized catch. Hunter had 106 victories over the last five seasons with the A's and was the reigning American League Cy Young award winner with a career-best 25 wins. As expected, an incredible bidding war among at least 20 teams broke out for Hunter's services for the 1975 season as team officials descended on the North Carolina law offices of Cherry, Cherry and Flythe in North Carolina, near Hunter's home in Hertford. But in the end, it was Steinbrenner who swooped in to grab Hunter with the richest deal in baseball at the time. Hunter signed with the Yankees on New Year's Eve for an unprecedented $3.5 million package over five years. The era of the big-contract superstar free agent had officially begun.

With one stroke of the pen, the Yankees became immediate World Series contenders. Hunter won 23 games in his first season in the Bronx in 1975, leading the American League with 328 innings, and no one since has come close to matching his amazing 30 complete games. By the next season, Hunter was helping propel the Yankees to three straight American League pennants (1976–78) and back-to-back World Series titles in 1977 and 1978. Catfish was a World Series starter in each of the team's three Fall Classic appearances.

Hunter was just 63–53 in five seasons for the New York Yankees from 1975 to 1979. But numbers don't measure Hunter's importance to the Yankees. "He was the first to teach us how to win, what it means to be a winner," said Steinbrenner.

During spring training of 1978, doctors diagnosed Hunter as a diabetic, but he still went on to be a 12-game winner and the winning pitcher in Game 6 of New York's World Series–clinching victory over the Dodgers. Arm trouble forced Hunter to retire at age 33 in 1979, or at least that's what his Hall of Fame plaque states. Hunter has a different explanation. "I wanted to start spending time with my family, and I told the Yankees when I signed that

I would only play for five years," adding, "I had no arm problems when I retired."

When he was inducted into the Hall of Fame in his third year of eligibility in 1987, Hunter was surprised.

"I didn't think I would make it," he said. "I figured I wasn't good enough. I figured the people in there were like gods."

To which commissioner Peter Ueberroth noted, "Catfish Hunter had the distinction of playing for both Charlie Finley and George Steinbrenner, which is enough to put a player in the Hall of Fame."

Hunter became the first player born after World War II to gain a spot in Cooperstown. He died in 1999 at age 53 of amyotrophic lateral sclerosis, the same disease that took the life of another Yankees legend, Lou Gehrig.

77 Recall the Polo Grounds Rivalry

When Babe Ruth joined the New York Yankees for the 1920 season, fans expected a World Series triumph to immediately follow. The Bambino clouted 54 homers his first year in pinstripes, yet it was the Cleveland Indians who went on to win the American League pennant. In 1921, Ruth established new marks for home runs (59) and runs batted in (171) in a season, while batting .378. Still, the Yankees could not run away from the rest of the American League. After a neck-and-neck race with the Indians in the final days of the 1921 season, the Yankees captured their first AL pennant after sweeping a doubleheader from the Philadelphia Athletics. It was the franchise's first pennant in its 19-year existence.

The Yankees would meet the National League champion New York Giants in the World Series. The dream of New York baseball fans came true: it was a Polo Grounds World Series. The Yankees were then playing their home games in the Giants' ballpark, and the first time that all the games were played at one stadium. This World Series provided other firsts, as well as a last. It was the first to be broadcast on radio, and the final best-of-nine series in Major League Baseball history.

The Yankees, playing their first World Series game in franchise history, sent Carl Mays to the mound and he tossed a complete-game shutout to defeat the Giants 3–0. The next day, Waite Hoyt matched his teammate Mays with another 3–0 complete-game shutout, and the Yankees took a 2–0 series lead. The Giants, who won the World Series in 1905 before losing their next four trips to the Fall Classic, rallied to beat the Yankees in eight games. Despite missing two games with knee and arm injuries, Ruth still was a key figure in the series, batting .313 and hitting his first World Series home run. By the time the Babe's career was done, he would hit 15 series homers.

The 1922 season was not a majestic one for Ruth. He was suspended five different times during the season for, among other things, barnstorming (playing non-approved games), throwing dirt in an umpire's face, and attacking a fan in the stands. Still, the season's odd twists and turns took baseball right back to where it had been the previous October. Once again, the Giants and Yankees met at the Polo Grounds, this time in a best-of-seven World Series. The Yankees, who had already announced they were moving into a new stadium across the Harlem River in the Bronx the following year, once again played patsy to their Polo Grounds landlords. Babe Ruth batted only .118 with no home runs, and the Yankees were swept by the Giants 4–0, with one tie. The National Leaguers had so dominated their American League rivals that the closest the Yankees came to winning a game was Game 2, which was cancelled on account of darkness in a 3–3 tie after 10 innings. The American League president, Ban Johnson, groaned, "The Giants have humiliated the American League in a way that cannot be forgotten."

After losing to the Giants the previous two Octobers, the Yankees finally got their revenge in 1923, downing the Giants in the World Series in six games. Ruth made up for his terrible 1922 showing by crushing three homers, a triple, a double, and three singles. Ironically, the Yankees clinched their first-ever championship in a Game 6 win on the very Polo Grounds field from which they'd been evicted.

The New York rival Giants and Yankees would meet three more times in the World Series before the Giants would move to San Francisco after the 1957 season. The Yankees won all three Series. In 1936, the Yankees won in six games; in 1937, it only took five. And in 1951, they won again in six games to send a retiring Joe DiMaggio out a winner.

78 Taunt a Red Sox Fan with the Curse of the Bambino

As decades go, the Roaring Twenties jumped out of the starting gate. On January 3, 1920, the Boston Red Sox sold perhaps the best baseball player of all time, Babe Ruth, to the New York Yankees. It was, without a doubt, the greatest transaction in Yankees history.

In 1920, the Yankees were a 17-year-old team that had never won a pennant. The Red Sox had won four World Series in the past eight seasons. Ruth, only 24, had already led the American League in home runs for the past two seasons. But Red Sox owner Harry Frazee, who was also a theater producer, was riddled with debt. In a deal that has haunted Boston baseball fans ever since, Frazee sold Ruth to New York for over $100,000 in cash and a $385,000 loan.

The Yankees immediately doubled Ruth's salary—at his demand—to a then-unheard-of $20,000 a year. No athlete had ever been paid so much. But the Babe was worth every penny. In his first season with the Yankees, Ruth hit 54 home runs. By July 19 he had already broken his own record of 29 homers, set the year before. *Ruthian* became a word to describe the Babe's extraordinary feats. No other major league *team* hit as many homers as Ruth did in 1920. He was primarily responsible for the Yankees becoming the first club to draw more than 1 million fans in a single season.

Once seen, the Ruthian homer was never forgotten. Most home run hitters power the ball into the seats or over the wall on either a line or a high arc. But Ruth's hits soared lazily skyward to dizzying heights, then carried farther and farther from the plate. When they dropped, they seemed to drop straight down. Even the shots that stayed in the park often amazed fans.

"No one hit home runs the way Babe did," said Dizzy Dean, a Hall of Fame pitcher for the Cardinals. "They were something special, like homing pigeons. The ball would leave the bat, pause briefly, suddenly gain its bearings, then take off for the stands."

The only thing Ruth failed to do in his first spectacular season in New York was lead the Yankees to the pennant. Still, the sale of Ruth became the single most important—and infamous—deal in sports history. It dramatically reversed the World Series fortunes of both teams. The Yankees would win 26 World Series by the end of the century, becoming the most successful team in professional sports. The Red Sox didn't even play in another World Series until 1946, and the team would not win a World Series for 86 years, often failing in heartbreaking fashion. Many fans believed it was Ruth's curse upon them.

The phrase "Curse of the Bambino" became ubiquitous following a 1990 book by the same title by *Boston Globe* sports columnist

Dan Shaughnessy. The book chronicles the classic BoSox debacles, from Johnny Pesky's holding the ball in the seventh game of the 1946 World Series, to Bucky Dent's deflating home run in the deciding game of the 1978 season, to the horrifying dribbler that slithered between Bill Buckner's legs one out away from a Series victory in 1986.

Mining such heartbreak led the author Stephen King to give one of publishing's all-time great book-jacket blurbs: "The quintessential New England horror story. Read it and weep."

Then in 2004 the world changed. Boston and New York met in the ALCS, with Boston becoming the first team in major league history to win a playoff series after being down 3–0. Then Boston defeated St. Louis in the World Series to win its first championship since 1918 and thus end the Curse of the Bambino. The Red Sox, who also won titles in 2007 and 2013 (bookending the Yankees' 2009 title), now boast having Reversed the Curse, but the curse is always fair game for a friendly taunt among fellow fans wistful for the good old days of baseball curses. Even the Chicago Cubs, those once-lovable losers, have ended their 108-year championship drought and finally laid to rest the Curse of the Billy Goat, which lasted 71 years, from 1945 to 2016.

79 Wells Ain't Perfect, but Game Is

Twenty-seven batters up. Twenty-seven batters down. No runner reaches base for any reason in any inning. It's a perfect game, one of the most difficult feats in sports.

On May 17, 1998, at Yankee Stadium, portly veteran left-hander David Wells pitched only the 15th perfect game in Major

League Baseball history, retiring all 27 Minnesota Twins he faced in a 4–0 Yankees victory.

Relying on pinpoint control of his fastball and curve, Wells was in total command on the mound. No Twins batter could touch him. Wells struck out 11 of the 27 Twins he faced, including Javier Valentin three times and Ron Coomer and Jon Shave twice.

Renowned for his excessive weight and excessive ways off the field, for at least one day everyone focused on Wells' pitching excellence. "Nobody can ever take this away from me, ever, no matter what," said Wells.

Hours earlier, Wells felt far less elated. Out until five o'clock in the morning, he arrived at his stadium locker in sorry shape, finding a quiet area in the player's lounge, drinking half a pot of strong coffee, and gulping a handful of aspirin. By game time, Wells recovered and began stringing together innings of three up and three down.

In the seventh inning, Wells' bid for history was anything but close to perfection. He got behind in the count on eight of the last nine batters he faced, including Paul Molitor, a member of the 3,000-hit club and a future Hall of Famer, who ran the count to 3-1 before fanning.

One of baseball's time-honored superstitions forbids a teammate to talk to a pitcher in the middle of his no-hitter for fear of jinxing him. Yet Wells, always one to buck tradition, was the one hoping to make conversation with someone in the dugout. "I just wanted to talk so it would ease my mind a little bit, but no one would come near me," Wells said later. Finally, pitcher David Cone joked that Wells should start throwing a new pitch. "Coney comes over to me before the eighth inning and said, 'Guess it's time to break out your knuckleball,'" said Wells.

Cone kept Wells relaxed, and Yankees second baseman Chuck Knoblauch kept him perfect, robbing Coomer of the only potential hit with a slick backhanded stab of a hard one-hop smash near second base in the eighth inning. It would be Wells' biggest scare. As he took the mound for the ninth inning, the crowd of 49,820 greeted Wells with a standing ovation. He continued his mastery, inducing a lazy fly ball from Shave and striking out Valentin.

"The fans were going crazy, which was great, but I kind of wanted them to calm down because they were making me nervous," Wells said. "By the end I could barely grip the ball, my hand was shaking so much."

Then the Boomer, as he's known, took a deep breath and threw a fastball to Pat Meares. When Meares' pop-up landed in right fielder Paul O'Neill's glove for the final out, Wells jumped high in the air, waving his arms in delight, then embraced his catcher, Jorge Posada, and screamed, "This is great!"

Then the 245-pound Wells was carried off the field by three teammates. He whipped off his cap and waved it at the crowd. To punctuate the historic moment, the voice of Frank Sinatra singing "New York, New York," which always signals a Yankees victory, filled the stadium. It was a poignant scene, coming just three days after the beloved crooner's death.

After the game Wells fielded a congratulatory call from fellow San Diego native Don Larsen, who had pitched the only other perfect game in Yankees history. Coincidentally, both men attended the same high school, Point Loma, in San Diego. Larsen graduated in 1947, Wells was Class of 1982.

The next call came from New York City mayor Rudy Giuliani, who invited Wells to City Hall to give him a key to the city. To which Wells jokingly replied, "Do you think that's a good idea?"

Hey, David Wells, New York is the city that never sleeps.

80 Yankees Owners

The first men to own the New York Yankees were Frank Farrell and Bill Devery. On January 9, 1903, they purchased the defunct Baltimore franchise of the upstart American League for $18,000, and then moved the team to Manhattan. Farrell was a big-time gambler and racehorse owner with associates in Tammany Hall. Big Bill Devery was a former New York City police chief known to look the other way, for a price, whenever trouble was around. He, too, was a wheeler-dealer with important political connections. Sadly, these were dismal days for Yankees fans as their ballclub was losing games on a regular basis. By 1915, owners Farrell and Devery had become extremely unhappy. Farrell was broke, and he and Devery were quarreling openly. They no longer had their own ballpark, as Hilltop Park had grown into disrepair, and crowds were small at the Polo Grounds for the Yankees. As the Yankees continued to fall in the standings, Farrell and Devery began looking around for a buyer.

They found as potential new owners two men with nothing in common except money and an interest in baseball. Colonel Jacob Ruppert was a New York socialite whose wealth came from his family's prosperous brewery. Captain Tillinghast L'Hommedieu Huston was from Ohio and had been a U.S. Army engineer who would go on to make a fortune in construction in Cuba after the Spanish-American War. Later, Huston would serve as a colonel in World War I, while Ruppert's rank was that of an honorary colonel on the governor of New York's staff. Together, Ruppert and Huston paid Farrell and Devery $460,000 and took command of the ballclub.

Four years later they made a better deal by acquiring Babe Ruth from the Red Sox for about $100,000. That deal forever altered the game's competitive landscape and would make the Yankees brand synonymous with winning. The team owners did not endear themselves to the rest of baseball. When a reporter asked Ruppert what he considered a perfect day at the ballpark, he replied, "When the Yankees score eight runs in the first inning and slowly pull away."

While Huston was off in France with the Army during World War I, Ruppert, acting on his own, hired Miller Huggins to take over as Yankees manager in 1918. Huston was furious when he heard the news, and a rift developed between him and Ruppert that never fully closed. The discord got worse in 1922 when Huston and Huggins argued over the manager's handling of the Babe. Huggins wanted to discipline his star player for his late-night carousing, but Huston was willing to look the other way. Ruppert sided with Huggins over Huston, which meant the end of Huston as co-owner. Huston asked Ruppert to buy his half of the club, and the Colonel agreed to end their uneasy partnership. One month after the new stadium opened for the 1923 season, Ruppert bought out Huston for $1.5 million, six times what he had paid for his share eight years earlier. Ruppert was sole owner of the team until his death in 1939.

Two years later, the United States would enter into World War II. With the national pastime so significantly affected by the war, ownership of a Major League Baseball team was suddenly a dubious business proposition. In New York, center of the baseball universe, two of the city's three teams traded hands in 1945. On January 26, 1945, the heirs of Jacob Ruppert sold the Yankees to a syndicate headed by Larry MacPhail, Dan Topping, and Del Webb. The price was estimated at a whopping $2.8 million. Later that year the Dodgers were bought by investors that included Walter O'Malley, who retained ownership for half a century. The Yankees won the 1947 World Series, and while soaked with champagne in the celebratory clubhouse, Larry MacPhail announced his decision to retire. He would sell his one-third interest in the Yankees to Topping and Webb for $2 million, which was not a bad return for MacPhail on his three-year investment.

The Yankees dynasty peaked from 1947 to 1964. During those 18 seasons, the Yankees won 15 American League pennants and 10 World Series. But after never having to wait more than four years to reach a World Series, the Bronx Bombers did not make it back again for 12 years. It was truly the end of an era. Dan Topping sold the Yankees to the CBS television network in 1964. The next year, the team, which had gone 40 years without a losing record, dropped to sixth place and in 1966 finished dead last.

It was a cautionary tale about the bad things that can happen when an absentee corporate owner takes over a sports franchise. CBS paid $11 million for 80 percent of the stock in the Yankees (they soon bought the other 20 percent), and then watched its

---

Memorize the List of Yankees Owners

January 9, 1903—Frank Farrell and Bill Devery purchase the American League's Baltimore franchise for $18,000 and move the team to New York.

January 11, 1915—Colonel Jacob Ruppert and Colonel Tillinghast L'Hommedieu Huston purchase the Yankees for $460,000.

May 21, 1922—Col. Ruppert buys out Col. Huston for $1.5 million.

January 13, 1939—Col. Ruppert dies.

January 26, 1945—The estate of the late Col. Ruppert sells the Yankees to Dan Topping, Del Webb, and Larry MacPhail for $2.8 million.

November 2, 1964—A television network, the Columbia Broadcasting System (CBS), purchases the Yankees for $11.2 million.

January 3, 1973—George M. Steinbrenner III heads a limited partnership that purchases the Yankees from CBS for $8.8 million.

July 13, 2010—George M. Steinbrenner III dies and his son Hal takes over the day-to-day operations of the team.

investment depreciate. The Yankees went to the World Series in 1964, but in eight full seasons under the network's ownership, they compiled a 636–649 record.

At the start of the 1965 season, Johnny Keane, who had won the World Series with the Cardinals the previous year, took over as the Yankees manager. He was not a success in New York, as the Yankees finished sixth. In 1966, the Yankees finished last in the American League for the first time in 54 years and Ralph Houk replaced Keane 20 games into the season. Houk managed the Yankees for the rest of CBS' stewardship. When CBS finally sold the team to George Steinbrenner in 1973, it got only $8.8 million in return. Steinbrenner was ecstatic at his good fortune. "Owning the Yankees is like owning the *Mona Lisa*," he said.

He also said he would be a hands-off owner. After that season, Steinbrenner replaced Houk with Bill Virdon, starting the revolving door of managers that finally stopped spinning in 1996 when Joe Torre arrived. Steinbrenner died in 2010, and his family now controls a franchise that is believed to be worth over $1 billion.

81 Cheer Godzilla, Conquer Gotham

A new era in the history of the New York Yankees began on April 16, 2009, when the team played its first game at the new Yankee Stadium against the Cleveland Indians. The ghosts of the old Yankee Stadium seemed to have moved across the street to the new stadium, because by season's end the Yankees would win their 27th world championship.

With offseason additions C.C. Sabathia, Mark Teixeira, and A.J. Burnett proving to be difference-makers, the Yankees won a major-league best 103 games in 2009 and then powered through the postseason. After sweeping the Minnesota Twins in three games to win the divisional series, and then winning their 40th American League pennant by defeating the Los Angeles Angels of Anaheim in six games, the Yankees advanced to the World Series for the first time since 2003. That year was Japanese home run champion Hideki Matsui's first season with the Yankees, which ended with a World Series loss to the Florida Marlins.

Six years later, the Yankees were back on baseball's biggest stage, where they would face the defending champion Philadelphia Phillies in the 2009 World Series. Since Matsui was the designated hitter, he didn't start any of the games played in Philadelphia, but that didn't lessen his impact. "Godzilla" had a huge series, going 8-for-13 for a .615 batting average with three home runs and eight runs batted in.

"My first and foremost goal when I joined the Yankees was to win the world championship," Matsui said through his interpreter. "Certainly, it's been a long road and very difficult journey. But I'm just happy that after all these years we were able to win and reach the goal that I had come here for."

In the series-clinching sixth game, Matsui almost single-handedly defeated the Phillies. He hit a two-run home run in the second inning, a two-run single in the third, and a two-run double in the fifth, helping lead the Yankees to a 7–3 victory. Matsui drove in six runs, tying the single-game World Series record, and he was the obvious choice for World Series Most Valuable Player, the first full-time designated hitter (and Japanese player) to earn the award. Bobby Richardson was the only other player with six RBIs in a World Series game, doing it for the Yankees in Game 3 against the Pittsburgh Pirates in 1960. Richardson hit a first-inning grand slam and a two-run single in the fourth.

"I guess you could say this is the best moment of my life right now," Matsui said.

"They're partying in Tokyo tonight," said teammate Nick Swisher.

Matsui finished the series with six hits in his final nine at-bats, including three home runs. Nothing, though, topped his Game 6 performance, when Matsui's history-making offensive output resulted in his raising of a championship trophy.

"He looked like he wanted it bad," Derek Jeter said. "Matsui is one of my favorite players. He's one of my favorite teammates. He comes ready to play every day. He's a professional hitter. All he wants to do is win."

"It's awesome," Matsui said. "Unbelievable. I'm surprised myself."

Veteran left-hander Andy Pettitte, pitching on three days' rest, threw 5⅔ solid innings, allowing three runs on four hits. He earned his fifth World Series ring with his second victory of the series. Pettitte's 2009 postseason was one for the ages: he became the first pitcher in baseball history to start and win the clinching games in the division series, championship series, and World Series in the same postseason. (He also won the regular season game that clinched the American League East.)

On his way to five World Series championships, Andy won 19 postseason games, more than any other pitcher in baseball history. He's also the all-time postseason leader in games started (44) and innings pitched (276.2). With a career record of 256–153, he is one of 13 pitchers since 1900 with at least 200 wins, a career winning percentage of .600, and a record more than 100 games above .500. Remarkably, he never had a losing season. As far as where he falls in Yankees history, he's the franchise's all-time leader in strikeouts (2,020), ranks first in games started (438, tied with Whitey Ford), and is third in wins (219, behind Ford and Red Ruffing).

Pettitte was an intense pitcher, standing on the mound glaring at opposing batters, cap pulled tightly down on his forehead, glove held up to shield his face from the batter so only his piercing eyes were visible as he looked in for a sign from the catcher.

"He had that ability to always dial it up when we needed him," said former Yankees manager Joe Girardi, an ex-catcher who was a teammate and manager to Pettitte. "That's a guy that you want on the mound in pivotal games."

82 Roger Clemens

The Yankees received quite a gift when the team traded for Roger Clemens on February 18, 1999, sending pitchers David Wells and Graeme Lloyd and infielder Homer Bush to Toronto in exchange for the game's premier power pitcher. "It's like Christmas in February," manager Joe Torre said of the deal.

The Yankees were already rich in pitching talent after winning the 1998 World Series, but as general manager Brian Cashman pointed out, "We're a pro-active organization and constantly looking to improve."

They sure did improve by landing Clemens, who had won 41 games and two Cy Young awards in the previous two seasons with the Blue Jays. But Toronto wasn't very competitive in the American League East, and Clemens, who had never been part of a world championship team, asked to be traded to a contender. The Yankees were only too happy to oblige, having failed to land Clemens as a free agent in 1996 after 13 seasons with Boston despite having been the highest bidder. Finally Cashman and the Yankees got their man.

In his first season in New York, The Rocket posted a 14–10 record with a career-worst 4.60 earned-run average. The Yankees won 98 games and the division title, and after steamrolling through two rounds of the playoffs, defeated the Atlanta Braves in a four-game sweep to win the World Series. Proving he could pitch when it counted, Clemens sealed the clincher by scattering four hits over 7⅔ innings. "Thank you, Boss. I did it for you," the Rocket said to owner George Steinbrenner as the champagne flowed in the winning locker room. For Clemens, celebrating his first World Series title, the taste was particularly sweet.

"I just loved the fact that you put your name right alongside the great Yankees players," Clemens said later. "It's one thing to play here, it's another thing to play on a World Series champion. That's why I said after that [clinching] game that I knew what it was to be a Yankee. It was being part of a championship team."

Roger Clemens' most dominant performance as a Yankee occurred in Game 4 of the 2000 ALCS against the Seattle Mariners at Safeco Field. Clemens pitched the first complete-game one-hitter ever in a National or American League Championship Series. He also struck out 15 Seattle batters with a nasty split-finger fastball in the Yankees' 5–0 victory. David Justice and Derek Jeter hit home runs to provide all the offense the Yankees, and Clemens, would need. Clemens had a no-hitter through six innings, but had to settle for a one-hitter when Al Martin's line drive caromed off Tino Martinez's glove for the Mariners' only hit. Because of the dominant way Clemens was pitching, Seattle was never a threat to score. "That was the best I ever caught him," said catcher Jorge Posada. "He had no-hit stuff. He was special today."

Clemens' next start came in Game 2 of the 2000 World Series against the Mets, and in the most surreal moment of any series, Clemens fired the barrel of Mike Piazza's broken bat in the direction of the Mets catcher. The incident aroused heated public debate in light of Clemens' beaning of Piazza in July. Four nights later, the Yankees won the first Subway Series in 44 years, finishing off the Mets in five games for their 26th championship and Clemens' second.

In 2001, Clemens, at age 39, became the first pitcher in major league history to start a season with a 20–1 record. He earned his 20th win of the season by allowing five hits and three runs in 6⅔ innings in Chicago on September 19, 2001, just days after driving his family for 23 hours from New York to Texas in the wake of the terrorist attacks the previous week. Clemens finished the season with a pair of losses to end his Yankees-record 16-game winning streak, but the Rocket still earned his first Cy Young award in pinstripes (and sixth overall), going 20–3.

Clemens joined a very exclusive club on June 13, 2003. In a 5–2 win over the St. Louis Cardinals at Yankee Stadium, Clemens notched both his 300th career victory and his 4,000th career strikeout. Clemens became the 21st pitcher in major league history to reach 300 wins, and the first since Nolan Ryan, another hard-throwing Texan, did it in 1990. Phil Niekro was the only other pitcher to win his 300th game while playing for the Yankees, but the knuckleballer did it at Toronto in 1985, making Clemens the first Yankees pitcher to win his 300th in front of the home fans. After the final out, Clemens ran onto the field as Elton John's "Rocket Man" played over the public address system. He raised both arms, tipped his cap to the fans, and touched his heart.

"I'm real fortunate that I had the opportunity to do it here in this stadium and in this uniform," said Clemens. "I just couldn't have drawn it up any better."

Clemens allowed two runs over 6⅔ innings and struck out 10 Cardinals batters, including Edgar Renteria for No. 4,000. Only Ryan (5,714), Randy Johnson (4,875), Steve Carlton (4,136), and Clemens have more than 4,000 strikeouts.

"To have these two milestones that I was able to attain on the same night here, it couldn't have worked out any better," said Clemens. "4,000 and 300 put me with some great men that have ever stepped on that mound."

83 Graig Nettles

In 1981, the Yankees outscored the Oakland Athletics 20–4 in the only American League Championship Series sweep in franchise history. Graig Nettles, the MVP of the series, drove in three runs in each of the three games, batting .500 (6-for-12) with a home run. Nettles keyed the Yankees' 3–1 Game 1 victory with the bases loaded in the first inning by hitting an 0-2 pitch into the left-center-field gap for a bases-clearing, three-run double. He went 4-for-4, including a three-run home run, to lead the Yankees in a 13–3 rout in Game 2. In the Yankees' seven-run fourth inning, Nettles led off the inning with a single, then became the first player in ALCS history to get two hits in one inning.

The third game was a 1–0 pitcher's duel until Nettles hit a three-run double in the ninth inning to clinch a 4–0 win as the Yankees captured their 33rd league pennant. At a team party later that night, a celebration turned to fisticuffs when members of Nettles' family claimed to be mistreated by some of Reggie Jackson's friends. A shoving match ensued, and before order could be restored, Nettles had thrown a punch at Jackson.

The atmosphere in the New York Yankees clubhouse had prompted Nettles to say, "When I was a little boy, I wanted to be a baseball player and join a circus. With the Yankees, I've accomplished both."

Nettles possessed an acerbic wit. When the Yankees replaced the reigning Cy Young award winner Sparky Lyle with Rich "Goose" Gossage as the team's new closer for the 1978 season, Nettles quipped that Lyle had gone "from Cy Young to Sayonara." Nettles, who was known as "Puff," is among the best third basemen in Yankees history. A five-time All-Star with the Yankees, he hit

Graig Nettles retired with the AL record for most home runs by a third baseman with 319. He was passed by Yankees' third baseman Alex Rodriguez.

GRAIG NETTLES

250 home runs in 11 seasons, and was the American League home run champion with 32 in 1976. In his best season of 1977, he set career highs with 37 home runs and 107 runs batted in and won the first of two consecutive Gold Glove awards, helping the Yankees win their first world championship in 15 years.

His sparkling fielding single-handedly turned around the World Series in 1978. The Dodgers won the first two Series games in Los Angeles, 11–5 and 4–3. The New Yorkers came home to the Bronx and sent left-hander Ron Guidry to the Yankee Stadium mound in a must-win game. Guidry, coming off an otherworldly 25–3 season, wasn't sharp; he allowed eight hits and seven walks, yet went the distance in a 5–1 victory. Guidry was bailed out by the glove work of Nettles, who made four dazzling stops at third base, including two with the bases loaded, to squelch the Dodgers' hopes. "Every time I put my glove down, a ball seemed to jump into it," said Nettles.

Proving that defense wins championships, the Bombers went on to win a second consecutive World Series championship in six games. They overcame a 2–0 deficit by winning four straight games for the title. No team in Series history had ever done that before.

Nettles retired with 390 homers in his six-team career, 319 as an American League third baseman—a record that stood until Alex Rodriguez came along.

84 Feel Empathy for Gil McDougald

Mickey Mantle was baseball's most touted rookie in 1951, but teammate Gil McDougald, who hit .306 with 14 homers, was the winner of the Rookie of the Year award. A timely hitter, McDougald belted the first World Series grand slam by a rookie, a bases-loaded home run off Larry Jansen of the New York Giants in Game 5 at the Polo Grounds.

McDougald excelled as a sure-handed fielder and productive hitter at whichever infield position the Yankees needed him to play. Alternating between second base, third base, and shortstop for Casey Stengel's clubs, he led American League infielders in double plays at third base in 1952, second base in 1955, and shortstop in 1957. It was as a shortstop that he helped preserve what turned out to be Don Larsen's perfect game in the 1956 World Series against the Brooklyn Dodgers when he threw out Jackie Robinson in the second inning after Robinson's hot smash deflected to him, caroming off the glove of third baseman Andy Carey.

The versatile and valuable McDougald was a member of eight pennant-winning teams and five World Series championship teams during his 10 seasons with the Yankees. Always a tough out, he twice hit over .300 in a season and had a career .276 batting average. He was a five-time All-Star, and his pinch-hit single won the 1958 All-Star Game. But what he is forever remembered for is the role he played in an accident that severely injured pitcher Herb Score, and which put a promising pitching career on hold.

The 23-year-old Score, in only his third major league season, was already rated as one of the best pitchers in the league. The Indians' brilliant left-hander was a 16-game winner as a rookie in 1955, and was coming off a 20-win season in 1956. His 245 strikeouts in 1955 and 263 in 1956 were the most by any pitcher in the majors. Coming into this game he had already fanned 39 batters in 35⅓ innings. It was the first inning of a night game between the Yankees and Indians at Cleveland's Municipal Stadium on May 7, 1957. The ballgame was barely three minutes old when a line drive drilled off the bat of McDougald struck Score in the face. Score fell to the ground and remained there for several minutes. A hush of tremendous concern overwhelmed the spectators. The public address announcer asked, "Is there a doctor in the stands?"

Score had retired the first Yankee he faced, Hank Bauer, on a grounder to third baseman Al Smith. McDougald was the second batter of the game. He slashed a line drive headed directly at the pitcher. Unable to get his glove up in time, Score was hit squarely on the right eye. Members of both teams rushed to Score's side. Ice packs were applied and a stretcher brought out.

His right eye closed, and bleeding from a broken nose, Score was carried off the field and taken to Cleveland's Lakeside Hospital. A prominent eye specialist examined him and reported hemorrhaging in the eye so severe it might permanently endanger Score's sight. After the game, McDougald told reporters, "If Herb loses the sight in his eye I'm going to quit the game."

Score did regain his vision, but he was sidelined for the rest of the season. When he did return the following year his unlimited career was effectively ruined. He never recovered his brilliant form, winning just 17 more games over five years with the Indians and White Sox. He then broadcast Indians baseball games for more than 30 years.

McDougald retired after the 1960 season at age 33, when it appeared that he would be picked by either the Los Angeles Angels or the Washington Senators in the first expansion draft in baseball history. Even though he had a few good seasons left, McDougald decided to retire rather than leave the Yankees.

85 1964 World Series: End of an Era

Both the New York Yankees and St. Louis Cardinals made it to the 1964 World Series after heart-pounding pennant races. The Yankees, skippered by Yogi Berra, rallied in September with an 11-game win streak to clinch the American League pennant on the next-to-last day of the season. The Cardinals stole the National League title on the season's final day after Philadelphia blew a 6.5-game lead with 12 games to go.

It was the second time in team history the Yankees had made it to five straight World Series. Mickey Mantle, playing in his final Fall Classic, batted .333 with three home runs and eight runs batted in, and Bobby Richardson collected a record 13 hits in the Series. But the Cardinals were not impressed, prevailing in seven tense games behind the overpowering pitching of Bob Gibson, who won two Series games and struck out 31 Yankees in 27 innings.

After the teams had split the first two games in St. Louis, Game 3 proved to be Mantle's defining World Series moment. The score was tied 1–1 going into the bottom of the ninth inning. Mantle was due to lead off against knuckleballing relief pitcher Barney

Schultz. As Mantle watched Schultz warm up, he turned to Elston Howard, the on-deck batter, and said, "You might as well go on in. I'm going to hit the first pitch I see out of the park." Sure enough, Mantle deposited Schultz's first pitch into the third deck of the right-field grandstand to win Game 3 and break a tie with Babe Ruth for career Series homers. The Mick hit two more in the games that followed to set a mark of 18 Series homers that will be hard to match.

The long ball was a big St. Louis weapon, too. Ken Boyer's grand slam provided all the runs the Cards needed in a 4–3 victory in Game 4, and Tim McCarver's home run in the 10th inning of Game 5 gave the Cardinals a 3–2 Series edge heading back to St. Louis. The home runs continued to fly in Game 6 for the Yanks, as Joe Pepitone's grand slam forced a deciding seventh game. The Bombers produced three home runs off Gibson in Game 7, but it was not enough to win the Series. Pitching on two days' rest, Gibson outlasted rookie Mel Stottlemyre, hanging on for a 7–5 win and the Cardinals' first championship since 1946. St. Louis executive Branch Rickey was ecstatic. "It's the most champagne I've had in four years," he said in the celebratory locker room. "I'd rather beat the Yankees than any other team in baseball."

In a stunning development, both World Series managers left their ballclubs after Game 7. The Yankees ownership was unhappy with Berra's performance and fired him, while Keane quit the Cardinals and then became the Yankees skipper.

The loss turned out to be a bad omen for the great Yankees dynasty that started in the 1920s with Ruth and Gehrig and peaked from 1947 to 1964. During those 18 postwar seasons, the Yankees won 15 AL pennants and 10 World Series. But after never having to wait more than four years to reach a World Series, the Bronx Bombers did not make it back again for 12 years. It was the end of an era. Within two years, the Yankees would tumble all the way to last place.

86 Joe McCarthy

Joe McCarthy never played a single game in the major leagues. His entire playing career was spent as a minor league infielder. He managed several minor league clubs before joining the Chicago Cubs as manager in 1926. McCarthy went on to become one of the most successful managers in major league history with a .615 career winning percentage.

McCarthy led the Cubs to five straight winning seasons and the National League pennant in 1929. Bitter fan disappointment and criticism over the Cubs' World Series loss to the Philadelphia Athletics that year caused McCarthy to resign in September of 1930.

In 1931, McCarthy took over as Yankees manager and began the most astonishing run any manager has ever had. His Yankees teams, led first by Babe Ruth and Lou Gehrig, and later by Joe DiMaggio, finished first or second in 12 of the next 13 seasons. McCarthy's Yankees won eight pennants and seven World Series, taking the championship in 1932, 1936, 1937, 1938, 1939, 1941, and 1943. When the Yankees beat the Cubs in the 1932 World Series, McCarthy not only got sweet revenge on his old team but also became the first manager in major league history to win pennants in both leagues. "I eat, drink, and sleep baseball 24 hours a day," said McCarthy. "What's wrong with that? The idea of this game is to win and keep winning."

But things were not always easy for the Yankees skipper. From the moment he arrived in New York, many Yankees veterans regarded him as a National Leaguer who had no business being in the AL. Many players and fans also felt that Babe Ruth should have been named manager in 1931 instead of McCarthy, and the Babe felt the same way. McCarthy never won Ruth's trust, and there was always conflict between them.

When Ruth left the Yankees in 1935 to finish out his career with the Boston Braves, McCarthy's greatest run began. A rookie named Joe DiMaggio joined the club in 1936, and from then until 1939, Joe McCarthy's Yankees were practically unbeatable. They won four championships in a row, often clinching the pennant in early September, a month before the season ended, and then crushing all opposition in the World Series.

Although McCarthy suffered criticism even after becoming the first manager to win four World Series championships in a row—some called him a "push-button manager" and said that anyone could manage those great Yankees teams—Joe DiMaggio said, "Never a day went by when you didn't learn something from McCarthy."

McCarthy shared a special bond with Gehrig, who he called "the finest example of a ballplayer, sportsman, and citizen that

Joe McCarthy's 10 Commandments for Baseball Success

1. Nobody ever became a ballplayer by walking after a ball.
2. You will never become a .300 hitter unless you take the bat off your shoulder.
3. An outfielder who throws in back of a runner is locking the barn after the horse is stolen.
4. Keep your head up and you may not have to keep it down.
5. When you start to slide, slide. He who changes his mind may have to change a good leg for a bad one.
6. Do not alibi on bad hops. Anybody can field the good ones.
7. Always run them out. You never can tell.
8. Do not quit.
9. Do not fight too much with the umpires. You cannot expect them to be as perfect as you are.
10. A pitcher who hasn't control hasn't anything.

(Published in the *Boston Herald* in 1949.)

baseball has ever known." When Gehrig decided on May 2, 1939, to end his incredible streak of 2,130 consecutive games played, he told McCarthy he wanted to sit down "for the good of the team" and his boss reluctantly complied with the request. At the tearful testimonial held in Gehrig's honor on July 4, 1939, McCarthy told Gehrig, "Lou, what else can I say except that it was a sad day in the life of everybody who knew you when you told me you were quitting as a ballplayer because you felt yourself a hindrance to the team. My god, man, you were never that."

Despite the loss of Gehrig, the Yankees captured three more American League pennants from 1941 to 1943 before McCarthy resigned in May of 1946 due to a personality clash with the team's new owner, Larry MacPhail. McCarthy returned as manager of the Boston Red Sox in 1948 and 1949, but suffered two terrible disappointments, losing a one-game playoff against the Cleveland Indians in 1948 and missing out on the 1949 pennant to the Yankees on the last day of the season. In June of 1950, he resigned as Red Sox manager.

McCarthy finished with 2,125 wins to rank eighth on the all-time list for managerial wins, and he ranks first all-time for the Yankees with 1,460 wins. He also holds the record for winning percentage in the regular season (.615) and in the World Series (.698). Only Casey Stengel has ever matched McCarthy's record of seven world championships.

87 Gooden's Unlikely No-Hitter

Of all the no-hitters in Yankees history, Dwight Gooden's gem on May 14, 1996, was probably the most unlikely. Two years out of baseball and making just his seventh start for the Yankees, the 31-year-old Gooden revived the magic of his early Mets years by pitching his only no-hitter in a 2–0 win against the Seattle Mariners at Yankee Stadium. The pitcher once known at Shea Stadium as "Dr. K" struck out five but also walked six batters.

The Mariners had knocked the Yankees out of the playoffs the previous October, and in their first meeting since Game 5 of the 1995 AL Division Series, the Stadium again had a playoff atmosphere. The Mariners boasted the best offensive attack in baseball with such sluggers as Ken Griffey Jr., Edgar Martinez, Jay Buhner, and Alex Rodriguez. With his father, Dan, going into the hospital the next morning for open heart surgery, no one could blame Gooden if his heart wasn't in the game. Yet batter after batter, the mighty Mariners went down, until Gooden had pitched the ninth no-hitter in Yankees history.

"I thought about [my father] all day; hopefully he knows about this," Gooden said. "This is sweeter than my first victory here. I think this is a great feeling, especially since it happened in New York."

Gooden was once the prince of the city, particularly in 1985 when he recorded a 24–4 record with a 1.53 earned-run average with the Mets. Soon after, he began struggling with drugs and alcohol.

Gooden's historic night got off to a rocky start, walking leadoff batter Darren Bragg, and it almost got worse. The next batter up, Alex Rodriguez, lined a shot to center field that had extra bases written all over it. But New York's Gerald Williams retreated

Dwight Gooden was carried off the field by his teammates after firing the only no-hitter of his career in 1996.

quickly, looked left, then right, and somehow made a spectacular catch. Certain the ball was going into the gap, Bragg was already rounding second base when Williams got the ball back quickly, doubling Bragg up at first. After a Ken Griffey walk, Gooden served up another hard shot by Edgar Martinez—this time, Paul O'Neill was there to make the running catch near the right field corner. Disaster averted.

After giving up another base on balls to Paul Sorrento in the second inning, Gooden settled into a nice rhythm and retired 11 of the next 12 batters until Bragg came to the plate in the sixth inning. Bragg grounded a hard shot toward Tino Martinez that bounced off his shoulder and into the first-base stands for a two-base error. Gooden recovered—after a Rodriguez ground-out that moved Bragg to third, Gooden broke off one of his signature curveballs to get Griffey out on strikes. Then Williams made another defensive save with a shoestring catch off the bat of Edgar Martinez. The gem was still intact.

After retiring the side in order in the seventh and eighth innings, the final test was yet to come. Well over 100 pitches, Gooden was showing signs of fatigue. Rodriguez led off the inning by working another free pass, and then the bullpen began stirring. With just a 2–0 lead, a win was still in question, let alone a no-hitter.

Next, Griffey sent a slow-hit ball toward Martinez at first. Gooden seemed to freeze up on his way to covering the bag, leaving Martinez to fend for himself. As Griffey raced down the line, Tino dove with his glove stretched toward the bag for the first out. Then Edgar Martinez walked again. Gooden stood on the mound, blowing on his right hand after every pitch as a way to release the tension. With Jay Buhner batting, Gooden let go a wild pitch—moving the runners up to second and third—and sending New York's pitching coach Mel Stottlemyre to the mound for a visit.

Whatever was said worked. Gooden pumped a two-strike fastball past Buhner for the second out, then got Sorrento to pop up to Derek Jeter on the infield. The miracle was complete, and teammates carried Gooden off the field, his arms pumping all the way. After losing time to drug rehabilitation and then to arm injury, Gooden turned baseball on its ear with a magical renaissance and a brilliant performance against an archenemy. In a fitting '80s flashback, the stadium's public address system blasted Tina Turner's song, "Simply the Best."

On this night, Dwight Gooden surely was.

88 Collect NFL Trading Cards of Yankees Draft Picks

The New York Yankees was also the name of a professional football team that played in the All-America Football Conference (AAFC) from 1946 to 1949. The baseball Yankees have had ties to professional football ever since George Halas played six games in the outfield for them in 1919, starting the myth that he was the Yankees right fielder before Babe Ruth. (Ruth actually replaced Sammy Vick in 1920.) By then, Halas would be hard at work helping to establish the National Football League. For nearly 50 years through 1968 he played and coached for the Chicago Bears, winning six NFL championships and eventually becoming a member of the Pro Football Hall of Fame.

Halas was not the last Yankee who could hit the horsehide and catch the pigskin. In perhaps his signature moment as a two-sport star, Deion Sanders returned a punt 68 yards for a touchdown in the first quarter of his first National Football League game with the Atlanta Falcons on September 10, 1989. Five days earlier, while playing as a rookie outfielder for the New York Yankees, Sanders hit a home run in a 12–2 win over the Seattle Mariners. Sanders made history as the first athlete to hit a home run in the major leagues and score a touchdown in the NFL in the same week. He is also the only athlete to play in a World Series (Atlanta Braves, 1992) and a Super Bowl (San Francisco 49ers, 1995; Dallas Cowboys, 1996). During the 1992 World Series, Sanders stole four bases and batted .533, the highest average ever in a six-game series.

Sanders would play baseball until the season ended in October and then join the Falcons to play football. The Falcons wanted him full-time or not at all, but Sanders refused to give up baseball. Before the 1994 season, the Falcons made him a free agent, and he signed with the San Francisco 49ers. In his only season with the 49ers, Sanders was a defensive force. He intercepted six passes and returned three of them for touchdowns. He became the first player in NFL history to have two interception returns for touchdowns of more than 90 yards in one season. The 49ers won the Super Bowl, and Sanders was named the NFL's Defensive Player of the Year.

Another Yankees farmhand would go on to accomplish outstanding feats on the gridiron. John Elway, who excelled as a football and baseball player while at Stanford University, was drafted by the New York Yankees in 1981. In his senior season, Elway batted .361 in 49 games with nine home runs and 50 runs batted in. By the time Elway was selected as the first overall pick by the Baltimore Colts in the 1983 NFL Draft, he had already played two summers of minor league baseball in the Yankees organization. Elway refused to play for Baltimore, and publicly stated that if the Colts did not trade him, he would play baseball instead. Eventually, the Colts traded Elway to the Denver Broncos, where he won two Super Bowls and went on to be inducted into the Pro Football Hall of Fame.

The Yankees used their 1982 second-round pick to select a shortstop from Bessemer, Alabama, named Bo Jackson, who instead chose to attend Auburn University on a football scholarship. He was the first pick in the 1986 NFL Draft by the Tampa Bay Buccaneers, but opted instead to play baseball for the Kansas City Royals. He would play baseball for the Royals and football for the Los Angeles Raiders. He hit three home runs in a game as a visiting player at Yankee Stadium on July 17, 1990. In his first at-bat against starting pitcher Andy Hawkins, Jackson hit a 410-foot home run over the center-field wall. Bo was just getting started. His second time up, he put a ball into orbit, an opposite-field shot that traveled more than 450 feet into the black seats of the right-center-field bleachers. Royals teammate George Brett called the monumental blast "colossal," adding, "I had to stop and watch."

As Jackson strolled toward the batter's box for his next plate appearance, Yankees manager Stump Merrill visited the mound to ask Hawkins how he intended to pitch Jackson this time.

"Outside," Hawkins said.

"It better be way outside," Merrill replied.

Hawkins' next pitch was indeed outside, but Jackson reached across the plate and knocked the ball over the right-field fence for his third consecutive home run of the game. Fans of the Bronx Bombers cheered for him as he circled the bases. Sadly, Bo never got the opportunity to try for four home runs that day. He hurt his shoulder while making a spectacular diving catch. As an injured Bo walked off the field and into the trainer's room, New Yorkers stood and cheered once again for a ballplayer with extraordinary physical ability.

"You know what?" said Kansas City teammate Frank White reflecting on his experience playing with Bo Jackson. "I really did play baseball with Superman."

89 Joe Girardi: From Catcher to Manager

The acquisition of Joe Girardi for the 1996 season was not a popular move with Yankees fans. He was replacing catcher Mike Stanley, who was an All-Star on the 1995 wild card team. Girardi had a tough start in New York. Three weeks into his career as a Yankee, he was batting just .228 with 2 RBI. Fans missed Stanley, whom Girardi had replaced, and Girardi got booed mercilessly.

Girardi said that Yankees fans stopped booing him after he caught Dwight Gooden's no-hitter at the Stadium on May 14, 1996. He also started hitting better, and finished the season with a .294 average. But as the Yankees rolled through the postseason, and moved to within a game of clinching the world championship, Girardi had yet to make a significant offensive contribution. He had only five hits in 28 postseason at-bats and had not driven in a single run.

That changed dramatically in Game 6 of the 1996 World Series. The Yankees had lost the first two games at home against the Braves, but then roared back to take the next three in Atlanta. Fans arrived in the Bronx stoked to celebrate what they hoped would be the Yankees' first World Series title since 1978. The Yankees struck against Atlanta pitcher Greg Maddux in the bottom of the third inning. Paul O'Neill led off the inning with a double and advanced to third on a groundout. Then Girardi sent a shot over the head of centerfielder Marquis Grissom. The ball landed on the warning track and bounced against the fence.

"I hit it and I thought I got a sac fly," Girardi said. "And then I saw it go over his head. I was just running as fast as I could."

As Girardi raced around the bases, O'Neill easily jogged home from third to give the Yankees a 1–0 lead. The fans in Yankee Stadium erupted.

"When I stepped on home plate, when I scored, I could actually feel the ground shaking," said O'Neill.

Girardi wasn't on third base for long. He scored on Derek Jeter's RBI single to make it 2–0, and the old Stadium got even louder. Television analyst Tim McCarver said to his broadcast partners Joe Buck and Bob Brenly, "Guys, our booth is shaking."

To which Brenly replied, "I think the whole city is shaking."

Bernie Williams then singled home Jeter and the Yankees led 3–0. Those were the only runs Maddux gave up in the series, but they were costly. The Yankees held on for a 3–2 victory and then popped the champagne corks to celebrate the franchise's 23rd world title.

Girardi's playing career with the Yankees lasted from 1996 to 1999, and during that time there was little disappointment, as the team won the World Series each year except 1997. Girardi was behind the plate to catch David Cone's perfect game at the Stadium on Yogi Berra Day, July 18, 1999. After the final out, Cone dropped to his knees, and was swarmed by Girardi, who joined the pitcher in a massive bear hug. Then Girardi pulled Cone down on top of him.

"I didn't want to let go," said Cone. "That's how good I felt about Joe Girardi and what he means to me not only professionally but personally."

Girardi retired as a player after the 2003 season. The following year, he became a television commentator for the Yankees' YES network, but missed being in uniform. In 2005, he joined the team as the bench coach under manager Joe Torre. A year later, at 41, Girardi was hired to manage a National League franchise, the Florida Marlins, and he was named the 2006 NL Manager of the Year award. This success, however, did not help him keep his job. Jeffrey Loria, the Marlins' owner, fired Girardi in October.

Girardi returned to the Yankees' broadcast booth for the 2007 season, Joe Torre's last as manager. Then Girardi took over as Yankees skipper with the goal to deliver World Series championship No. 27. "I expect to be playing in the fall classic next October. I think that's everyone's expectation," Girardi said.

Girardi was well aware of the lofty expectations he would face replacing Torre. Undeterred, he put the bull's-eye on his back, taking uniform No. 27 in recognition of the fact the Yankees were chasing their 27th title. The Yankees broke a string of 13 straight postseason appearances in 2008, Girardi's first year in the Bronx, but hard work prevailed. Two years later, he redeemed himself with a 2009 team that won 103 games and cruised to a World Series title with an 11–4 playoff record. Following the team's 2009 World Series triumph over the Phillies, Girardi changed his number to 28, signifying a new goal. He guided the Yankees to postseason appearances in 2010, 2011, and 2012, averaging nearly 96 wins per season, and also claimed an AL wild card in 2015 and 2017. The 2017 season was supposed to be a rebuilding year, but Girardi guided the Yankees into the American League Championship Series, one win shy of reaching the World Series.

Despite six postseason appearances and a World Series title in ten years at the helm, Girardi's contract was not renewed following the 2017 season. He ended his run with a 910–710 record as Yankees manger, the sixth-most wins in franchise history behind Joe McCarthy (1,460), Joe Torre (1,173), Casey Stengel (1,149), Miller Huggins (1,067), and Ralph Houk (944). Girardi also posted a .562 winning percentage, the best mark among managers during that time. The Yankees never had a losing season during his tenure.

90 Mark the Spot of Former Yankees Ballparks

The New York Yankees were born in 1903. The team was transplanted from Baltimore to give the upstart American League a team in New York to compete with the established National League's New York Giants. The original home of the Yankees was Hilltop Park, a small, hastily built wooden ballpark with a grandstand to seat 15,000 fans and a center-field fence 560 feet away from home plate. The park was located in Harlem along upper Broadway between 165th and 168th Streets, one of the highest spots in New York City.

This new American League team still needed a name. At first, the team was going to be called the Americans, but then most people called them the Highlanders because of their home ballpark's high elevation. Newspapers introduced the nickname

Yankees to reference the club's location, to the north of the Giants. A majority of sportswriters at the time were loyal to the Giants and viewed the new competition as the enemy. By 1904 the name Yankees was already popular in the papers and commonly abbreviated as Yanks, but the name was not yet official.

The Highlanders lost the first game they ever played 3–1 to the Senators in Washington, D.C., on April 22, 1903. The next day, with Harry Howell on the hill, the Highlanders beat the Senators 7–2 to capture the first win in franchise history. Seven days later, back in New York, the Highlanders beat the Senators 6–2 to record a win in their home opener at Hilltop Park. The team finished its inaugural season in fourth place; it would take another 20 years for the first World Series title. The Highlanders played in Hilltop Park until 1912. When the team's lease on Hilltop Park ran out, they worked out a deal with the Giants to sublet the Polo Grounds. Prior to moving into the Polo Grounds for the 1913 season, the Highlanders officially changed their name to the Yankees.

The Polo Grounds was originally built in 1876 to be used as a field for the sport of polo. After moving from its original location at 110th Street in Manhattan, the Polo Grounds was built at a permanent site at the northwest corner of 155th Street and Eighth Avenue. Overlooking the ballpark to the northwest is a steep hill called Coogan's Bluff, which is why Bobby Thomson's famous home run to win the 1951 NL pennant is often called "The Miracle at Coogan's Bluff."

On April 14, 1911, a fire at the Polo Grounds burned down the grandstands. The Giants shared Hilltop Park with the Yankees during the two-month renovation period. Two years later, the Giants returned the favor and allowed the Highlanders—now the Yankees—to become tenants at the Polo Grounds. The Yankees played their home games at the Polo Grounds from 1913 to 1922. The Yankees' lease arrangement with the Giants owners ended in 1923 with the opening of Yankee Stadium—The House That

Ruth Built—across the Harlem River from the Polo Grounds in the Bronx.

The Giants called the Polo Grounds home until relocating from New York to San Francisco after the 1957 season. In their 75 years playing at the Polo Grounds, the Giants won 17 National League pennants and five World Series championships. Before dying its ultimate death, the Polo Grounds hosted the expansion New York Mets in 1962 and 1963. After a legal battle between the city and the Coogan Family, which still owned the property, the City of New York claimed the land, which allowed them to condemn the stadium and pave the way for the eventual building of high-rise apartments on the site where the Polo Grounds stood.

The Yankees also played home games at Shea Stadium, the home of the New York Mets, in 1974 and 1975 during the renovation of the original Yankee Stadium. Shea Stadium was torn down in 2009 to make way for Citi Field near the same spot.

91 Managers of the Yankees and Mets

Four men have filled out the lineup card as manager of both the Yankees and Mets: Casey Stengel, Yogi Berra, Dallas Green, and Joe Torre.

As manager of the New York Yankees from 1949 to 1960, Casey Stengel knew only success, winning 10 pennants and seven World Series titles in his 12 seasons at the helm. His experience as inaugural manager of the expansion New York Mets from 1962 to 1965 was dreadful. Stengel's Mets posted horrific records of 40–120, 51–111, and 53–109 in the franchise's first three years, prompting the manager to ask, "Can't anybody here play this game?" Despite

Coaches' Corner

There have been 115 men who have served as a coach for the New York Yankees. Ten coaches—Bob Shawkey, Ralph Houk, Yogi Berra, Bob Lemon, Dick Howser, Gene Michael, Stump Merrill, Lou Piniella, Buck Showalter, and Joe Girardi—have then been promoted to manage the Yankees. Houk went on to skipper the Yankees to World Series triumphs in 1961 and 1962. Girardi skippered the Yanks to the 2009 title.

Former Yankees coaches who have won a World Series managing other teams include Joe Altobelli (Baltimore Orioles, 1983), Dick Howser (Kansas City Royals, 1985), Bobby Cox (Atlanta Braves, 1995), and Lou Piniella (Cincinnati Reds, 1990).

finishing in the cellar of the 10-team National League in all four seasons under Stengel, the Mets attracted large crowds to the Polo Grounds and Shea Stadium (opened in 1964) due to Stengel's showmanship.

Of his Amazin' Mets, Stengel was fond of saying, "I've been in this game a hundred years, but I see new ways to lose I never knew existed before." On his three catchers, he quipped, "I got one that can throw but can't catch, one that can catch but can't throw, and one who can hit but can't do either."

Just three weeks after playing in his final World Series game in 1963, Yogi Berra was named the Yankees manager, taking over a team that had just won four American League pennants in as many years. "If I can't manage, I'll quit," said Berra. "If I'm good, I'll stick around a little longer."

In 1964, with Berra at the helm, the Yankees won the pennant but lost the World Series to the St. Louis Cardinals in seven games. The day after the Series ended the Yankees fired Berra. The team finished sixth in 1965, and didn't appear in the World Series again until 1976—when Berra came back as a coach. In the meantime, the Mets had hired Berra as a coach, reuniting him with Stengel. Berra remained with the Mets long after Stengel retired, and when manager Gil Hodges died unexpectedly in 1972, Berra took over as skipper. In 1973 he managed the Mets to their second National League pennant and became only the second manager in major league history to win pennants in both leagues. (The first was Joe McCarthy.) Those "Ya Gotta Believe" Mets came from last place in the final month of the season to win the NL East with the lowest winning percentage of any division winner in history. That year Berra had said, "It ain't over 'til it's over."

Berra returned to the Yankees as a coach in 1976 and then as a manager again in 1984 and part of 1985. George Steinbrenner fired him 16 games into the 1985 season. Steinbrenner had promised before the season that Berra would be the manager for the entire '85 season "no matter what." But when the White Sox swept a three-game series from the Bombers, Steinbrenner fired Berra and hired Billy Martin for a fourth time. Berra was so hurt that he stayed away from Yankee Stadium for 15 years. The two men made up during the winter of 1998, and Berra returned to the Bronx to throw out the first pitch on Opening Day in 1999. Later that summer, on Yogi Berra Day, David Cone pitched a perfect game as Berra and Don Larsen looked on.

Dallas Green managed the Philadelphia Phillies to its first world championship in team history in 1980, but could not repeat his success with the Yankees. Green managed the Yankees for part of one season in 1989, posting a record of 56–65 (.463 winning percentage), and complaining often of the cantankerous owner George Steinbrenner, who he called "Manager George" for his insufferable meddling. The Boss, noting that the team had finished nine games over .500 the prior year but fell to nine games under .500 during Green's tenure, fired Green during that one season. With the Mets from 1993 to 1996, he was 229–283 (a .447 winning percentage).

Joe Torre was the Mets manager from 1977 to 1981. He was fired after five losing seasons. After mediocre stints managing the Atlanta Braves (1982–85) and St. Louis Cardinals (1990–95) his hire as the new Yankees manager in 1996 was met with derision by the New York tabloid press. But Torre had the last laugh while managing in the Bronx from 1996 to 2007—the longest tenure for any manager in the Steinbrenner Era, and the second-longest to Joe McCarthy of any Yankees manager. The Yankees reached the post-season each year under Torre and won 10 American League East titles, six AL pennants, four World Series titles, and compiled a .605 regular season winning percentage. With 2,326 career wins as a manager, Torre ranks fifth on the list of all-time managerial wins.

92 Herb Pennock

Herb Pennock was one of the game's most studious and scientific pitchers. He constantly analyzed his delivery to improve it. His smooth, unhurried left-handed motion was fine-tuned over 22 major league seasons, during which he posted a 241–162 record. Pennock developed such a seemingly effortless windup that sportswriter Grantland Rice said he pitched each game "with the ease and coolness of a practice session."

Pennock came to the New York Yankees in 1923 at the age of 29 after winning 77 games in 10 seasons for the Philadelphia Athletics and Boston Red Sox. During his 11-year stint with the Yankees from 1923 to 1933, he posted an excellent 162–90 record. Known as a big-game pitcher, Pennock was a member of four World Series winners and five American League pennant winners with the Yankees. He boasted a perfect 5–0 record in World Series play and pitched to an enviable 1.95 earned-run average.

Tall and reed-thin at 6'0" and 160 pounds, Pennock did not intimidate opponents with his fastball, instead relying on breaking balls and off-speed pitches to keep hitters off balance. He also studied the hitters and observed their tendencies. New York manager Miller Huggins marveled at Pennock's detailed knowledge of opposing hitters. "If you were to cut that bird's head open, the weakness of every batter in the league would fall out," said Huggins.

Nicknamed the "Knight of Kennett Square" after his hometown in Pennsylvania, Pennock made the jump right from high school to the Philadelphia Athletics in 1912. Three years later, he was sold to Boston. Pitching in a game for the Red Sox in 1921, he hit an inside-the-park home run to beat the Yankees. Two years later, he was traded to the Yankees, where he reunited with former Red Sox teammate Babe Ruth.

Pennock flourished in New York, where he was backed by the imposing offensive firepower of the famed Murderers' Row lineup. In his first season with the Yankees, Pennock went 19–6, leading the league in winning percentage. His first World Series appearance for the Yankees was against the New York Giants, who had beaten the Yankees eight games in a row in World Series competition while winning back-to-back titles. Pennock defeated the Giants in Game 2 of the 1923 Series with a nine-hit, 4–2 win. He came back two days later to save Game 4, escaping a bases-loaded jam in the eighth inning by getting Frankie Frisch to pop out. Then, on just one day of rest, he got the win in the clinching sixth game to give the Yankees their first World Series championship. It was, according to umpire Billy Evans, "the greatest pitching performance I have ever seen."

Pennock won 20 or more games in two of the next three years, and then 19 in 1927. In his first six seasons with New York his average record was 19–10, and he helped the Yankees capture three straight American League pennants in 1926, 1927, and 1928. Pennock was nearly unhittable in World Series play. He allowed just three hits while beating the St. Louis Cardinals 2–1 in Game 1 of the 1926 Series. He won again in Game 5, allowing seven hits in a 10-inning complete-game victory to give the Yankees a 3–2 series edge. However, the Cardinals won the next two games to hoist the trophy. In the deciding Game 7, with New York trailing by one run, Pennock pitched three scoreless innings of relief on two days' rest. Unfortunately, the Yankees could not tie the game against Grover Cleveland Alexander, who dramatically struck out Tony Lazzeri with the bases loaded in the seventh inning and then matched Pennock inning for scoreless inning.

The Yankees beat the Pittsburgh Pirates in a four-game sweep in the 1927 Series, and Pennock was masterful in his Game 3 starting assignment at Yankee Stadium, retiring the first 22 batters to face him before Pie Traynor broke up the no-hitter with a single with one out in the eighth inning. Pennock developed a sore arm in 1928 and became a less frequent starter, though he still averaged almost 10 wins per season for the next five years. New York manager Joe McCarthy used the skinny left-hander as a relief pitcher as his career wound down. Pennock's final World Series appearances were saves in Game 3 and Game 4 of the sweep over Chicago in 1932, limiting the Cubs to a mere two singles in four innings.

A fan favorite, Pennock was often the choice as starting pitcher on holiday games, such as Memorial Day, the Fourth of July, and Labor Day, when the stadium was packed to capacity. His personal career highlight was a complete-game 1–0 win over Lefty Grove in a 15-inning marathon at Yankee Stadium in the first game of a doubleheader against the Philadelphia Athletics on the Fourth of July in 1925. Pennock allowed just four hits and did not walk a batter, showing off his trademark control. "You can catch Pennock sitting in a rocking chair," said catcher Bill Dickey.

The Yankees released Pennock after the 1933 season. He appeared in 30 games for Boston in 1934 and then took over the team's minor league system in 1940. In 1944 he became general manager of the Philadelphia Phillies, and helped build a youth movement that culminated in the NL pennant-winning 1950 team known as the Whiz Kids. Sadly, Pennock never got to see that team's success. He died in 1948 at the age of 53. Three weeks later, he was elected to the Hall of Fame.

93 Raul Ibanez's Power Move

New York Yankees manager Joe Girardi made the gutsiest decision of his managerial career late in Game 3 of the 2012 American League Division Series. Trailing the Baltimore Orioles 2–1 in the bottom of the ninth inning, the Yankees were two outs from finding themselves on the brink of elimination. That's when Girardi called on 40-year-old Raul Ibanez to come off the bench and pinch-hit for Alex Rodriguez, who was 1-for-12 in the series with eight strikeouts. Girardi's decision paid off, and Ibanez became an unlikely hero in Yankees postseason lore.

Facing Orioles closer Jim Johnson in the bottom of the ninth inning with one out, Ibanez launched a game-tying solo home run into the seats in right field. Three innings later, in the bottom of the 12th, Ibanez came up once more with lefthander Brian Matusz on the mound. And again, this time on the first pitch, Ibanez knocked the walk-off winner toward the same short porch in right for a stunning 3–2 victory, sending the Bronx crowd into frenzy.

Ibanez's feats were unprecedented. He became the first Major League Baseball player to hit a home run in the ninth inning and another in extra innings of a postseason game. The two home runs also marked the first time in playoff baseball history that a player who didn't start a game hit multiple home runs.

PINCH ME! screamed the front-page headline of the *Daily News* under a photograph of Ibanez's amazing heroics in a victory that gave New York a 2–1 lead in its best-of-five-game series.

"It's been a blur," the lefty-slugging Ibanez said about all the big games and the part he has played in many of them in the season's pennant drive.

The bald and muscular veteran, who played in Seattle, Kansas City, and Philadelphia before joining the Yankees, had already made his presence felt in two other key comeback wins late in the season.

On September 22, Ibanez, who earlier in the game had belted a pinch-hit home run, blasted a game-tying, two-run home run in the 13th inning to cap a comeback that erased a four-run lead taken by the Oakland Athletics and allowed New York to win the game in the 14th inning.

Then, on October 2, in the penultimate game of the regular season with the Yankees battling Baltimore for the American League East title, Ibanez blasted a two-run pinch-hit homer in the bottom of the ninth against Boston to tie the game and then won it in the 12th inning with a run-scoring single.

Ibanez, who hit 19 home runs and drove in 62 runs during the 2012 season, provided some insight into his clutch hitting.

"I think the tendency late in the game when the game is tied, we try to do a little too much," he said. "I was trying to fight that feeling, trying not to do too much. And fortunately it worked out."

The homers by Ibanez turned the tide in a series the Yankees could have easily lost to the Orioles and provided a career highlight for a player who hit 305 home runs during his 19-year career. But he wasn't done yet. Ibanez hit another dramatic and clutch home run in the next playoff round, continuing his emergence as an unlikely October hero.

With the Yankees down to their final strike against the Detroit Tigers in Game 1 of the American League Championship Series, Ibanez turned around a Jose Valverde pitch for a game-tying, two-run home run that landed in the seats behind the wall in right field. The two-run blast capped a four-run inning for the

Yankees, who had been trailing 4–0 through eight innings. Sadly, the Yankees would end up losing the game in extra innings, and eventually, the series.

But Ibanez's postseason heroics had become a delight for Yankees fans. With his ninth-inning blast against Detroit, Ibanez joined Johnny Bench and Alex Rodriguez as the only players to hit two game-tying postseason home runs in the ninth inning or later. Counting his walk-off blast against the Red Sox on October 2, Ibanez had hit four home runs in the ninth inning or later in the month of October. Even more impressive, he became the first player in MLB history to slug three home runs in the ninth inning or later in a single postseason.

Although he spent just one season in pinstripes, Raul Ibanez left a legacy of clutch hitting that Yankees fans will long remember. "I really don't think about it. I'm just trying to help the team win any way I can," he said about his October spree of hitting three homers in a span of 10 at bats. "The only thing that matters is that we win games. That's the only thing that matters. It doesn't matter how we win them, but as long as we win them."

94 Bullpen Aces

Yankees fans have been spoiled by the consistent greatness of Mariano Rivera, the most dominant relief pitcher in baseball history. Even before Rivera and Dave Righetti began saving games for the Yankees, fans at the Stadium have been blessed to cheer for several quality relievers.

Johnny Murphy was baseball's first real relief pitcher. His nickname, "The Fireman," is still used today as a moniker for the game's best closer. A big right-handed curveballer with excellent control, Murphy held the record for saves (107) and relief wins (73) until the mid-1960s, when bullpens and closers became much more specialized. Murphy led the big leagues in saves four times, with a career-high 19 saves in 1939. Twice, he won 12 games coming out of the bullpen (1937 and 1943). His best overall season was in 1941, when he had 15 saves and an 8–3 record to go with a stellar 1.98 earned-run average. So integral to the Yankees' success was Murphy that during spring training when starter Lefty Gomez was asked by reporters to predict how many games he would win in the coming season, Gomez replied, "Ask Murphy."

Joe Page took over for Murphy as the Yankees bullpen ace in 1947. Page struggled for three years as a starter before manager Bucky Harris put him in the bullpen. Page, a happy-go-lucky left-hander who would rear back and fire the ball toward the plate as hard as he could, proved to be a durable reliever. He led the league twice each in saves, relief wins, and appearances. Page picked up 14 relief wins in 1947, setting an American League record. In the 1947 World Series, Page saved the first game, took the loss in Game 6, and came back to win the clincher, holding the Dodgers to one hit in five scoreless innings. In 1949 he was even better, saving a record 27 games to go along with 13 wins. In the 1949 World Series, Page won Game 3 and again saved the clincher.

Luis Arroyo broke Page's relief records in 1961. That season, the screwballing lefty had a hand in 44 of the Yankees' 109 regular season victories with 15 relief wins and 29 saves. Arroyo also added a win in the 1961 World Series triumph over the Cincinnati Reds.

Sparky Lyle was a gregarious and mustachioed left-handed reliever who pitched just before the era of the modern closer. Acquired in 1972 for first baseman Danny Cater in yet another lopsided trade with the Boston Red Sox, Lyle relied on a sharp-breaking slider to save 141 games in seven seasons with the Yankees from 1972 to 1978. He never started a major league game. Though his save numbers would be surpassed by Righetti and Rivera, Lyle was instrumental in helping the Yankees return to their winning ways in the 1970s.

In his first season in the Bronx, Lyle led the American League with 35 saves while recording a 1.92 earned-run average. He saved 27 games in 1973, and posted a career-best 1.66 ERA in 1974. He led the AL with 23 saves in 1976 as the Yankees won their first pennant in 12 years. In 1977, Lyle was even better, pitching an astounding 137 relief innings, winning 13 games with 26 saves (second in the AL), and becoming the first relief pitcher to win the Cy Young award. He then added a win in the World Series as the Yankees beat the Los Angeles Dodgers in six games for their first title in 15 years. In 1979, Lyle authored a book about his experiences with the Yankees titled *The Bronx Zoo*.

The Yankees signed Rich "Goose" Gossage as a free agent in 1978. Gossage made an immediate impact with the Yankees, winning 10 games and saving 27 more. Gossage was a workhorse; in 1978 he pitched 134 innings, fourth-highest on the staff. Then he saved the American League East division playoff game against the Red Sox, and he was on the mound when the Yankees won the ALCS against the Kansas City Royals and the World Series against the Los Angeles Dodgers.

Goose spent about half of the 1979 season on the disabled list following a locker room brawl with teammate Cliff Johnson, but he returned in 1980 to save a career-high 33 games. The Yankees won 103 regular season games, but were swept by the Kansas City Royals in the ALCS, with Gossage allowing the series-clinching home run to George Brett. Gossage was at his overpowering best during the strike-shortened 1981 season. Limited to just 32 appearances, Gossage still managed 20 saves and allowed just 22 hits in 47 innings to go with 48 strikeouts. He gave up only four earned runs for a 0.77 ERA, and didn't give up a run in 14 postseason innings. He saved all three wins over the Milwaukee Brewers during the

ALCS and both Yankees wins over the Dodgers in the World Series. Following 52 saves over two more seasons in New York, he signed with the Padres as a free agent and helped them reach the World Series in 1984.

No bullpen was better than the Yankees' three-headed monster in 2016. Dellin Betances, Aroldis Chapman, and Andrew Miller comprised a powerful force, combining for 41 saves and a 2.35 ERA over 148 appearances. They registered a 41.8 percent strike-out ratio, and the Yankees were 19–2 when all three relievers appeared in the same game. In the 21 games where each member of the trio appeared for the Yankees, the group posted a combined 1.36 ERA and a 13.70 K/9 ratio, while allowing a .148 BA (34-for-230) in those games.

"In an era where sabermetrics and analytics rule, I think the most impressive thing for me was the eye test," said Yankees third baseman Chase Headley. "These guys were just filthy. I was thankful that I got to play with them and didn't have to face them."

The Merry Prankster

In addition to being one of the most effective relief pitchers ever, Sparky Lyle was famous for his practical jokes. He once showed up at spring training camp with his pitching arm in a cast, just to scare his manager and teammates.

One of his favorite pranks was dropping his pants and sitting naked on a teammate's birthday cake. According to Red Sox pitcher Bill Lee, Lyle's cake-sitting was what prompted his trade from Boston to New York. "He sat on [Red Sox owner] Tom Yawkey's cake, and Yawkey found out," said Lee. "The next day Lyle is shipped off to the Yankees, and here comes Danny Cater—all because of sitting on a birthday cake."

Lyle wrote that Yankees teammate Ron Swoboda defecated on a cake which he then had delivered to Lyle. Lyle claimed the reason he stopped sitting on cakes was because he feared someone might try to "put a needle in the cake" to teach him a painful lesson.

It wasn't long before New York's dominant bullpen trio got a catchy nickname. It's "No Runs DMC," with each letter of DMC referencing the relievers in the order that they take the mound. While clever, it did require a licensing agreement with the hip-hop group Run-D.M.C.

The Yankees broke up the crew in July 2016, trading Chapman to the Cubs and Miller to the Indians, helping those clubs to a World Series matchup while swiftly restocking a Yankees farm system that is now rated among the best in baseball.

Betances took over as the Yankees' closer through the final two months of the 2016 season, but he slid back into a setup role after the flame-throwing Chapman re-signed with New York as a free agent prior to the 2017 season.

95 Visit the Babe Ruth Museum

Nearly seven decades after his death, Babe Ruth still remains the game's most memorable and dynamic figure. His image has graced postage stamps, and his name is included in most American history textbooks. His birthplace has also been turned into a museum.

George Herman Ruth Junior was born on February 6, 1895, the oldest of eight children born to Kate Schamberger and George Ruth. The nickname Babe was given to him at the start of his professional baseball career. Growing up, he was called Little George; his father was Big George.

The Babe Ruth Birthplace and Museum is located on the second floor of a three-story brick house in Baltimore, Maryland, at 216 Emory Street, just a three-block walk northwest of Oriole Park at Camden Yards, the ballpark where the Baltimore Orioles

The Babe Ruth Birthplace and Museum in Baltimore, Maryland, houses an impressive collection of memorabilia and artifacts from the Babe's legendary career.

play their home games. Just follow the 60 baseballs painted on the sidewalk from the stadium to the museum.

Ruth never actually lived in the house, which was rented by his maternal grandparents, Anna and Pius Schamberger. Ruth and his family lived two blocks away in a cramped three-room apartment above the saloon Big George opened at 426 West Camden Street. The barroom was called Ruth's Café. It was located on the spot that is now center field at Oriole Park. The building was located in a rough-and-tumble neighborhood near the Baltimore Harbor District. The specific area where Ruth grew up was called Pigtown. The district got its name from the herds of pigs that ran through the neighborhood alleys on their way from the stockyard to the slaughterhouse. The sounds of pigs squealing were ever present.

In the late 1960s, two decades after his death, Ruth's birthplace was in disrepair. The building was going to be demolished when Baltimore officials stepped in to save the house as a national landmark. The building was restored, and with the help of Ruth's family, it became a museum.

The celebrated row house officially became a museum for Babe Ruth and was opened to the public in 1974. Exhibits include:

- **The Historic House:** Visitors to the museum can see the upstairs bedroom where Ruth was born, furnished just as it was in 1895.
- **Babe Batted Here:** Ruth learned to play baseball at St. Mary's Industrial School for Boys in Baltimore. This exhibit displays artifacts of Babe's ballplaying youth, including the St. Mary's jersey he wore and the catcher's mitt he used.
- **The 500 Home Run Club:** On his way to slugging 714 home runs—a feat only two men have matched—Ruth was the first to hit 500 career home runs. This exhibit honors Ruth and the 26 other major league players (through the 2017 season) to have reached the 500 home run milestone.
- **Babe: Husband, Father, Friend:** Here we learn about Ruth's many personal relationships with family and friends. The Babe married twice, first to Helen Woodford and then to Claire Hodgson, and had two daughters, Dorothy and Julia.
- **Playing the Babe:** Ruth's life was the subject of several movies and television shows. This exhibit features memorabilia from those productions. Ruth also played himself in 1920 in the film *Heading Home*, and he played a fictionalized version of himself seven years later in the movie *The Babe Comes Home*, as the character Babe Dugan. In retirement, Ruth played himself in the 1942 movie *The Pride of the Yankees*, based on Lou Gehrig's

life. To look athletic for the part, Ruth lost 45 pounds in two months. This made him so weak he ended up in the hospital, but he did look good in the film.

- ***The Ruthian Legend:*** An exhibit touting Ruth's numerous records as a slugger and pitcher.

The Babe Ruth Birthplace and Museum is open every day but New Year's Day, Thanksgiving, and Christmas from 10:00 AM to 5:00 PM (7:00 PM on dates of Orioles home games). Admission is $10 for adults, $8 for seniors, and $5 for children under 17.

96 Jeter Passes Gehrig

Derek Jeter became the Yankees' all-time hits leader when he picked up his 2,722nd career hit, passing legendary Hall of Famer Lou Gehrig's mark. Jeter's milestone hit came at 8:23 PM on September 11, 2009, in the third inning of a 10–4 loss to the Baltimore Orioles on a drizzly Friday night at Yankee Stadium.

With two balls and no strikes on Jeter, Baltimore pitcher Chris Tillman threw a 94-mph fastball and Jeter swung the familiar swing Yankees fans have seen so many times before, hitting a clean single to right field. The Yankees—the most storied franchise in all of baseball—had a new hits leader. Jeter had finally caught Gehrig, his storied predecessor as team captain, who had held the record for 72 years. Appropriately, Jeter's record-breaking hit skipped past Gehrig's old position, first base, for a single. Jeter dashed from the batter's box, as he always does, rounded first swiftly, then scooted back to the bag. Swatting a base hit to the opposite field is Jeter's signature hit, and as is his signature way of celebrating, he spread his arms wide and clapped his hands. The game was stopped as flashbulbs went off all over the new Yankee Stadium.

Suddenly, 46,771 fans were raucously chanting Jeter's first and last names. *DER-ek Jee-tah! DER-ek Jee-tah!* The players on the Yankees bench leapt from the dugout and bounded onto the field to take turns hugging him. Even the players who had only recently joined the Yankees understood the importance of the record. The Yankees shortstop, known for his calm, cool, and confident nature, and always a team-first guy, appeared uncomfortable with the adulation, unsure what to do next.

"I never imagined, I never dreamt of this," said Jeter, referring to the adoration. "Your dream was always to play for the team. Once you get here, you just want to stay and try to be consistent. So this really wasn't a part of it. The whole experience [was] overwhelming."

Finally, and somewhat awkwardly, Jeter doffed his helmet, waved it from foul line to foul line to all the fans in the stadium, and pointed to his family sitting in the stands. The grateful spectators continued chanting Jeter's name, and Nick Swisher, the next batter, stepped out of the box to allow the moment to continue. The crowd cheered for two and a half minutes. Right then, being the Yankees' all-time hits leader was satisfaction enough for the player known as Captain Clutch.

"I can't think of anything else that stands out more so, and I say that because of the person that I was able to pass," said Jeter. "Lou Gehrig, being a former captain and what he stood for, you mention his name to any baseball fan around the country, it means a lot."

As the electricity of the cheers echoed around the ballpark and the adulation cascaded over him, Jeter clapped his hands in the pitcher's direction, hinting to all that it was time to get back to work, which for Jeter means getting back to the task of winning baseball games and, ultimately, World Series titles.

Principal owner George Steinbrenner would often praise Jeter's character, comparing him favorably to Gehrig, who died in 1941, a little more than two years after his final hit. Gehrig was far more prolific as a run producer, but Jeter surpassed his hit total in 64 fewer plate appearances. Steinbrenner's failing health did not allow him to be present at the stadium when Jeter broke the record, but he did issue a statement afterward. "For those who say today's game can't produce legendary players, I have two words: Derek Jeter," Steinbrenner said. "As historic and significant as becoming the Yankees' all-time hits leader is, the accomplishment is all the more impressive because Derek is one of the finest young men playing the game today."

97 Party at the Copacabana

Whenever he put on the Yankees uniform as a player or as a manager, Billy Martin instilled a fiery emotion in his teams. Unfortunately, he is best remembered as a hard-drinking brawler whose battles during the 1970s with Reggie Jackson and George Steinbrenner turned Yankee Stadium into the Bronx Zoo.

Martin's passion for drinking and fighting overshadowed a brilliant career as a clutch performer. His lifetime batting average of .333 in five World Series is one of the best for players with at least 75 Series at-bats. He made a terrific running catch in 1952 to save Game 7 for the Yankees. The following year he hit .500 to lead the Bombers to their fifth straight title. As a manager, his burning desire to win helped propel the Yankees to the American League pennant in 1976 and a World Series championship in 1977.

Martin's defining on-field moment came during Game 7 of the 1952 World Series against the Brooklyn Dodgers at Ebbets Field. With the Yankees holding a tenuous 4–2 lead in the seventh inning, the Dodgers had the bases loaded with two outs and Jackie Robinson at bat. That's when the scrappy second baseman made the play of the series. Robinson hit a seemingly innocent little pop-up on the infield, but first baseman Joe Collins looked up and lost the ball in the sun. Pitcher Bob Kuzava stood transfixed on the mound. Third baseman Gil McDougald was too far away to catch it. Martin, the second baseman, realized that no one was going for the ball. It looked as if it might fall safely to the ground—with disastrous results for the Yankees. But Billy Martin came to the rescue for New York. He darted in and made a game-saving knee-high catch between the pitcher's mound and first base. Their rally snuffed out, that was it for the Dodgers. Kuzava got out of the inning and got Brooklyn out in the eighth and ninth to save it. The Yankees were champions of baseball for the fourth consecutive season.

In 1953, for the second year in a row, Martin was one of the heroes as the Yankees again defeated the Dodgers, this time in six games. Martin hit a single in the bottom of the ninth inning of Game 6, breaking a 3–3 tie and driving in the Series-clinching run. The winning hit capped a brilliant series for Martin. He batted .500 with 12 hits, two homers, two triples, and a team-leading eight runs batted in.

Martin's defining off-field moment prompted the Yankees to send him packing. Martin and six teammates were involved in a late-night brawl with members of a bowling team during a Sammy Davis Jr. show at the Copacabana nightclub in Manhattan on May 16, 1957. (The Copa, then at 10 East 60th Street, is now located in Times Square at 268 West 47th Street.) Martin along with teammates Mickey Mantle, Whitey Ford, Yogi Berra, Gil McDougald, Johnny Kucks, and Hank Bauer were at the club to celebrate Billy's 29th birthday when the altercation occurred. A reputation for post-midnight alcohol-fueled donnybrooks had followed Martin around since 1952, so it came as no surprise, despite manager Casey Stengel's affection for Martin, when the Yankees held him responsible for the incident. Four weeks later, Martin was traded to the Kansas City Athletics in a deal generally acknowledged to have stemmed from the brawl.

Martin's playing career ended in 1961, and after brief and turbulent stints in the manager's office in Minnesota, Detroit, and Texas, the combative former Yankee was hired by new owner George Steinbrenner. Martin's tenure in the Bronx under Steinbrenner began on a high note, with the Yankees winning the American League pennant in 1976 and the World Series in 1977. That season, two and a half months into his Yankees playing career, Reggie Jackson was already in Martin's doghouse. In the sixth inning of a nationally televised game between the Yankees and the Boston Red Sox at Fenway Park on June 18, 1977, Martin thought Jackson had been loafing when he failed to hustle on a Jim Rice blooper that landed for a double. When Martin made a pitching change, he also sent Paul Blair to right field to replace Reggie. Jackson was understandably unhappy when he returned to the dugout. The manager and slugger exchanged heated words in the dugout and were separated by coaches Elston Howard and Yogi Berra before any punches landed.

The Martin vs. Jackson feud came to a head in July of 1978, when Reggie bunted despite Martin's order to swing away. Martin suspended Jackson for five games for insubordination, but Steinbrenner ordered his star slugger reinstated, prompting Martin to fire back with this notorious quip: "The two of them deserve each other. One's a born liar, the other's convicted." Martin quit the next day. He would eventually be rehired four more times.

During his five separate stints as New York's skipper, Martin became involved in several highly publicized drunken fights that each time led to his undoing. "Billy the Kid" got bounced from a Texas strip club; threw punches at pitcher Ed Whitson in the parking lot of a Baltimore drinking establishment; and flattened a marshmallow salesman at a hotel bar in Minnesota, to name but a few incidents.

"Lots of people look up to Billy Martin," said former Yankees pitcher Jim Bouton. "That's because he just knocked them down."

The Steinbrenner Managerial Merry-Go-Round

George Steinbrennner made 21 managerial changes between 1973 and 2007, including the hiring and firing of Billy Martin five times. The Martin-Steinbrenner relationship bordered on comical, with Martin being fired four times as the Yankees manager (he resigned once).

September 30, 1973	Ralph Houk resigned.
January 3, 1974	Bill Virdon hired.
August 1, 1975	Virdon fired. Billy Martin hired.
July 24, 1978	Martin resigned.
July 25, 1978	Bob Lemon hired.
July 29, 1978	Martin hired for 1980.
June 18, 1979	Lemon fired. Martin hired.
October 28, 1979	Martin fired. Dick Howser hired.
November 21, 1980	Howser's resignation announced. Gene Michael hired.
September 6, 1981	Michael fired. Lemon hired.
April 26, 1982	Lemon fired. Michael hired.
August 3, 1982	Michael fired. Clyde King hired as interim manager.
January 11, 1983	Martin hired.
December 16, 1983	Martin fired. Yogi Berra hired.
April 28, 1985	Berra fired. Martin hired.
October 27, 1985	Martin fired. Lou Piniella hired.
October 19, 1987	Piniella promoted. Martin hired.
June 23, 1988	Martin fired. Piniella hired.
October 7, 1988	Piniella fired. Dallas Green hired.
August 18, 1989	Green fired. Bucky Dent hired.
June 6, 1990	Dent fired. Stump Merrill hired.
October 7, 1991	Merrill fired.
October 29, 1991	Buck Showalter hired.
October 26, 1995	Showalter's resignation announced.
November 2, 1995	Joe Torre hired.
October 18, 2007	Torre rejects new contract offer.
October 30, 2007	Joe Girardi hired.

Alcohol also played a part in Martin's death on a snowy Christmas Day in 1989. The 61-year-old was a passenger in a car driven by his friend when the vehicle slid off the road and crashed in upstate New York, less than a mile from Martin's home. Both men were drunk at the time of the accident. The driver survived, but Billy did not.

98 1981 World Series: Down Goes Frazier

The New York Yankees made headlines during the 1981 World Series for all the wrong reasons. It appeared the Yankees would breeze to a Series triumph against the Los Angeles Dodgers when they won the first two games at Yankee Stadium by scores of 5–3 and 3–0. But then the roof caved in on the Yankees and they blew the next four games by scores of 5–4, 8–7, and 2–1 at Dodger Stadium, and by a lopsided 9–2 score in Game 6 at Yankee Stadium. Luckless Yankees reliever George Frazier, done in by ground-ball singles and bloopers, was charged with the loss in three of those games, setting an ignominious record for most losses in a six-game Series. High-priced free agent Dave Winfield had troubles of his own in the Series as he managed just one single in 22 at-bats for an almost invisible .045 average, and was forever labeled Mr. May by owner George Steinbrenner for his ill-timed slump. And an angry Boss was allegedly involved in a fracas with Dodgers fans in a Los Angeles hotel elevator after his team lost the fifth game.

The Series had gotten off to a promising start for the Yankees. Bob Watson hit a first-inning three-run home run to stake Yankees starter Ron Guidry in the opener. In Game 2, Tommy John, who had pitched for the Dodgers against the Yankees in the 1977 and 1978 Series and now was pitching for the Yankees, stymied his old teammates for seven innings and Rich Gossage completed the shutout for his second save in two days. "Every Series win is satisfying," said John, "but there was something very special getting back at the Dodgers after they decided I couldn't help them anymore."

The Yankees had an aura of invincibility as the Series moved to Los Angeles, and the Dodgers were reeling. Manager Tommy Lasorda turned to rookie sensation Fernando Valenzuela in Game 3, and although he allowed nine hits and seven walks, Valenzuela came away with the victory. "He didn't have good stuff, but it was one of the gutsiest performances I've ever seen," said Lasorda.

Frazier had won a game for the Yankees in the American League Championship Series against the Oakland Athletics, and during the regular season he compiled a 1.63 earned-run average over 16 appearances. But in Game 3 at Dodger Stadium, pitcher Rudy May allowed the go-ahead run to score, which was charged to Frazier, saddling him with the loss.

The next day the Dodgers evened the Series with another close win. This time, Frazier entered the game in the seventh inning of a 6–6 tie, and his back luck continued. Dusty Baker reached base on an infield single, and after Rick Monday's soft fly ball dropped for a double, Frazier was relieved by John, who allowed a sacrifice fly to Steve Yeager for the eventual winning run. The loss was again charged to Frazier. In Game 5, for the third day in a row, the Dodgers overcame a Yankees lead to grab a one-run victory. The Dodgers were one win away from the title, but Yankees manager Bob Lemon was not conceding.

"All we need is a two-game winning streak at home," said Lemon. "We've done that before."

The final game was tied 1–1 in the fourth inning when Lemon decided to pinch-hit for John, his dependable starter, with two on and two out. The controversial decision backfired when Bobby Murcer flied out, and the Yankees did not score. Then Frazier came in to pitch, and again, he could not catch a break. A single, a sacrifice bunt, and another single gave the Dodgers the lead. Then the bullpen imploded as the Dodgers made it four wins in a row to take the Series, handing Frazier his third loss.

"It looks like the voodoo lady was against me in this Series," said Frazier.

In the locker room, Frazier answered every question from reporters after the game.

"I felt, at that time, I can go sit in the trainer's room, go hide somewhere, but what's that going to accomplish?" said Frazier, later a broadcaster for the Colorado Rockies until his retirement in 2015. "If I go with this and stand out at this locker and just answer every single question somebody fires at me, once it's over, I won't have to worry about it anymore."

Afterward, an irritated Steinbrenner issued a public apology to all Yankees fans. Despite the mea culpa, the 1981 World Series loss put the Yankees in a postseason funk that would keep them away from the World Series for 15 seasons, the longest drought in team history since their first World Series in 1921.

For his part, Frazier did redeem himself in the 1987 World Series with the Minnesota Twins. He pitched two scoreless innings and helped the Twins win the championship.

99 All-Star Games at Yankee Stadium

The first All-Star Game was staged in 1933 at Chicago's Comiskey Park in conjunction with the city's Century of Progress Exposition. The idea came from Arch Ward, sports editor of the *Chicago Tribune*.

Ward persuaded the league owners to agree to a game between stars from the American and National Leagues to build up interest and attendance, which had been slipping. Baseball, like every other commercial enterprise, had felt the aftershocks of the 1929 stock market crash. With millions of Americans out of work and with so little money, Americans were not spending their few dollars on entertainment. Between 1930 and 1933, Major League Baseball attendance plummeted by 40 percent.

At the inaugural All-Star Game in 1933, John McGraw, who had recently resigned as manager of the New York Giants, was selected to manage the National League squad. The leader of the American League team was the ageless Connie Mack. Fittingly, it was legendary Babe Ruth—still a force at 38 years old—who left the biggest mark on the first contest. The future Hall of Famer slammed a two-run homer in the third inning off "Wild" Bill Hallahan (the first home run in the game's history) and made a nice running catch in right field to rob the Reds' Chick Hafey of a hit in the eighth. Ruth's exploits helped the Americans capture a 4–2 victory over the Nationals. For the game, American League players wore their individual team uniforms, while the National Leaguers wore specially designed league uniforms.

Ward's proposal was for a onetime event, but the All-Star Game proved so popular it has been played every year since—except in 1945, when the game was called off because of travel restrictions during World War II. (There were two All-Star Games played each season from 1959 to 1962 to raise extra money for the players' pension fund.)

Since the inaugural All-Star Game in 1933, the Yankees have had the most All-Star players (129) and the most All-Star selections (308) of any major league team through 2017. Lefty Gomez of the Yankees is the only pitcher in All-Star Game history to earn three wins. Derek Jeter became the first All-Star Game MVP in Yankees history, taking home the trophy in 2000 after going 3-for-3 with a double and two RBIs to help the American League to a 6–3 win at Atlanta's Turner Field. Mariano Rivera won the award in 2013.

Yankee Stadium has been the host site of the All-Star Game four times. Here is a summary of those games:

July 11, 1939: 7th All-Star Game
American League defeats National League 3–1
Winning Pitcher: Tommy Bridges
Losing Pitcher: Bill Lee
Yankee Stadium was host to the 1939 All-Star Game because the World's Fair was held at Flushing Meadows in Queens that year. Joe McCarthy, the Yankees manager, skippered the AL All-Star squad which boasted 10 Yankees, including six players in the starting lineup. Joe DiMaggio hit a solo home run and Lou Gehrig, who had retired in May of that year, was an honorary member of the AL team.

July 13, 1960: 29th All-Star Game
National League defeats American League 6–0
Winning Pitcher: Vern Law
Losing Pitcher: Whitey Ford
Pitcher Whitey Ford, catcher Yogi Berra, outfielders Mickey Mantle and Roger Maris, and first baseman Bill Skowron of the Yankees were all in the American League starting lineup. The 38,000 fans at the game witnessed four National League home runs, hit by Willie Mays, Eddie Mathews, Ken Boyer, and Stan Musial. The four home runs equaled the All-Star Game record.

July 19, 1977: 48th All-Star Game
National League defeats American League 7–5
Winning Pitcher: Don Sutton
Losing Pitcher: Jim Palmer
A newly renovated Yankee Stadium was host to the 1977 Midsummer Classic. Yankees skipper Billy Martin managed an American League squad that included Yankees outfielder Reggie Jackson and second baseman Willie Randolph as starters.

July 15, 2008: 79th All-Star Game
American League defeats National League 4–3
Winning Pitcher: Scott Kazmir
Losing Pitcher: Brad Lidge

The 2008 All-Star Game marked the first time the game was played in the host team's final season at its ballpark. The 15-inning affair—won by a walk-off sacrifice fly by Texas' Michael Young— took 4 hours and 50 minutes, making it the longest All-Star Game by time and equaling the 15-inning contest in 1967. Forty-nine Hall of Fame players took part in the pregame ceremonies, making it one of the largest gatherings of living Hall of Famers ever.

100 Waite Hoyt

Waite Hoyt spent the years from 1921 to 1930 as part of a great Yankees pitching staff that was supported offensively by the likes of Babe Ruth and Lou Gehrig. Together they propelled the Yankees to greatness. The Yankees won six pennants and three world championships between 1921 and 1928.

Hoyt got the nickname "Schoolboy" when he signed with the New York Giants at the age of 15. The Brooklyn high school pitching star had been throwing batting practice at the Polo Grounds when Giants manager John McGraw signed him to a major league contract. Hoyt was one of the youngest players ever to turn professional.

But Hoyt would not achieve his greatest success as a Giant. After one brief appearance for the team, he made the big leagues as a member of the Boston Red Sox. After two mediocre seasons

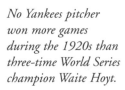

No Yankees pitcher won more games during the 1920s than three-time World Series champion Waite Hoyt.

in Boston he was traded to New York, where he was reunited with his friend and former teammate Babe Ruth. Hoyt held the Babe in high esteem. "Babe Ruth found baseball lying in the gutter as a result of the Chicago White Sox World Series scandal in 1919," Hoyt said. "He reached down with his bat and lifted it to the status of America's national pastime."

In his first season as a Yankee in 1921, Hoyt won 19 games and gained national attention in the World Series with his superlative pitching done in a losing cause against his former Giants teammates. Hoyt pitched three complete games, winning two and losing one, and gave up just two unearned runs, thus equaling Christy Mathewson's 1905 series performance by going 27 innings and posting a perfect 0.00 earned-run average.

Waite Hoyt held interesting off-season jobs. In winters during the late 1920s, the Yankees hurler took to the stage as a vaudeville song-and-dance man, appearing with many famous performers, including Jack Benny, Jimmy Durante, and George Burns. He also opened a funeral parlor with a friend. "I'm knocking 'em dead on Seventh Avenue while my partner is laying 'em out up in Westchester," Hoyt often said.

In 1927, "the Merry Mortician" led the American League with 22 wins, and followed that with a 23-win season and a league-leading eight saves. Starting pitcher Herb Pennock missed the 1928 World Series with a sore arm, so the Yankees decided to go with a three-man starting rotation. Hoyt beat the Cardinals twice in the 1928 World Series, both times pitching complete games, including the clincher, allowing just three earned runs in 18 innings of work. In all, Hoyt won six World Series games for the Yankees. Over his career, Hoyt was a member of seven pennant-winning teams (six with the Yankees and one with the Philadelphia Athletics).

Hoyt won 157 games with the Yankees and compiled a lifetime record of 237–182 and an ERA of 3.59. During his 21-year career, he won 10 or more games 12 times, 11 of them consecutively. Hoyt pitched for eight years after leaving the Yankees in 1930, but never with the same success. By the time he retired in 1938, he had won more World Series games than any other pitcher. Today his six Series victories ranks third-most in history.

When his playing career ended in 1938, Hoyt became a broadcaster for the Cincinnati Reds, a job he kept for 24 years. He was inducted into the Baseball Hall of Fame in 1969.

Sources

Books

Allen, Maury. *Yankees World Series Memories*. Sports Publishing L.L.C.; Champaign, Illinois, 2008.

Anderson, Dave; Chass, Murray; Creamer, Robert; and Rosenthal, Harold. *The Yankees: The Four Fabulous Eras of Baseball's Most Famous Team*. Random House, New York, 1979.

Creamer, Robert W. *Babe: The Legend Comes to Life*. Simon and Schuster; New York, New York, 1974.

Falkner, David. *The Last Hero: The Life of Mickey Mantle*. Simon & Schuster, New York, 1995.

Gershman, Michael. *Diamonds: The Evolution of the Ballpark*. Houghton Mifflin Company, Boston, 1993.

Honig, Donald. *The World Series: An Illustrated History from 1903 to Present*. Crown Publishers, New York, 1986.

Hoppel, Joe. *The Series*. The Sporting News Publishing Company; St. Louis, Missouri, 1990.

Krantz, Les. *Yankee Classics: World Series Magic from the Bronx Bombers*. MVP Books, Minneapolis, Minnesota, 2010.

O'Connor, Ian. *The Captain: The Journey of Derek Jeter*. Houghton Mifflin Harcourt, New York, 2011.

Pietrusza, David; Silverman, Matthew; and Gershman, Michael (editors). *Baseball: The Biographical Encyclopedia*. Total/Sports Illustrated, New York, 2000.

Smith, Ron. *The Sporting News Chronicle of 20th Century Sports*. Mallard Press, New York, 1992.

Publications and Websites

2010 Yankees Media Guide
New York Daily News
The New York Times
Sports Illustrated
www.baberuthmuseum.com
www.baseball-almanac.com
www.baseballhalloffame.org
www.baseballlibrary.com
www.baseball-reference.com
www.espn.com
www.newyork.yankees.mlb.com